JESUS' STRATEGY FOR SOCIAL TRANSFORMATION

To the Lay Ministry Program
and Its Leaders

Jesus' Strategy for Social Transformation

Emerito P. Nacpil

ABINGDON PRESS
Nashville

JESUS' STRATEGY FOR SOCIAL TRANSFORMATION

Library of Congress Cataloging-in-Publication Data

Nacpil, Emerito P.
    Jesus' strategy for social transformation/Emerito P. Nacpil.
        p. cm.
    Includes bibliographical references.
    ISBN 0-687-07136-4 (alk. paper)
    1. Sociology, Christian (Methodist) 2. Jesus Christ—Political
and social views. 3. Bible. N.T. Gospels—Criticism,
interpretation, etc. 4. Sociology, Biblical. I. Title.
BX8349.S65N33   1999
261.8—dc21   99-31490
                                                                  CIP

99 00 01 02 03 04 05 06 07 08 —10 9 8 7 6 5 4 3 2 1

MANUFACTURED IN THE UNITED STATES OF AMERICA

CONTENTS

FOREWORD

As modern men and women preparing to enter the new millennium, we look into ourselves and around us, and, to our dismay, discover that despite technological breakthroughs, we have remained, as in the time of our foreparents, enmeshed in deep human turmoils—spiritual, economic, political, and social.

The need for personal transformation is timeless.

Philippine society is beset with the same evils that have hounded humanity since time immemorial—greed, injustice, cruelty, and inhumanity. In our midst abound the hungry, the sick, the lost, and the victims of injustices. God's people are called to a mission to bring healing to the wounded, wholeness to fragmented lives, and hope to despairing and violated communities. And this could be done only through a transformation of persons and society, through Jesus Christ, the Savior of the world.

The laypersons of The United Methodist Church have heard this call. Three years ago, we launched a lay ministry program as an expression of our growing vision to see God glorified in the world through our effective witness and service for Christ. The work has just started, and only a handful of Methodist laity have been actively involved in it. There is still much to do.

As we grapple with the *hows, whys,* and *wherefores* of lay ministry as a tool for changing society, Bishop Emerito P. Nacpil's book, *Jesus' Strategy for Social Transformation,* provides us a wealth of insights, thoughts, guideposts, and inspiration that could strengthen us in spirit and resolve to follow Jesus in ministry. Bishop Nacpil's prose is both powerful and brilliant.

This book strikes me as a textbook on theology for laypeople, which every member of The United Methodist Church should read to acquire a better understanding of the ministry of Jesus and of mission evangelism in our time. This could also serve as a basic resource material for the laity spearheading or participating in lay ministry in society.

We glorify the Lord for this book and for the time and dedication He has given to the author.

Brig. Gen. Roland I. Pattugalan (Ret.)
Chairperson, Lay Ministry Congress '98
January 14, 1998

PREFACE

This book originally is a part of a much larger study which was begun some seven years ago and to this day remains unfinished. The larger study deals theologically with the grounds, motivations, and strategies of mission evangelism. This book represents the portion of that study dealing with the strategy of social transformation.

The reason for publishing this portion of the larger study now is an urgent request from the clergy and lay leaders in my area of supervision to illustrate a way of reading Scriptures missiologically which I had suggested to them in a lecture. Basically a missiological reading of Scripture or Christian doctrine or church history focuses on the encounter between gospel and world and seeks to discern the transformation in the human situation that takes place as a result of such encounter. Outlining the method did not seem adequate to those who made the request. Showing how the method works in terms of a specific example of interpreting Scriptures is what they asked for. This request prompted me to look at what I had written earlier, which hitherto remained filed away in the shelves of my private library. To my surprise, I discovered that the portion of the unfinished manuscript published here (chapters 1 to 9) was the most ready for publication and, with minor revision, could meet the need expressed in the request. Three new chapters (10 to 12) were added to complete the manuscript.

Moreover, two developments in the Philippine scene make the publication of this book with its particular theme timely. One is occurring in the larger society, and the other among "the people called Methodists." Social reform in the Philippines today has taken on an urgency that is comparable to its birth as a nation in the revolutionary years at the close of the nineteenth century. In 1898 the Filipino people in a daring act declared their independence from Spain and gave themselves a new basis for their nationhood in terms of the Malolos Constitution. Reflection on what "constitutes" them as a people has continued unabated since then. This is indicated by the series of constitutional revisions, which seems unfinished to this day. The Filipino people are asking what defines their identity and character. They are searching for what would order their life-together in peace, freedom, justice, and prosperity. They are seeking to improve the quality of their life with ideals, values, norms, and practices that will fit them as a people for genuine nationhood in the family of civilized nations. They work at overcoming poverty and the pervasive culture it has spawned. They are reforming their social structures and their institutions in the hope that they will prevent their further perversion and make them more responsive to the efforts of national development and expressive of their aspirations for a better future. A social reform agenda has been launched by the present government to help this process.

At the same time, the Methodist people in the Philippines have launched a program of lay ministry in Philippine society. They have reached a degree of maturity in their spiritual growth that prompts them to address significant local and national social issues in the light of their Christian faith. Quite a few of them are placed in various positions in the many sectors of Philippine society where they can wield decisive influence through Christian witness and service. They want their Christian faith to bear significantly on many aspects of daily life: on the family, the economy, the professions, the streets and marketplaces, the affairs of government, the administration of the justice system, the care of the environment, and so forth. And they are raring to do just this, knowing that they can make a significant difference!

It is the fervent hope of the Methodist people in the Philippines that through the lay ministry program they can contribute significantly to the realization of the social reform agenda. This book is being sent out in the hope that it can help stimulate discussion and generate action programs by which the Methodist people—both clergy and laity—may participate in the national effort at social reform.

The book is designed as a help in Bible study groups. It is a theological exposition of some texts from the synoptic Gospels dealing with the theme of social transformation. The expert in New Testament studies will not find anything worth his/her while in this book. The reflections on social issues presented here will be found to be too elementary by the professional social ethicist. Neither one of these two groups of experts is the target audience of this study. I hope the pastors and lay leaders seeking some light from Scriptures on the issue of social transformation will benefit from this study.

Since I became a Bishop in 1980, it has not been easy to find any significant length of time to do serious research, reflection, and writing. The little time that I could avail of in producing this book is what I could snatch from a busy schedule of administration, endless meetings and conferences, and travel. I therefore would like to thank the people in my area of supervision for understanding why sometimes I am in my study at home and not in my office. I am also grateful to my family, particularly my wife, Angelina, for knowing what I am about when I am home and for leaving me undisturbed, except when my two grandsons, Emy II and Joaquin, are delightfully around. Finally, I want to thank Vilma May Fuentes, my editor, for greatly improving the quality and readability of what I have written, and most specially my secretary, Dolly Ocampo, for her patience and diligence in preparing the manuscript for publication.

January 1998

ACKNOWLEDGMENTS

I want to acknowledge gratefully my indebtedness to the authors and works cited in the footnotes and the bibliography. I also owe plenty to scholars and thinkers whose names do not appear on the pages of this book. My reading has suffered from neglect of careful documentation since I gave up an academic career in 1971 in favor of administrative work. I deeply regret this. The best I could do now is to acknowledge my indebtedness to these unnamed scholars and thinkers whose ideas may have found their way into this book.

I also want to thank Prof. George R. Holcombe, the Rev. Toribio C. Cajiuat, and Brig. Gen. Roland I. Pattugalan, all of whom read the manuscript and suggested ways of improving it. None of the mistakes or shortcomings of this work is to be attributed to the scholars, authors, and readers whose work has provided resources for the production of this book.

INTRODUCTION

The message proclaimed by the Christian Church in mission evangelism through the witness and service of word, deed, and a life of discipleship in community is the salvation wrought by God through Jesus Christ in the power of the Holy Spirit. Salvation is multidimensional. Its scope includes the personal, the social, the cosmic, and the eternal. The aspect of salvation that is singled out for consideration in this volume is the social.

Human beings are created to relate not only to God but also to one another. The same text which speaks of the human being as created by God in His image also speaks of human beings as created male and female (Gen. 1:27). Human sexuality and gender—being male and female—are undoubtedly basic to human sociality. By being an other who is meant to relate to another human, interaction becomes possible, and thus human community and its various forms emerge. Moreover, it is precisely in this interaction that human otherness is acknowledged and given the matrix for its development. And so life-together comes to exist.

Moreover, the social relation is from the same source (i.e., God) and on the same level (i.e., in creation) as the religious relation (i.e., being made in the image of God). Human life is not only a being-with-God in the world; it is also at the same time a being-with-fellow-human beings in the same world. This affirms that there is a profound inner relationship between being with God and being with another human being in the world. This relationship is the basis for the mutual interaction of these two relations in social and historical life. The religious relation inevitably has an impact on the social relation in a variety of ways; the social relation presupposes and, in some measure and form, expresses the religious relation.

It is absolutely important that the mutuality of these fundamental relationships is understood at the levels in which they interact decisively. Both the religious and social relations interact in the way things are (creation), in the way things are saved (salvation), and in the way they are brought into consummation in their final destiny (eschatology). Such an understanding of their mutuality can go a long way in avoiding the deplorable practice of separating the religious and the social dimensions of salvation in mission evangelism. This separation has been the bane of contemporary mission. In this separation, the religious relation is sometimes given the primary emphasis at the expense, or to the neglect of, the social relation. At other times, the social relation is seen as all-important and is pursued as though the religious relation has nothing at all to do with it. It is obvious that this separation must be overcome in both Christian understanding and practice. But how?

I do not think that this separation can be overcome if the traditional way of understanding the relationship of mission and church persists. In this view, the church is seen as prior in order and dignity to mission, and so mission is premised upon the church. Mission is here understood as an activity of the church through which it expresses its witness and service and is the way by which it propagates and perpetuates itself. This puts mission completely under the authority of the church, and the church may not easily resist the temptation to use mission as a means for its self-perpetuation. In the end mission is seen as a self-serving activity of the church, when the church is supposed to bear its cross and deny itself for the sake of the world.

This understanding of the relationship of church and mission must be reversed, and for good reason. It is the mission which is prior in order and dignity to the church and is, therefore, logically the premise of the church.[1]

The reasons for this reversal follow. First, mission is first and foremost the mission of God *(missio dei)*. It is for mission that God sent His Son into the world in the power of the Holy Spirit (Jn. 3:16; 20:21; Gal. 4:4-6). Jesus himself understood his life and ministry as something he was sent out to do (Mk. 1:35-38; Lk. 4:42-44). In its fullest sense, mission is an activity of the Triune God (Mt. 28:19).

Second, the purpose of the mission and the burden of its message is the salvation of the world. This is what God in the power of the Spirit accomplished in the mission and achievement of Jesus (cf. 2 Cor. 5:19). An essential dimension of salvation is the social relation. This is evident in the career of Jesus Christ, as will be shown in the rest of the book.

Third, the church is called into being precisely as the "first fruits" of the mission (cf. Rom. 8:23). Undoubtedly it is the church which is the product of the apostolic mission. Without the mission being achieved, there is no church. But the purpose of the mission is not primarily the calling of the church. It is rather the salvation of the world. It is as the world is saved that the church comes into existence precisely as sign that the world is saved in Christ.

Fourth, the church comes to "have" a mission only as it participates *in* mission, and what it does in mission is to witness to the salvation of the world in Christ through its life as a saved and saving community. And so the purpose of the church is precisely to be in mission and for mission in the world. The church is defined and judged in terms of the mission and not the other way around.

Fifth, the burden of the message and purpose of mission evangelism, as one of the many ways in which the church serves the mission, is the gospel of salvation in Jesus Christ. This gospel affects social reality because it is social salvation. Mission evangelism cannot avoid having a "strategy" for social transformation in relation to the concrete ways in which social reality is encountered. That strategy cannot be one of detaching the social relation from its grounding in the religious relation and vice versa; otherwise, the church"s participation in the mission through mission evangelism becomes distorted and ineffectual. It cannot also be one of ignoring blithely the essential elements of social reality needing to be transformed in the light of the gospel of salvation.

We must inevitably have to ask the question how social reality is affected by the Christian experience of, and witness to, this gospel. Can mission evangelism play a significant role in the reformation of society, as Methodists, among many others, claim? May such a role include a plan or strategy of social transformation that is grounded in the religious relation, that is, in *missio dei* as an activity of God in His relation to the world? If so, what would such a strategy look like?

In taking account of the concrete forms of social reality, mission evangelism needs only to consider those basic elements that require transformation in the light of the gospel of salvation. It is not necessary to offer a full-blown theory of society, nor offer a fully developed Christian social ethic, for this purpose. But it would be helpful to indicate those aspects of social reality which are amenable to change and could be the target of deliberate social transformation in the light of the gospel.

It is these social factors that must be addressed in any effective strategy of social transformation. What might these factors be?

Human interaction and life-together in contemporary experience is a diverse and complex phenomenon. Social interaction is carried out through attitudes, values, norms, and modes of behavior by persons in community. There is an enormous variety of these. They are also amenable to deliberate change. If there is to be social transformation of some significance, this is one aspect of social reality on which deliberate efforts at change might be focused.

Moreover, these forms of social interaction are not isolated elements. They interconnect and together they are expressed through social structures, systems, institutions, and traditions passed on from generation to generation. These systemic structures are themselves brought together into some measure or degree of social order and are undergirded with some sense of meaning by culture itself. This implies that social transformation must go beyond the merely personal and subjective. It must also affect the systemic patterns of human interaction and the form that orders them and invests them with some measure of meaning. In short, social transformation must also be structural in depth and scope. Change at this level is more difficult and requires more wisdom, effort, and time. But it is possible. It should also be taken into account in any strategy of social transformation in mission evangelism.

Furthermore, a society's views and practices on the religious and social relations mutually influence each other for good or ill. The distortions of one affect the other. Since the human being is formed socially and culturally, the distortions of society and culture and their consequences are internalized by the human being, through the socialization process, and so the person embodies, operates, and perpetuates them. Today, social sins have become entrenched and institutionalized, not only through structures and systems, but in and through people who have been conditioned and shaped by them. And so people and system are mutually involved in the vicious circle of social evil. If social transformation is to make a difference at all, it must affect decisively the entrenched and institutionalized forms of social distortion and evil embodied in social systems and in people.

Any attempt at reform must deal with both system and people. It is not enough to change people and leave the system out. Nor is it enough to change the system and expect the people to change accordingly.

Moreover, both people and system rest on some fundamental beliefs embodied in an ideology or in a constitution or a religious vision. Such basic beliefs "constitute" them as a people, defining their identity as persons-in-community, providing them with a basic sense of selfhood, and rendering the structures of their life-together with some measure of plausibility and legitimacy. Because of the "constituting" and conditioning power of such basic beliefs, they carry an aura of ultimacy; they express some measure of transcendence or a sense of the "sacred." Any attempt at change in both people and system cannot neglect this level of depth that is somehow presupposed in life-together in the variety of its forms. Can change take place at this paradigmatic level and scope, given the difficulty and magnitude of transformation that is entailed? Why not?

Given the complexities of human community, does it seem possible to change people, transform systems, and alter perceptions of ultimacy? Traditional evangelism has sought to change primarily individual persons. It has shied away from reforming communities. Revolutions have sought to change social systems, but they are unable to change human nature as such.

Ideologies have sought to provide alternative perceptions of ultimacy without realizing that their alternatives suffer just as much from having feet of clay. So where does this leave us? Can the radical change represented by the gospel mission and the experience of social salvation it offers provide a better handle?

On the assumption that Christianity is a unique form of human experience, and therefore represents a radical change in the way human life is lived and understood, it would seem helpful to look for an answer to our question in the primal sources or roots of this experience in the life and career of Jesus. A cursory reading of the portrait of his public ministry as it is presented in the synoptic Gospels gives the indelible impression that Jesus had a profound experience of God which was quite different from the way the Jewish people and society of his day had come to know God and apply that knowledge in personal and social life. Jesus came to know God in His reign as a Father who in love sought to be with His people to share with them the benefits of His loving care. His experience of God was at the same time a vision of what human life can be in God, and so he proceeded to reshape human life and community accordingly. In the course of doing this in his public ministry, he came into conflict with the guardians of the status quo of his day, and that conflict cost him his life.

That conflict could not have been avoided, given the constraints of the circumstances that came into play, the importance of the issues involved, and the strength of the convictions surrounding them. Jewish society experienced God in terms of His power to rule by Law. The dimensions of personal and social life were seen in the light of Law and so were organized accordingly. In this view, justice was understood as retributive rather than redemptive. Salvation was by way of obedience to the Law and not through mercy and forgiveness. The Jewish authorities saw Jesus and his "program" as a dangerous threat to the way things were. If he were allowed further opportunity to continue doing his work, he would turn the whole "establishment" upside down. And so to be rid of him, he was executed. Surprisingly enough, his way of reorganizing human life in the light of his vision of God came to endure and to spread and became a power, a program, and an inspiration for the transformation and reshaping of human experience.

This study seeks to probe the interplay of three major factors which seem responsible for transforming Jewish society in Jesus' day. These are the vision of God's coming reign as having drawn near, the impact of this reign upon Jewish social reality through the ministry of Jesus, and the resistance it provoked from the status quo as structured by Mosaic Law.

Jesus' message about the kingdom of God contains both his experience of God and his vision for human life in the light of that experience. His message has profound conceptual implications for an understanding of God and the human condition. Jesus, however, did not fully develop conceptually these implications. Instead, he straight away applied his vision upon the social realities of his time. One can discern basic elements in his understanding of the kingdom of God which functioned as working assumptions in applying his vision. They include the following:

1. God expresses His deity by *reigning*. But His reign is yet to come. It is expected to come from the future. And so His reign is *coming*. This much Jesus shared with his fellow Jews at the time.

2. However, Jesus believed that the coming reign of God has indeed *come near at hand*. Three critical points must be noted here. One is that the coming reign of God *has come*, and it has come *so near* as to be *in*

the midst of the present. This means that God's reign has come and has come near enough so that it can alter the way things are decisively. This view is unique to Jesus. Moreover, although the kingdom of God has come so close as to be in the midst of things, it is not yet fully and wholly present. There is more to it than what has come near. This conviction of Jesus was not shared by his fellow Jews in his time simply because they could not accept Jesus' claim that the coming Kingdom has indeed drawn near!

3. God's coming reign has come near at hand *in Jesus* in what he said and did and in what he was. His life and ministry were in fact signs of God's reign in and through him. Jesus may in fact be said to constitute "the sphere" of the kingdom of God, or more directly, following Origen, Jesus *is* the kingdom of God. This claim was rejected by the authorities of his day. This set of three interrelated notions we have tried to express in terms of the phrase, the coming reign of God as having drawn near in Jesus, throughout this study.

A second major factor is the sort of change Jesus sought to effect in the light of his vision upon the social realities of his time. They include the following:

1. He sought change in the basis or foundation of Jewish society by putting a new one in its place;

2. He ministered to the various classes of people of this society according to the new basis;

3. He sought fundamental change in the social structures of this society;

4. He provided a new working ethos for this society;

5. He founded the nucleus of a new community that reflects the new lifestyle that he sought to foster.

This book is organized in order to highlight the way Jesus sought to transform these aspects of the society of his day. Chapters 1 to 4 deal with the first three of these social issues; chapters 5 to 12 with the last three. The last three chapters develop the implications of the main portion of the book for lay mission.

The third major point to note is the tension that escalated into open conflict between the "program" of the kingdom of God as "implemented" by Jesus and the resistance it provoked from the defenders of the Law and of the status quo of his time. This is indicated in all the critical areas in which Jesus sought to realize his vision.

It is the dynamic interplay of these three sets of factors—the coming kingdom of God having drawn near, the social realities in Jesus' time, and the strong resistance of the Law and its defenders—which is denoted by the phrase "Jesus' Strategy for Social Transformation." The phrase is *a way of putting together* various elements of the ministry of Jesus as *it affected the social reality of his day*. It is a construal of the significance of his public career from one possible unitary perspective. For this reason, whether or not Jesus deliberately designed such a "strategy," historically speaking, is beside the point. One hopes that what is more or less beyond dispute historically are the basic elements of the public ministry of Jesus, which are here put together in the light of a possible interpretation of their social significance. Since the phrase "Jesus' Strategy for Social Transformation" describes the theme of the book, it seems fitting to make it also serve as its title.

Note

1. Cf. Adrian Hastings, a Roman Catholic historian in Oxford University: "In truth it is because of the mission that there is a Church: the Church is the servant and the expression of this mission. The mission consequently dictates the nature of the Church and insofar as the Church fails to live up to the demands of mission, it is effectively failing to be the Church. In this perspective it is quite misleading to say that the purpose of the mission is the expansion of the Church; in the fullest sense of mission the church cannot possibly be its end. Rather, it is the Church called into being by mission for the sake of salvation" (*Encyclopedia of Theology*, New York: Crossword, 1975, p. 968). Also Jurgen Moltmann, A Reformed theologian in Tubingen, Germany: "What we have to learn . . . is not that the church 'has' a mission, but the very reverse: that the mission of Christ creates its own church. Mission does not come from the church; it is from mission and in the light of mission that the church has to be understood. . . . Mission comprehends the whole of the church, not only parts of it" (*The Church in the Power of the Holy Spirit,* SCM Press, 1977, p. 10).

CHAPTER 1

A NEW FOUNDATION FOR SOCIAL LIFE

Jesus and the Law

In Matthew's Gospel, Jesus appears as defining his position in relation to the Law (the Torah, originally the Ten Commandments given by Yahweh to Moses, and then the first five books of the Old Testament attributed to Moses) very early in his public ministry. As a Jew engaged in a public career as a teacher (he was perceived as a rabbi), he would be judged by his people and their leaders by his attitude towards the Law. The reason for this is obvious. The Law is the foundation of Jewish life and society, of Jewish religion and culture, of Jewish hope and destiny, and so of Jewish identity and self-consciousness. It is what founds the Jewish nation and shapes its social structure. To the Jew the Law represented the will of God; it was viewed as a whole as having come from God and all of its parts are equally binding. The Law is formative and normative in Jewish life. Its authority combined legal, moral, social, cultural, and religious dimensions! Given this importance of the Law in the Mosaic dispensation, did Jesus have an attitude towards it? If so, was it positive or negative? Or was it a combination of both? Jesus could not have avoided giving an answer in public to this question early in his career.

It is not surprising that in Matthew's Gospel, Jesus, himself formed by the Law, affirms the value of the Law in very clear terms: Do not think that I have come to abolish the law; I have come to fulfill it (5:17). He also says that not only the important matters of the Law, but even the least points and smallest details, will be observed and fulfilled by him (5:18). Then he goes on to define his attitude towards those who obey or disobey the Law. One may obey the Law, but would he also require others to do so? If he does not counsel others to do the same, that leaves in doubt his sincerity in valuing the Law. And so Jesus, to forestall any possibility of doubt about his attitude toward the full validity of the Law not only for himself but for others and for society as a whole leaves no question whatsoever about the way he values the Law and his obedience to it: "Whoever breaks one of the least of these commandments, and teaches others to do the same, will be called least in the kingdom of heaven; but whoever does them and teaches them will be called great in the kingdom of heaven" (5:19).

Finally, he turns directly to his disciples and tells them: You notice the scribes, the teachers of the Law, and the Pharisees. They are the most faithful, the most assiduous, the most strict fulfillers of the requirements of the Law. You can hardly find anyone who can surpass their obedience to the Law. But now, if you wish *to enter the kingdom of God,* your fulfillment of the Law must surpass that of the scribes and Pharisees: you must be more faithful, more righteous, more saintly than the scribes and Pharisees (Mt. 5:20). You must live by a "new righteousness" that "exceeds" that of the scribes and Pharisees!

Judging from these remarks, it would seem that there is nothing more important to Jesus than the Law; that fulfilling the Law is the mission of his life! But this is clearly not the case, of course. *Jesus defined his mission in terms of an entirely different reality, namely, the coming kingdom of God as having drawn near* (Mt. 4:17, 23; Mk. 1:14; Lk. 4:43; cf. Mk. 1:38-39). The centrality of the gospel of the Kingdom in the mission and achievement of Jesus may be discerned unmistakably in the Gospels in a variety of ways. If *prayer* is understood as expressing the deepest aspiration of a person before God, then the aspiration for the coming of the Kingdom is what is most important for Jesus, for this is what he prayed for and taught his disciples to pray for (Lk. 11:1-4; Mt. 6:9-13). If we look at the characteristic *language* of Jesus, which is the parable, we discover that the main burden of the message of his parables is the gospel of the coming kingdom of God at hand (Mt. 13:1-52). Many of his *sayings* had for their theme the drawing near of the coming kingdom of God (Lk. 11:20; 17:20-21; Mt. 11:12, etc.). The "mighty works" that he performed are best interpreted as signs of the power of the Kingdom drawn near. Finally, the *good news he proclaimed and taught* is none other than the reality of the coming kingdom of God drawn near. There is absolutely no doubt that what is most historically genuine and important to Jesus—what he lived and died for—is none other than the kingdom of God!

Even when Jesus was affirming the validity of the Law, the reality of the coming Kingdom as already at hand was not far away from his thoughts. The status of those who obey or do not obey the Law of Moses is defined, not in terms of fulfillment of the Law itself, but in terms of their response to the kingdom of God as having come near. The "higher" righteousness demanded of the disciples is also not with reference to the Law in itself but with "entry" into the Kingdom of heaven (Mt. 5:19-20). This means—does it not?—that the Law and its fulfillment are already here *relativized* by the reality of the coming Kingdom drawn near. Put differently, obedience to the Law is not here understood as an end in itself; it is only a means to a higher end, namely, entry into the kingdom of God!

But fulfilling the Law through obedience is a human achievement. If it were accomplished, it would be human achievement which would bring in the kingdom of God! On the contrary, from all that can be gathered about the movement of the kingdom of God, it is God who, in grace, freedom, and love, initiates the coming of His royal rule. The gospel that Jesus proclaimed asserted that God did not wait for repentance and faith to take place for God to bring in the Kingdom. Rather, God has taken the initiative of drawing near in His Kingdom; therefore, people must repent and believe! (Mk. 1:14). It is the drawing near of the Kingdom that makes repentance and faith possible. Put differently, it is the coming near of the Kingdom which makes repentance and faith possible and in turn provides the condition for the fulfillment of the Law. It is not human obedience to the Law that makes the Kingdom come; rather, it is the Kingdom already at hand which makes it possible to obey the Law and so fulfill it.

Jesus' treatment of the Law of Moses has a three-tier progression. First, negatively, he did not transgress it; and positively, he fulfilled the Law by completely realizing its essence as love of God and neighbor. After carefully considering the material in the Gospels, including those in which Jesus appears to be transgressing the Law (Mk. 2:23-28; 3:1-6; 7:1-13), the learned Oxford scholar E. P. Sanders has concluded that except in one instance the evidence indicates no transgression of the Law by Jesus.[1] He adds that "nothing which Jesus said or did which bore on the Law led his disciples after his death to disregard it."[2] This means that Jesus is remembered as having affirmed the validity of the Law and did not transgress it.

The one exception found by Sanders in his considered judgment was Jesus' admonition to the man whose father had died, "Let the dead bury their own dead" (Mt. 8:21f.; Lk. 9:59f.). The obligation to bury one's dead father is not a mere custom, and the injunction to do so is not a mere proverb. The Jews of Jesus' day understood this obligation as a command to have been given by God Himself. But Jesus deliberately admonished its transgression as a requirement of discipleship (Mt. 8:21f.; Lk. 9:59ff.), thus suggesting that something more important than burying a dead father has come upon the human scene, namely, his call to discipleship.

This brings us to the second tier in Jesus' handling of the Law. *Jesus did not regard the Mosaic dispensation as final and absolutely binding.*[3] While Jesus affirmed the validity of the Law and fulfilled it, he nevertheless did not regard it as ultimate and absolutely obligatory as the scribes and the Pharisees did. The evidence that establishes this conclusion is as follows: Jesus spoke of the destruction of the old Temple, which was absolutely central under the Law to Jewish life and society, and its replacement by something new (Mt. 26:60f.; Mk. 13:1f.; John 2:18-22); he admitted sinners into the Kingdom without requiring them to repent as the Law required (cf. Mt. 21:31-32; Lk. 7:22-30, 36-50); he promulgated at least one law for the new order, namely, the prohibition of divorce (Mk. 10:2-12; Mt. 5:31f.; 19:3-9; Lk. 16:18).[4]

We come to the final and most critical point in Jesus' attitude towards the Law. Having fulfilled it but not regarding it as final and absolutely binding, *Jesus went the further step of replacing Law as a constitution of Jewish society with an alternative foundation, namely, the coming kingdom of God as already at hand.* This is clearly expressed in the well-known antithesis sayings in Matthew 5 (21-22, 27-28, 31-32, 33-34, 38-39, 43-44). The formula is structured antithetically: "You have heard that it was said to the men of old . . . But I say to you." This leaves no doubt that what was said to the men of old was being superseded by what Jesus was saying to his disciples. The words of Jesus, however, are not to be interpreted as another law being substituted for the Mosaic Law. Rather, they express the dynamic judgment of the reign of God upon the Mosaic Law as a way of relating to God and of organizing human life. As Jesus put the matter, God's reign appears to be antithetical to the Law.

The first part of the antithesis reveals three elements which need to be clearly distinguished and grasped together at the same time. For one thing, what was heard to have been said to the men of old is nothing less than the *Torah*, the Law as given to Moses in its original form—as an oral word directly from God. The authority of the Torah derives directly from God as expressing His will. But this authority is mediated through Moses. The authority of Moses is thus linked mediately with that of Yahweh.

Moreover, there developed a tradition of interpretation and application of the Law through the authoritative teaching of the "elders," hence the so-called "tradition of the elders" (Mk. 7:3, 5, 9, 13). The intent of this tradition was to teach the Law and apply it upon all aspects of life. Since it intended to mediate the authority of Moses, it soon took on the same authority as that of Moses.

Finally, it was this tradition of the elders which was interpreted and applied by the teachers of the Law in Jesus' day (Mk. 7:1-13). There was therefore a line of continuity which ran from Yahweh to Moses to the "elders" and to the scribes and Pharisees of Jesus' day as far as the authority of the Law was concerned. Although theoretically a distinction was made between the Torah as revealed by God through Moses, on the one hand, and the "tradition of the elders," on the other hand, in practice there were virtual identity and continuity between the one and the other. The one cannot be had without the other!

Jesus attacked this confusion of the authority of Torah with the authority of the tradition of the elders. As he saw it, the confusion had the effect of setting aside the authority of the Torah and replacing it with that of the tradition of the elders (Mk. 7:8-9). It is substituting the interpretation of a text for the text itself and invoking the authority of the text for the interpretation. This resulted in "making void the word of God" through the tradition which the scribes and the Pharisees sought to hand on (Mk. 7:13). This consequence is precisely the opposite of what was intended. And so Jesus doubted strongly the claim that the Law as the will of God was expressed in the tradition of the elders (cf. Mt. 15:1-20; 16:11-12; 23:1-36).

Replacing the Law with the Kingdom as the Basis of Society

But now it is not enough merely to make the proper distinction between Torah and tradition. Someone greater than Abraham and

Moses has burst upon the human scene (cf. Jn. 8:53-59). Since the Torah, its tradition and its current interpretation (What was heard to have been said to the men of old) together undergirded and regulated all of Jewish life and society, the whole package has now to be superseded and set aside by that which is "greater" than Abraham and Moses (cf. 2 Cor. 3:7-11). And so Jesus with the aura of royal majesty and incredible boldness says: "But I say unto you . . ." The word "but" here is not meant merely to oppose or contradict, but rather to relativize, surpass, supersede, and replace. The "I" who speaks here is one who reveals his will through what he says; his word and his will are identical; and together they reveal who he is. Whereas Moses was only an intermediary between Yahweh and the people in the revealing of His will through the giving of the Law, Jesus directly reveals and speaks his will. What he says directly flows from his person and authority; it has no need of an intermediary. Whereas the "elders" only interpreted and applied what they had received, Jesus directly says what he means and applies it himself. He has no need of an interpreter. He speaks the truth with the force of law. And so what he says on his own authority replaces what Moses and the elders had said before him. The total effect of Jesus' "But I say unto you . . ." is to provide a new basis for Jewish life and society, and eventually give rise to and constitute a new people of God! It alters the condition of peoplehood: a new covenant replaces the old!

But what is the source of Jesus' radical boldness? For an answer we must look at the relationship of Jesus to the kingdom of God. For Jesus the more original, immediate, overwhelming, and inescapable reality is not the Law but the kingdom of God. His experience of God is more directly of God actively exercising His royal power to rule, that is, God reigning, which is a reality more primal than the Law itself. In fact it is God as King exercising His royal prerogative which is the primal basis and source of the Law. It is the reality of God as active royal sovereign and ruling power, and not merely the authority of the Law, which is basic to the faith of Jesus.

Moreover, one can go so far as to say that Jesus experienced God more in terms of God's altering the situation created by the Law than by adhering to the order of the Law. It is as the Law is surpassed and set aside that the reality of God as royal power comes through! In short, God's reality for Jesus comes through more forcefully not through the

Law but against it. This is the point of "But I say unto you . . ." (cf. Mt. 5:3-11; 23:1-39). Whereas the ordinary Jew experienced God through the order of the Law, Jesus experienced God through the power of God over the Law. This is what made him different from the ordinary Jew and offensive to the Jewish leaders of his day.

Furthermore, for Jesus the reality of God as active royal power and, therefore reigning, is more genuinely experienced through his compassionate power to save in mercy than through his power to rule by Law. In this perception, Jesus was only being true and faithful to Israel's primal experience of God. In the Exodus, Israel experienced God originally and primarily as redeemer and liberator. In fact it would be more consistent with the experience of the Israel of the Exodus to view deliverance, liberation, and salvation as creating the conditions for the giving of the Law, and to regard the promulgation of the Law within the framework of the covenant as a continuing expression of the saving activity of God. The giving of the Law is premised logically upon the character of God as the covenanting, redeeming, and liberating God, and historically upon the deliverance of Israel from Egyptian oppression: "I am the LORD your God, who brought you out of the land of Egypt, out of the house of slavery" (Ex. 19:20; Deut. 5:6). God's covenanting and saving activity is presuppositional to His law-giving activity. Jesus was merely seeking to recover the primal experience of God as Savior. In what he said and did, he is demonstrating that God's active exercise of His royal power is primarily as compassionately saving rather than legally ruling power.

To be sure, the Jew of Jesus' time also believed in the reign of God. He or she could not have sung the psalms or the liturgy of the Temple unless he or she affirmed that "God reigns" (Ps. 97:1; 99:1). But it was also firmly believed that the condition for God's reign to come is the complete fulfillment of the Law. Thus, the kingdom of God will not come until the Law is fully and finally fulfilled. But the complete fulfillment of the Law is by human achievement. This implies that the human failure to fulfill the Law holds God hostage and prevents Him from exercising His reign. Until the Law is obeyed completely by the Jew, the Kingdom will not come. Human failure effectively stands in the way of God exercising His reign. And so the coming of the Kingdom is permanently relegated to the unforeseeable future!

Jesus reversed this timetable. He experienced God's reality in His coming from the distant future into the near present. God reigns by coming. He comes by breaking through the wall of human failure to obey the Law completely! He sovereignly sets aside obedience to the Law as a condition for coming redeemingly in His reign. He comes as reigning precisely by shattering the deadly grip of the Law upon God's people. He comes so near as to be in the midst of God's people to the point that His nearness can decisively alter redeemingly their life conditions. And so Jesus sought to realize his vision of God concretely in human terms by reshaping the social realities of his time! It is this experience of the coming reign of God as having drawn near to His people that seems to be the source of Jesus' boldness in declaring, "But I say unto you."

In conclusion, it is clear from what has been said that the reign of God in the experience and perspective of Jesus is a reality more primordial than the Law. The reign of God is in fact the basis of the Law and it must come to expression in human society through the Law. It is only the reign of God and none other that transcends the Law, and for this reason it alone can evaluate it. The Law is to be judged only by the One who reigns sovereignly over it and through it. And when God reigns by coming near at hand where the Law operates, as in the society of Israel, it inevitably seeks to find out whether it has indeed come to full expression through the workings of the Law. Jesus found out that this was not the case. Israel's obedience to the Law was found wanting both in the way its people had been treated and in the kind of social structures that it established. In the light of his vision of the coming reign of God drawing near, Jesus sought to bring about social change that would radically affect both the people and the social structure of Jewish society. What follows in the next three chapters seeks to describe these changes.

Notes

1. E. P. Sanders, *Jesus and Judaism* (London: SCM Press, 1985), p. 267.
2. Ibid., p. 268.
3. Ibid., p. 267.
4. Ibid., pp. 245-69.

CHAPTER 2

SAVING THE VICTIMS OF SOCIETY

Finding the Lost

The exercise of divine power as typically saving is amply illustrated by the character and thrust of Jesus' ministry, which was primarily to save. He spoke of his mission in terms of seeking and saving the lost (Lk. 19:10). He explained to the scribes and Pharisees who criticized him for receiving sinners and eating with them (Lk. 15:2) that his mission is like that of a sheep-owner who, having lost one sheep, leaves the ninety-nine in the wilderness to "go after the one that is lost until he finds it" (Lk. 15:3-4); or that of a woman who, having lost one of her ten silver coins, lights up a lamp, sweeps the house, and diligently looks for the lost coin until she finds it (Lk. 15:8). And when what was lost is found, the owner not only rejoices by herself but calls her friends and neighbors to rejoice with her (Lk. 15:5-7, 9-10).

What Jesus said about his mission, he went about doing. Who are the "lost" whom Jesus sought? The root sense of the word "lost" denotes someone or something that is not in its proper place and relationship, as a sheep which has gone astray and is not with the rest of the flock under the watchful eye of a shepherd (Lk. 15:4; cf. 11-32); or something that is not in its proper place, such as a coin that is not in the place determined by its owner as all the rest are (Lk. 15:8). Something is "lost" by reference to an order of relationship that is presumed to be right or proper, such as a flock with a shepherd, a son with his father, a coin with the others. What is "lost" if not found and restored to its rightful relationship or returned to its proper place will eventually perish or be destroyed. And so to find it is to save it by restoring it to its rightful place and proper order of relationship. Finding and saving it are a cause for great rejoicing.

In the synoptic tradition, the "lost" generally refers to "the sinners," and they include among others tax collectors (Mk. 2:17; Lk. 18:13; 19:7; cf. 6:32; 15:7, 10), harlots (Lk. 7:34, 37, 39), and the Gentiles (Mk. 14:41; Lk. 6:33; Mt. 5:47). "Sinners" are those who live outside the order framed by the Law. It is by reference to the Torah that a person is judged a sinner or righteous. A tax collector is a sinner because he serves a foreign master and engages in dishonest business. A harlot is a sinner because she violates the law against adultery and lives an immoral life. And Gentiles are outside the pale of the Law. Because "sinners" live "outside" the order of the Law, their lives and persons have taken on features that have "dirtied" or blemished them. A life that has become "dirty" is therefore unclean. It stinks and pollutes. And so it must be treated as outcast; or one must stay away from it.

Contrary to common practice based on the Law, Jesus deliberately sought a tax collector to be his friend and disciple (Mk. 2:14; Lk. 5:27-29), he sat at table fellowship with tax collectors and sinners (Mk. 2:15; Lk. 19:1-10), and allowed himself to be ministered to by a prostitute (Lk. 7:36-50). The scribes and Pharisees (the "righteous ones") were scandalized by this behavior of Jesus and they complained about it to his disciples (Mk. 2:16; Mt. 11:19; cf. Lk. 7:39; 15:1-2). In Jewish culture, table fellowship is the most socially intimate and direct kind of communion. The prayer uttered at table united those who ate of the same bread (cf. 1 Cor. 10:16-17). For Jesus to have table fellowship with sinners is to violate legal instructions which forbid association with evildoers (cf. Ps. 1; Isa. 52:11; cf. 2 Cor. 6:14-18). And so for Jesus to express solidarity with sinners is to treat lightly their contempt of the Law and to make oneself unclean with them.

Strangely enough, it is precisely those who were adjudged to be "sinners" and "unclean" under the criteria of the Law and were therefore "outcasts" from the order of the Law and so outside of the pale of salvation, who were the very ones brought into the sphere of the kingdom of God. Jesus brought them into the Kingdom by seeking and befriending them, by calling them to follow him, by expressing solidarity with them, and by forgiving their sins. He was thereby restoring them to their rightful status as members of the people of God, as children of Abraham (cf. Lk. 13:16; 19:9). The only condition for their entry into the Kingdom was their actual entry into it—as they were. This already constituted their repentance, their return to God. Their turning to Jesus was precisely their entry into the sphere of the Kingdom, which Jesus was because the Kingdom was at hand in and through him. Salvation now is no longer by reference to the Law but to the coming Kingdom of God which is at hand in and through Jesus. The coming Kingdom drawn near supplants the Law as the order of salvation. This, too, is part of the meaning of "But I say unto you."

Ironically, Jesus observed that it was the tax collectors and the harlots who were going into the Kingdom; whereas the "righteous ones" refused to enter (Mt. 21:28-32; cf. Lk. 7:28-30). In the parable of the Pharisee and the publican, it was the publican (i.e., tax collector) who went home "justified," that is, accepted by God; whereas the Pharisee who trusted in his own righteousness in the eyes of the Law was not (Lk. 18:9-14). In the parable of the Great Banquet, those who were formally invited did not come; instead, the "outcasts"—the poor, the maimed, the blind, the lame—were brought in (Lk. 14:15-24; Mt. 22:1-14). The rich young ruler who had observed the Law from his youth refused the invitation of Jesus to follow him (Mk. 10:13-16; Mt. 19:13-15; Lk. 18:18-30). The prostitute who washed the feet of Jesus, wiped them with her hair, kissed them, and anointed them (the unmistakable symbolic act of acknowledging Jesus as Lord and so of confessing discipleship) was forgiven of her many sins because "she loved much," while the Pharisee who invited Jesus to table was forgiven little because "he loved little" (Lk. 7:36-50).

Jesus reserved his most biting criticism against the scribes and Pharisees for their blatant hypocrisy (Mt. 23:1-36). He specially scorned them for deliberately shutting the Kingdom of heaven against people, while they neither entered themselves, nor allowed those who would enter to get in (Mt. 23:13-14). The tragic irony about the Pharisees is their twofold failure: by their hypocrisy they failed to fulfill the Law which they sought to obey assiduously, and by their lack of trust in Jesus they failed to enter the kingdom of God which they awaited so fervently. They sinned against both the Law and the kingdom of God. The "sinners" were saved while the "righteous" were left in limbo (Mk. 2:17).

Healing the Sick

Jesus did not come only to save sinners but also *to be a physician to the sick* (Mk. 2:17). With this we come to the so-called "miracle stories" in the Gospels. The Gospels tell of miracle stories *that happened to Jesus* (his birth, his baptism, his transfiguration, his resurrection, his ascension) and those that *he himself performed*. Of the latter, which is our concern here, there are generally four types: (a) the healing of the physically disabled or sick; (b) the liberation of the demon-possessed; (c) the bringing back to life of those who had just died (Mk. 5:21-43; Lk. 7:11-17; Jn. 11); and (d) the nature miracles, which include the feedings (Mk. 6:30-44; 8:1-9), the stilling of the storm (Mk. 4:36-41), the walking on the water (Mk. 6:45-52), the miraculous catch of fish (Lk. 5:1-11), the cursing of the fig tree (Mk. 11:12ff.), the turning of water into wine in Cana (Jn. 2:1-11).

Our main interest here is to describe the significance of the miracle stories as signs demonstrating the saving power of the kingdom of God. We shall not engage in a discussion about the nature of miracles as such, whether they are naturally or historically possible. Theologically our interest is in what is savingly possible with God. Nor shall we investigate their transmission in the history of tradition. Important as these issues are, we cannot discuss them as they entail complex, philosophical, scientific, and historical considerations that we cannot go into here. We shall here assume the truth of the canonical record that the miracle stories of Jesus form a significant part of his ministry. We shall also follow the judgment of most New Testament scholars that the healing ministry of Jesus was unique to him in the context of his Jewish and Hellenistic environment.

What constricts human life and so distorts and stunts it is not only the sins of the spirit, such as the failure to take seriously the will of God which results in the kind of unprincipled life or loose living that has no transcendent reference or standard by which it is guided and evaluated. This sin is exposed by the Law. A more subtle sin of the human spirit is blind hypocrisy, vaunted self-righteousness and lack of basic trust in Jesus Christ. This sin is disclosed in its gnawing emptiness by the coming of the kingdom of God.

It is a fact that there are also the more mundane yet deadly forces that restrict the growth of life, limit its possibilities, deprive it of meaning, and slowly but inevitably strangle it. The Gospels reveal what is universally suffered: physical want, infirmity, and disease; psychological phobias, emotional disorders, and mental dementia; natural catastrophes and senseless yet death-dealing happenings, such as injuries or fatal accidents; and mindless suffering of all sorts. There are evil forces abroad in the world which are inimical to human life and its future. The human being and his/her communities are in profound and desperate need of salvation from these forces, just as he/she does from the perversions of the spirit which have been indicated above.

The synoptic portrait of Jesus, especially in the Gospel of Mark, presents him as waging a battle against these evil forces (Mt. 11:2-7; Lk. 7:18-23). He saves those who have fallen victim to these forces. He suffers with them in their condition, delivers them from it, sets them on the way towards a whole and fuller life, and builds up their confidence in the life-giving power of God. He reveals himself not only as able to save victims but as having power over what victimizes them. He heals diseases, overcomes demons, forgives sins, stills the storm, gives life to the dead. He wields the power of good over the power of evil; he overcomes the power of destruction and death with the power of life.

The synoptic stories about this activity of Jesus have certain characteristics which demonstrate the saving power of the kingdom of God. For one thing, the term used most typically in the synoptics to designate this activity is *dynameis*, translated "mighty works" in the Revised Standard Version of the Bible (Mt. 11:21, 23; Lk. 10:13; Mk. 6:2; Mt. 13:54; Mk. 6:5; cf. Mt. 13:58). The word denotes what is at work in this activity of Jesus, namely, the mighty power of God. In the Old Testament the power of God was experienced by Israel in its most basic form, as the power to redeem and liberate, especially from the powers that oppress and enslave. Israel's primal experience of this power in its saving quality is, of course, the deliverance from Egypt (Ex. 6:26; 7:4; Deut. 3:24).

In the ministry of Jesus through his "mighty works," the same power is encountered in its most basic form as saving power: the power that heals, liberates, revivifies; the power of good that overcomes the power of evil. It is the saving power of the kingdom of God that Jesus supremely wields in his mighty works. He was intensely conscious of this: "But if it is by the finger of God [a metaphor for the power of God] that I cast out the demons, then the kingdom of God has come to you" (Lk. 11:20; cf. Mt. 12:28). He wields that power not merely to save the victims of evil, but to assault and overcome the center or concentration of the powers of evil, namely, Satan himself. Upon receiving the report from the seventy whom he sent out on a mission that "even the demons are subject to us in your name," Jesus exclaimed: "I saw Satan fall like lightning from heaven" (Lk. 10:17-20 RSV; cf. 11:14-23).

Another characteristic of the "miracle stories" that brings out the saving thrust of the kingdom of God is their *literary form*. The essential elements include the following: (a) it describes an aspect of human need such as a disease, a demon possession, hunger, fear, death; (b) it indicates a desire of the victim to be helped by Jesus by a move towards him with the confidence that one will be healed; (c) it denotes what Jesus says and does in dealing with the condition of human need; (d) it points to the results of what Jesus says or does—the disease disappears, the lame walk, the blind see, the storm is stilled; (e) finally, it describes the response which the mighty work evokes from those upon whom it is done, or who witness it. People are struck by the authority of Jesus, they are amazed by the healing deed, and so forth.

This literary pattern or form may be discerned in most of the miracle stories in the synoptic Gospels. While one example may not suffice, it can illuminate. A typical miracle story is the healing of the leper in Mark 1:40-45. This story divides itself into the following elements:

1. There is a nameless person suffering from leprosy; his condition includes not only suffering what was believed then to be an incurable and contagious disease but also bearing the pain of being an outcast (Lev. 13:45-56).

2. This person nevertheless comes to Jesus with the plea that Jesus heal him: out of hopelessness there emerges a glimmer of hope that Jesus could cure him, and so he goes to Jesus and seeks help.

3. Jesus cures him: instead of recoiling from the ugly disease, Jesus takes pity on him; instead of withdrawing and fleeing from him, Jesus stretches out his hand and touches him; and instead of telling him to keep his distance and casting him out farther from human community, Jesus speaks the healing word.

4. There is evidence of the cure: the leprosy disappears immediately.

5. There is the twofold restoration: the individual is healed in body, and at the same time returned to society.

6. There is a response from the person healed; he talks freely about his cure even though Jesus forbade him.

There are two points in this pattern worth noting as they bring out the saving thrust of the kingdom of God. One is the complete change in the condition of the person who comes to Jesus: he is changed from being sick to being whole. The story begins with a sad picture of human pain and suffering; it ends with a picture of healing and wholeness! This is a vivid and powerful portrayal of salvation. The other point is the disclosure of Jesus as having the power to save, which he wields effectively upon concrete human need and suffering. That power is not his own; it is the power of the kingdom of God that has come at hand and is at work in and through him.

There is a third characteristic of Jesus' exercise of the power of the Kingdom that underscores its saving thrust. It is the *refusal of Jesus to use this power to punish*. An incident in his ministry illustrates the point. In his final journey to Jerusalem, he sent messengers to Samaria to make ready his reception there. But the people refused to receive him (Lk. 9:51-53). The Samaritans would have liked Jesus to recognize Mt. Gerizim as the holy mountain where God is worshiped (Jn. 4:19-20), but Jesus was dead set on going to Jerusalem. Whereupon two of his disciples, James and John, suggested to him that they bid "fire to come down from heaven and consume them" (the Samaritans). This suggestion recalls Elijah as a man of God calling down fire from heaven to punish the soldiers sent to capture him by King Ahaziah (2 Kgs. 1:1-16). The suggestion of the two disciples included two notions that Jesus did not like. One is to prove his status as Son of God by a demonstration of divine power; the other is to use divine power to punish. Jesus rejected the suggestion of his disciples and he rebuked them (Lk. 9:54-55; cf. 13:1-5; Jn. 9:13). His refusal is consistent with his belief that the nature of the power of the Kingdom is love, and love is at its best when it is love of the enemy and seeks to do good to him (Lk. 6:27-36). Jesus came not to condemn and punish, but to save (cf. Jn. 3:17).

A fourth characteristic of Jesus' use of the power of the Kingdom is *its connection with faith*. Where his power was sought for display to elicit faith, he refused to use it (Mk. 8:11ff.; Mt. 12:38ff.). Where there was faith in his power to help, to heal, to save, he readily used it precisely to honor such a faith (Mk. 2:5; 5:34, 36; 10:52; Lk. 17:19; 18:42; Mt. 8:10; Mk. 9:23ff.). According to Leonard Goppelt, the formula, "Your faith has saved you" is "new and unique" to Jesus; he alone has connected salvation as a promise to faith.[1] The faith that receives the power that saves is one that trusts exclusively and absolutely in Jesus' readiness to help. It eschews any vestige of self-help or confidence in any other source of help except that of Jesus. It is faith in the power of God to save. It is in this power of God to save that Jesus enabled people to see who he was and in what he was doing. Pressed by helplessness in the face of what strangles life whether in the form of disease or demon possession or natural calamity, and impressed by the ministry of Jesus as unquestionably saving, people came to Jesus and quite simply trusted in his readiness and power to save! This is faith, the faith that saves!

Liberating the Poor

Jesus did not only seek and find the lost and heal the sick; he also preached the good news to the *poor,* proclaimed release to the *captives,* set at liberty those who are *oppressed,* and proclaimed the acceptable year of the Lord (Lk. 4:18-19; 7:22; Mt. 11:5). The poor, the captive, and the oppressed represent another form of human misery and suffering, the kind that comes from the evil that human beings do to their fellow human beings. People get "lost" by their own doing; the sick and infirm become victims of inimical forces—often nonhuman—about which there is little they can do, if anything. On the other hand, the poor, the captives, and the oppressed have their affliction inflicted upon them by their fellow human beings within the human community itself. Here we are dealing with social evil in its many forms: injustice, exploitation, oppression, marginalization, violence, war; in short, man's inhumanity to his fellowmen.

The "poor" in Luke's Gospel, following traditional usage, refers not only to the economically destitute but to the "politically powerless."[2] They cannot expect any help from the political establishment! In fact they are rendered poor precisely because of injustice in the political order. The only source of help they can look up to in hope is God. Following this usage in Luke, we will use the term "poor" to denote all those who suffer because they have been "marginalized" by the social order and do not have the political power to better their condition or make a significant difference in society and its order. We shall include in this term those who are captives and oppressed because they are victims of superior political power. And to the extent that the "lost" and the "sick" have become "outcasts" of society and cannot make any political difference in it because they are excluded from it, they also belong to "the poor."

The one thing all these types of people share in common is their political destitution by virtue of the fact that they are social "outcasts." It is not merely their economic deprivation but their social marginalization and political destitution that make them poor, although misery due to economic want is not denied. Zacchaeus was rich, but he was an "outcast" from his community and so he was "lost"; that is to say, he was in a wrong relationship to his community and so had no place in it. Because of this, he was not in a position to make a political difference in its order, and so he was "poor." To him and his household, Jesus brought the salvation of the Kingdom (Lk. 19:1-10).

From a prophetic perspective, it is best here to understand poverty as a condition brought about by injustice *in* or *of* the sociopolitical order. There are at least four basic components of this perspective. For one thing, it is considered the will of God that there shall be no poverty among His people (Deut. 15:4). While the Hebrews were in bondage in Egypt, they were all poor primarily because they had no rights as a people. In fact they were no people at all. It was from this *political poverty,* with its accompanying economic deprivation and suffering, that they were redeemed and liberated by God and made into a people of God through covenant and law and were promised a land of their own. It was this primal memory of what they once were in Egypt and of what God did to them to save them that constituted them as God's people and should be the basis and motivation for their treatment of "strangers" and "slaves" (Ex. 22:21-22; 23:9; Lev. 19:24; Deut. 10:18-19).

Following the conquest of Canaan and with the formation of the Hebrew amphictyony, all the tribes, except the Levites who were provided for in a special way, received a portion of the promised land so that none got started in a position of advantage over the others (Josh. 13:1–21:45). The "laws of the covenant" that came into effect in governing the community sought to prevent the deprivation of rights and to envisage a nation where poverty was absent (Deut. 15:3-4). Israel was to become a nation that lends to other nations but does not herself borrow from them; it shall rule over nations but it shall not itself be ruled (Deut. 15:6). Until this blessing happens those Israelites who are poor and needy must be treated unselfishly and generously and be redeemed from their deprivation (Lev. 25:35-38). If they are not given this due, they will cry out to the Lord against those who oppress them and the Lord will hold their oppressors guilty and punish them, as the Israelites in Egypt cried out to God and were redeemed by God by destroying their oppressors (Deut. 15:9). Every seventh year creditors are to release their debtors from their loan obligations, and every fiftieth year (the year of

Jubilee) all properties acquired through leases or defaults shall be returned to their original owners (Deut. 15:1; Lev. 25:1-24). Judges and rulers are to judge the people impartially, and they are not to accept bribes "for gifts blind the eyes even of wise and honest men, and cause them to give wrong decisions" (Deut. 16:18-20 GNB; 17:14-20; Ex. 23:6-8; Lev. 19:15-16). In other words, there is to be no oppression in the land, for God wills as His blessing the liberty of His people (Deut. 15:15). It is oppression and the deprivation of rights that are the root causes of both political and economic poverty!

The second component of the prophetic perspective follows from the first. If it is the will of God to prevent poverty, and His blessing is to redeem and set at liberty those who are oppressed, then it follows that *any emergence of poverty in the human community is of human making! It is socially and politically caused.*

With the rise of the monarchy in Israel, social conditions changed, economic development took place, the laws were not fully kept, and social stratification emerged. There arose a new social class—the landowners who also had political power. Some of them functioned as judges, that is, as rulers. This provided them with the opportunity to use their economic and political power to judge or rule unjustly and so to oppress. Injustice and oppression which render people poor in the sense of depriving them of their rights and so rendering them powerless are the makings of the rich and powerful. Injustice and oppression are evils that powerful people do to their less powerful brothers and sisters.

It is this phenomenon of poverty as humanly caused and as perpetrated by the powerful which is a major emphasis in prophetic thought. Some of the unjust practices in Israel have been vividly described by the prophets. Amos (760–750 B.C.) wrote about the righteous being sold into slavery for silver and of the needy for a pair of sandals; of the weak and helpless being trampled upon and of the poor being pushed out of the way; of justice being twisted and of people being cheated out of their rights (Amos 2:6-7; 5:7). Isaiah (742–687 B.C.) accused the powerful in Israel of making unjust laws that oppress people and keep the poor from having their rights and getting justice (Isa. 10:1-2; cf. Job 24:2-12).

Some of the ways by which the powerful oppressed the weak and the poor include the following: fraudulent commerce and exploitation (Amos 8:5; Mic. 6:10-11; Isa. 4:14; Jer. 5:27; 6:12), the forcible and illegal acquisition of lands (Mic. 2:1-3; Ezek. 22:29), dishonest courts (Amos

5:7; Jer. 22:13-17; Mic. 3:9-11; Isa. 5:23; 10:1-2), violence (2 Kgs. 23:30, 35; Amos 4:1; Mic. 3:1-2; 6:12; Jer. 22:13-17), slavery (Neh. 5:1-5; Amos 3:6; 8:6), unjust taxation (Amos 4:1; 5:11-12), and unjust functionaries (Amos 5:7; Jer. 5:28).

From this list one can see the sort of tools the powerful used to oppress the weak. They include among other things: (a) economic power, which is derived from land, commerce, and taxes; the sort of weapons only the wealthy can wield; (b) political power in the form of ruling, adjudicating, administering, allocating resources; the sort of power only the politically dominant are privileged to have; and (c) sheer and blatant abuse of power by those who are in a position to perpetuate injustice and oppression!

A third basic element in the prophetic perspective is God's response to the situation of political and economic poverty as humanly caused, particularly by the powerful. God's attitude is revealed by the way the prophets fiercely and uncompromisingly denounced it. God's judgment falls most severely upon the powerful: "The LORD has taken his place to contend, he stands to judge his people. The LORD enters into judgment with the *elders* and *princes* of his people: '*It is you* who have devoured the vineyard, the spoil of the poor is *in your houses*. What do you mean *by crushing* my people, *by grinding* the face of the poor?' says the Lord GOD of hosts" (Isa. 3:13-15 RSV; emphasis added). In this text it is the elders and princes, the powerful rulers who are responsible for administering justice, who stand accused by God for "grinding the face of the poor" (cf. Isa. 3:14-15).

Moreover, since poverty is humanly caused, it can also be humanly corrected by those who perpetrated it by returning to God (repentance) and hearing and doing his Word. In Isaiah 1:10-20 the "rulers" of Israel are compared to the rulers of Sodom and Gomorrah for the way they have misgoverned. They are asked to "hear the Word of the LORD" and to listen to the "teaching," that is to say, the Torah. The word and teaching that is spoken to the rulers is twofold. First, it expresses the Lord's disgust over the hypocrisy of their "solemn assemblies" and the iniquity of the leaders. Second, it exhorts the leaders *to do what they can* to correct the situation of injustice and oppression. "Wash yourselves; make yourselves clean; remove the evil of your doings from before my eyes; cease to do evil, learn to do good; seek justice, rescue the oppressed; defend the orphan, plead for the widow" (vv. 16-17). The subject of the verbs in this text are the rulers of Israel. The activity that is enjoined is *what they can and must do.* It is twofold: it is both a reformation of self (v. 16) and a reformation of society (v. 17) (cf. Amos 5:14-15).

Finally, a fourth aspect of the divine response to poverty is that God *takes up the cause of the poor.* This is best shown in a general way by describing God's attitude towards the stranger, the widow, and the orphan. These three symbolize poverty vividly and unmistakably.

The "stranger" is one who comes into a foreign land—as the Hebrews once were in Egypt—where he/she is of course a "foreigner." As a stranger in a foreign land, he/she has no family or relatives to welcome or help him/her, no resources of food and shelter; and no rights to anything, nor can he/she appeal to anyone for protection. He/she is the *helpless one* who has to depend entirely upon hospitality. The "stranger" in a foreign land typifies *the poor who is without rights* and is helpless and is entirely dependent on the hospitality and goodwill of others!

The "widow" is one who through the death of her husband has been deprived of her means of support and protection. She has been rendered poor, and no one would provide for her. And so the widow symbolizes the *deprived one,* the one who has been *made poor* through no fault of her own, and for whose care, provisions, and protection no one is under any obligation to render. She is completely dependent also on the goodwill of others who would voluntarily help.

Finally, there is the "orphan." He/she is not only the helpless one, not only the deprived one and rendered without means of support through the death of his/her parents, but also *the abandoned one,* the one left to fend for himself/herself in a harsh world with which he/she cannot yet cope. Who would love him/her as their own and adopt him/her into a home and nurture him/her into adulthood?

The combination of being a sojourner, widow, and orphan was precisely the condition of Israel in Egypt and God took special care of her. As God looked after Israel so now the Bible pictures God as especially concerned about the condition of the sojourner, the widow, and the orphan within Israel and looks after their welfare. He protects them, cares for them, and vindicates them (Ex. 22:22; Deut. 10:18; 16:4; 24:19-21; Isa. 1:17; Jer. 7:6; 22:3; Ezek. 22:7). And in so doing God shows Himself as taking up the cause of the poor passionately and generally.

The situation became a lot worse in the time of Jesus. The paying of taxes to Caesar (Mk. 12:13-17; Mt. 22:15-22; Lk. 20:21-26) was especially galling to the ordinary Jew because it represented political and economic deprivation. Following the Exile in 587 B.C. Israel lost her political independence and was ruled by a succession of pagan rulers (Persians, Greeks, Syrians, Romans and Roman vassals) to which she paid taxes which were onerous and heavy. There were only two social classes, the few rich and the vast majority of poor people. There was no middle class. The rich were relatively few, and except for a few among them such as the House of Herod, which was exceptionally rich by the standards of the time, their wealth appears vast only in comparison to the appalling poverty all around. Most of the wealth of the rich was derived from the land, wholesale trade and banking, and those who by birth were associated with the ruling class. The vast majority were working people: slaves, day laborers, skilled workers, shopkeepers, agricultural workers, fishermen, and so forth. Unemployment was a chronic problem and especially acute during the time of the ministry of Jesus and shortly after his death. Work on the Temple was being completed and some ten thousand workers were losing their jobs. Agricultural crisis was a constant threat. The poverty of the Jews at this time was quite well-known throughout the Roman Empire. In pagan comedies they were portrayed as beggars, with only one shirt apiece, obliged to feed themselves on carobs. One rabbi sadly said: "The daughters of Israel are beautiful; it is a pity that they should be made ugly by poverty."

The determination of social class was not only through political and economic means; it was also done religiously. Israel understood herself as a "chosen race." Religion and race were intertwined. To guarantee purity of religion, purity of racial pedigree was absolutely necessary. Moreover, purity of race was also absolutely required for the enjoyment of civil rights within the Jewish community. Within these parameters there were mainly two classes of people who enjoyed full civil rights: the priestly class (priests and Levites), and the nonpriestly but pure Israelites who could trace their pedigree to the original tribes of Israel. The rich were to be found among the priestly and leading families of the tribes. The vast majority of them however were poor.

Outside of these parameters of pure religion and race and full enjoyment of rights, there was a special class of people called the *am-ha-arez.* Who were they? Originally the word meant "people of the land" or "people of the earth." But in the course of time the term came to cover a wide variety of human groups that had one common feature among them, namely, they were originally foreigners who occupied Jewish land and intermarried with the Jews. Their descendants were a mixed race, such as the Samaritans. The *am-ha-arez* were impure Jews both by race and religion, for they did not follow the Law strictly. Accordingly they were despised, rendered outcasts, and did not enjoy civil rights and so were politically and economically marginalized. Commerce, marriage, and hospitality to them were strictly forbidden! The contempt of the rabbis for this class of people was cruel and severe. Rabbi Hillel regarded them as anything but human. Rabbi Jonathan hoped that every one of these wretches might be split into two like a fish. A Jew was forbidden to marry the daughter of an *am-ha-arez* in compliance with Deuteronomy 27:21, which states: "Cursed be he who lies with any kind of beast" (RSV; cf. Ex. 22:19), apparently including an *am-ha-arez* within the category of "beast."

Here was a class of people who were the unfortunate victims of a systemic and merciless marginalization process carried out through racial, political, economic, and religious structures that had been entrenched institutionally through generations. They were even below the "proletarian" class. They were the poorest of the poor, "the least" of the brothers of the Son of Man (Mt. 25:31-46). They consisted of ill-paid workers, day laborers, slaves, beggars (which abounded in Jerusalem at the time), "all who labor and are heavy-laden" (Mt. 11:28 RSV). They had been cast out by Jewish society and so they could not hope to improve their lot within or through this society. They were laden with a twofold burden: public contempt and exclusion, and life without hope of salvation. How can they be helped?

Why Preaching Is Connected with the Poor

We must now note that Jesus connects the preaching of the good news directly with "the poor" (Mt. 11:5; Lk. 4:18). The *good news* meant is obviously the coming Kingdom of God drawn near (Lk. 6:20; Mt. 5:3). Does this mean then that the preaching of the good news of the kingdom of God drawn near is indeed the answer to the twofold burden of the poor who have been described above? Is this not rather an impertinent answer to a very desperate situation? How can the poor who are marginalized by an inhuman and oppressive society be delivered from their dispossession by the mere proclamation of an apparently religious event with a message? Can a political problem be solved by a religious proclamation?

To get a handle on the beginnings of an answer to this question, we must note first that the statement that connects the preaching of the good news with the poor is a quotation from the Old Testament (Isa. 61:1). We must, therefore, trace the significance of this practice to its roots in the Old Testament. An analysis of the early usage of the Hebrew word *basar* ("proclaim the news"), for example, in 2 Samuel 18:20-31, reveals several important structural elements, which include the following:

1. What is "told" or "proclaimed" is some *happening* or *event*, not some opinion or idea or theory or worldview. In the case of 2 Samuel 18, the event has to do with the victory of King David's forces over the rebellion led by his son, Absalom, which resulted in the death of Absalom himself (18:9-16). This is an event with two dimensions. On the one hand, it is a victory in battle, and so it is a reason for rejoicing. On the other hand, it is a victory with a tragic element, namely, the death of the king's son, and so it is also a reason for mourning.

2. News of this event must be *told* to the persons or the community that has an interest or stake in it, but who has not heard about it yet. In the example under consideration, the news about the battle and its outcome has to be told to David and his people. The king himself was at the gate of the city anxiously awaiting news about the battle (18:24).

3. For the news to be told to the interested party, a runner must be commissioned officially to bring the news to those who must hear it. If the news about the event is straightforward, there may be no difficulty about communicating it. But if the event is ambiguous, containing a reason for both celebration and mourning, it is not easy to tell the news about it. The telling of the news can have implications for both the teller and the hearer. One cannot predict with certainty the impact of the proclamation of the message. In the case under consideration, a non-Israelite was chosen by Joab so that if anything happens to him as a result of telling the news, he will not be a loss to the community itself (18:21). The official runner was forbidden to bring the news to the king precisely because of what the king might do to him. The official herald voluntarily went to tell the news just the same, ready to face the risk (18:19-20, 22-23).

4. Here we come to the most critical element: *it is as the news is told that the event makes an impact upon those who hear about it.* The event

did not make an impact yet upon the interested party when it happened, but only when the news about it was told. It happened earlier than when news about it was told, and where it happened was different from where news about it was told. News about it needed to be brought to where it was to be told. Yet, it was only when news about it was told that the event became real and meaningful to, and evoked a response from, the people who heard it. *It is not so much the happening of the event as the telling of the news about it that makes an impact and produces a response!* David wept in profound grief not at the moment when Absalom died, but when he received the news about his death (18:28-33). And the victory in battle which was to have been celebrated became an occasion for mourning for all the people because the king grieved over the loss of his son (19:1-2). *The event becomes real and makes an impact that alters the status quo through the telling of the news about it.*

5. Since the event has to be told in the form of news about it, the runner/teller of the news about the event has a critical role. *He must tell the truth about the event.* He must therefore be an eyewitness to the event. The instruction of Joab to the Cushite was: "Go, tell the king what you have seen" (18:21). But it is what *he has seen* of the event that he must tell. He may not have seen all that must be seen to tell the whole truth about the event. And what he may have seen, because it is fragmentary or partial, may only distort the truth about the event. In any case, his responsibility is to tell what he has seen. Moreover, *he has to tell* what he has seen. This makes of him an "interpreter" of the event. *It is what he understands and can tell in his own words of what he has seen that becomes news about the event.* And finally, he has to tell the news about the event to another audience and place different from where the event happened. This makes of him a "translator" of the event: he transfers the news from one audience to another! He bears the burden of truth and its impact. *What he tells of the event is what will be heard as news and could make a critical difference to the way things are!*

In the prophecy of Isaiah, "proclaiming the good news" has become almost a technical theological term (see Isa. 40:9; 41:27; 52:7; 60:6; 61:1). It is now used to denote (a) God's activity, (b) which is almost always saving for Israel, (c) thus bringing about a change in the way things are when it is told, and so (d) giving rise to public rejoicing and festival. Isaiah 52:7 enshrines the theological substance of the use of *basar.* "How beautiful upon the mountains are the feet of him who brings good tidings, who publishes peace, who brings good tidings of good, who publishes salvation, who says to Zion, 'Your God reigns'" (RSV). As in Samuel, there is an event—a deed of God—that has happened. It has to do with peace and salvation. Therefore, it is good. It has to be told, and it has to be told as *good news.* A runner/teller has been officially commissioned to publish the good news, and he runs from the place of happening to the place of telling. *It is when the message is told that it makes its impact and evokes a response. It is the telling of the news about the event through the witness of the teller that alters the course of things in a saving way!*

The same structure and meaning are presupposed in the New Testament language about the preaching or proclamation of the good news of the coming kingdom of God drawn nigh. There are, of course, some new things about its usage here. We must note them. First, it is not simply about some event of God's doing that is proclaimed, but God Himself as coming in His reign by drawing near to His people. What is told is *the event of His coming near* in exercise of His royal power. He reigns by coming to His people himself. In the process of His coming, He does certain things that signify His coming. And His coming itself is the primal expression of His reign. *That He reigns by coming near* is the good news.

Second, God comes to His people directly in the person and activity of Jesus Christ. He reigns precisely by coming in Jesus Christ through who he is and what he says and does. God does not stay put and do something in some place and time and then send a runner/messenger to bring the good news to His people. Rather, He comes directly in reality, presence, and power in the person and activity of Jesus Christ. His coming in Jesus Christ does not happen elsewhere and then is told somewhere. Rather, in Jesus Christ both the event of His coming and its telling happen at the same time and in the same place in who Jesus is and what he says and does. Both the reality and impact of His reign in His coming are simultaneous; there is no intervening time and space between the one and the other. The reason for this is that what God in Christ *says* happens, and what *happens* is what He says. The "Word" of God's reign in His coming happens by the "act" of proclaiming it.

Third, the purpose of God's coming is to save. His intention is to assault and overcome the evil powers and structures that oppose Him and marginalize and dehumanize His people, and to rescue their victims and bring healing and wholeness to them. The aim of God in His coming in Jesus Christ is to transfigure human life and alter its conditions so that it may fulfill its full potential in being created in His image and saved and fulfilled for His glory.

Fourth, the coming of God who reigns by saving takes place among those most in need of salvation. And these are "the poor," the outcasts of society and of history who cannot expect any hope of salvation from society and history because both are irresistibly working against them. Any possibility of hope for them must come *to* and *not from* their condition of dispossession. This is precisely the point of the coming kingdom of God drawing near by being preached as good news to the poor!

Fifth, the impact of the reigning presence of God in the midst of the poor is precisely the fall of Satan like lightning from heaven (see Lk. 10:18; 11:20). This means that all the evil forces that render people poor, whether physical, political, economic, racial, and religious, and the ways they are systematically organized into centers of oppression through social structures, processes, and institutions and through "man's inhumanity" to his fellow human beings are to be overcome and destroyed. There is to be a reordering of power structures in such a way that the mighty are put down from their thrones and those who are of low degree are exalted, and the hungry are filled with good things while the rich are sent away empty (Lk. 1:52-53). At the same time there is to be a restoration of the outcasts to the dignity that is proper to them as members of the people of God.

The impact of the coming of God who reigns in a saving way is precisely what Jesus told the disciples whom John the Baptist sent to inquire of Jesus whether it was he who is to come: "In that hour he cured many of diseases and plagues and evil spirits, and on many that were blind he bestowed sight. And he answered them, 'Go and tell John what you have seen and heard: the blind receive their sight, the lame walk, lepers are cleansed, and the deaf hear, the dead are raised up, the poor have good news preached to them. And blessed is he who takes no offense at me' " (Lk. 7:21-23 RSV; cf. Mt. 11:2-6). *In short, through what Jesus said and did, the conditions that make for poverty are altered, the victims of poverty are redeemed, and the powers of marginalization are overcome.*

Finally, the language of proclaiming the good news of the Kingdom through preaching and teaching and healing is essentially parabolic or symbolic (Mt. 13:3-50; Mk. 4:2-34). The metaphor is the mode in which Jesus characteristically spoke of the coming near of the kingdom of God. What is characteristic about the parables of the Kingdom, among other things, is their open-ended character: they invite the hearer to participate in effecting what the parable intends (cf. Mt. 13:44-46). The hearer is drawn into the narrative and challenged to participate in its plot and its decisive events. Since the coming of the Kingdom effects a reversal in the order of things, such as when a man finds a treasure hidden in a field and then "*goes* and *sells* all that he has and *buys* that field," the hearer is challenged to effect such a reversal in his life and condition. This is the decisive point about repentance and believing as the proper response to the Kingdom drawn near: to repent is to reverse the usual order of things and the normal direction of life, it is to return to God by seeking His Kingdom first; to believe is to have faith not in the power structures operative in society, nor in any other power, but in the power of the Kingdom that is already altering in a redeeming way those power structures which up till now only oppress and marginalize!

If all this is what is entailed in the preaching of the good news of the Kingdom to the poor, then the poor have reason to rejoice and to hope. The coming near of the Kingdom makes them "blessed" because it is the power that can alter their situation, redeem them from their poverty, and restore them to the dignity and vocation and hope that are proper to them in God's Kingdom. God reigns precisely in the preaching of the good news to the poor. No wonder it was the faceless "crowds" or "multitudes" consisting mainly of the poor who thronged to hear Jesus (Mk. 3:7-12). He gave them a reason for rejoicing by enabling them to catch a vision of hope in the reign of God who has come to save and redeem His people. Does the religious reality of the kingdom of God drawn near through proclamation alter the order and structure of society by repentance and faith? The ministry of Jesus seems to provide the basis for a positive answer to this question. *A religious revolution is the presupposition of a sociopolitical one!*

Notes

1. Leonard Goppelt, *Theology of the New Testament,* Vol. 1 (Grand Rapids, Mich.: E. B. Eerdmans Publishing Company, 1981), p. 151.
2. Frederick W. Danker, *Jesus and the New Age: A Commentary on Luke's Gospel* (Philadelphia: Fortress Press, 1988), p. 106.

CHAPTER 3

SAVING THE ELITES OF SOCIETY

The "Righteous" Need Salvation Also

We have now dealt with three types of people in Jewish society as ordered by the Mosaic dispensation. These are "the lost," "the sick," and "the poor." These people represent the victims of this society, and so they are also evidence of the victimizing power of its order and structure. Jesus ministered to them by both redeeming them and overcoming the powers that victimized them. He did this out of resources not available in the Mosaic dispensation but out of the coming near of God's reign in who he was and in what he said and did.

We now come to a fourth type of people, quite different from the other three. These are "the rich" and "the righteous." These people represent the best of what can be attained in human life and destiny through the resources available in the Mosaic dispensation. Obviously, their need, if there was any, was not the same as those of the victims of this society. Did they have any need at all? If so, what was it? Did the kingdom of God as proclaimed by Jesus have any saving significance to them at all? Did Jesus minister to these people also? After all, did he not say that "those who are well have no need of a physician, but those who are sick; I have come to call not the righteous but sinners"? (Mk. 2:17). These people were apparently "well" and "righteous." They did not need the kind of saving ministry that Jesus rendered to the lost and sick and poor! But did that mean that they had no need of salvation at all or that Jesus simply consigned them to limbo and did not offer salvation in the Kingdom to them? Did the call to repent and believe apply only to sinners but not also to the righteous? (Lk. 15:7, 10).

An answer to this question has critical significance for mission theology and the task of evangelism. If the answer is that Jesus offered salvation only to those who have need of a physician, then mission is no more than simply the search for "the dregs of society" and the task of evangelism is no more than simply to save them from the "gutter" and reform their lives by offering them Christ as a personal Savior and Lord to be appropriated in faith as a personal decision. If this were the *only* truth—and we do not deny this truth—then we confine mission evangelism only to the victims of a society and may even ignore the victimizing power of a society.

But a society also produces not only the "worst" but also the "best" among its people. There are those in it who attain to the best it can offer, those who reach the top as measured by its own standards and so can serve as models of its virtue. Does the gospel of the kingdom of God have nothing to say to those who have already achieved the best of human potentiality in a given society and its culture? Do the paragons of virtue in a society lack nothing at all? Does the best of a society and its culture already represent the "best" of the kingdom of God? Does not "the least" in the kingdom of God transcend and surpass even "the best" in any society and culture? If this be so, then clearly the elites in any society have need of salvation too, and the society that produces them has need of transformation as well simply because it produces good people who are not good enough by the standards of the kingdom of God!

The Elite Rich

And so we ask: In what sense were "the rich" of Jesus' day rich but not rich enough? In what sense were "the righteous" righteous but not righteous enough? We must distinguish between one who is rich but not righteous and one who is righteous but poor, and one who is both rich and righteous! A good example of the former is Zacchaeus. He was rich but not righteous because he was a tax collector and so a sinner; he belonged to "the lost sheep of the house of Israel"! An example of one who is poor but righteous is the poor widow who gave to the Temple all that she had out of her poverty, and so gave more than all those who gave out of their abundance (Mk. 12:41-44; Lk. 21:1-4). A good example of one who is both rich and righteous is the rich young ruler who came to Jesus in search of eternal life (Mk. 10:17-22; Mt. 19:16-30; Lk. 18:18-30). These three Gospels agree that this man was rich materially: "he had great possessions." These three Gospels testify to the fact that he had observed the Law. Luke adds that this man had observed the Law from his youth (Lk. 18:21). This means that this man was not only educated but he had the right education. And so he knew the Law. But not only did he know the Law, he practiced it, he lived by it, he conformed to its standards! Therefore, he was "righteous" by the standards of the Law. Moreover, Luke notes that this man was "a ruler." He had reached a position of political and social power. Matthew observes that this man was still "young" and so was healthy and strong (Mt. 19:22). In short, this man had all that is best: youth, health, wealth, education, virtue, and power! All this was available in his society and he had all of them.

Did Jesus decry his possession of all this? By no means! Mark has noted the attitude of Jesus: "And Jesus looking upon him *loved* him" (10:21 RSV; emphasis added). Jesus "loved" him not only for his earnestness and achievement, but also for his apparently sincere search for something better than the best that he had already attained. He wanted to "inherit eternal life" and in his perception this was a good quite different from, and better than, all the good that he already achieved and possessed! What else should he "do" to attain it? With all the good that he already possessed—youth, health, wealth, education, virtue, and power—he still believed that he was not "saved," for salvation here is equivalent to "inheriting eternal life." He wanted to add "eternal life" to the string of good that he already had. He believed he could have it by "doing." Jesus saw in the rich young ruler a desire "to be perfect" by self-achievement (Mt. 19:21). And this was something that must be appreciated by all means! By the same token, societies and cultures that make it possible for their people to attain the best they can offer and still foster the search for something better than the best they can give must be commended and affirmed. But does this mean that there is nothing lacking in its best anymore? How did Jesus handle this rich young ruler? We will return to this question later.

The Elite Righteous

Our concern is not with the rich but unrighteous, nor with the righteous but poor, but with the elite righteous and with the elite rich and righteous. We turn first to "the elite righteous" of Jesus' day. Who were they and in what sense were they righteous? The standard by which "righteousness" was measured was, of course, the Law of Moses and the tradition which sought to apply it. It was the same standard by which the lost, the sick, and the poor were measured. It was also the same standard by which "the righteous" were to be measured. In the time of Jesus, there were three kinds of people who made the claim that they were "righteous" by the standard of the Law. These were the priests, the scribes, and the Pharisees.

The meaning of the root word in Hebrew from which the word translated "priest" is derived means "to stand." A *priest* is one who stands before God as His servant and minister. He represents God to God's people, and he stands to represent the people in their vocation as God's people to God. Therefore, he must represent the holiness of God to God's people, and the holiness of God's people to the Holy God. He must be holy both to God and to the people (Lev. 21:6-8). Priesthood enshrines one cardinal principle: to serve God, one must be "like" Him in character and purpose. Because of this, the priest's being and function are most strictly regulated by the Law.

The position of priest is hereditary: he must be a member of the tribe of Levi (Ex. 28:1, 41; 29:9; Lev. 1:5, 7-8, 11; Num. 3:10; 18:7). Purity of Levitical pedigree was absolutely required. Moreover, the priest must be free from any physical defects (Lev. 21:16-23). He must be consecrated according to a prescribed ritual (Ex. 29:1ff.; Lev. 8:5ff.) and must wear officially prescribed vestments (Ex. 29:27ff.). He must marry only a virgin from his tribe, not a racially impure or divorced woman (Lev. 21:7). He must be clean and without blemish. All this has one purpose: to symbolize the sanctity of God and the priest's high calling to serve Him.

His functions as priest carry the same meaning and purpose. This task includes, among other things, the conduct of public worship according to the system of sacrifice, for only the priest may sacrifice (Num. 18:5, 7); giving instructions in the ways and requirements of God (cf. Mal. 2:67; Jer. 18:18); maintaining the institution of the Temple; and after the Exile fiscal administration of Judah was handed over to the Temple authorities (Ezra 8:33-34). The last two functions form the background for the activities in the Temple which Jesus denounced (Mk. 11:15-17).

What was the attitude of Jesus towards the priesthood? Despite the fact that some of his enemies came from this class of people, including the chief priests (Mk. 11:18) and whatever he may have thought about the character of some of the members of the priesthood, it is safe to conclude that Jesus on the whole did not repudiate the priestly system, which was a subsidiary part of a much larger system or institution, namely, Temple worship. He respected it as evidenced, for instance, by his instruction to the lepers whom he cured to show themselves to the priests in the Temple and do the customary offerings and ceremonies for purification (Mk. 1:44; Lk. 7:14). Is there nothing wrong then with the priests and the priesthood and, by representation, with the institution of Temple worship? We will deal with this issue below.

The *scribes* were a different class of people, although their vocation was primarily related to the Law, as well. Unlike the priests, scribes came from all sectors of Jewish society. The position was not hereditary. There was one qualification that was absolutely required: a study of the Law under competent teachers. The education of a scribe followed strictly a prescribed course. During a long period of training, the would-be scribe lived permanently with his teacher, who was a professional scribe. He heard and studied his lectures, he observed how his teacher carried out the duties of his profession, how he obeyed and applied the precepts of the Law. The purpose of this training was twofold: to master the tradition of the Law and to learn how to apply it. When he was deemed ready, he was then ordained and joined the professional class of interpreters and teachers of the Law. A scribe was one who by vocation and training knew the Law, interpreted it, taught it, applied it, defended it, and perpetuated it. This group of people grew as a professional class only after the Exile when the Law became "the soul of Judaism." The scribes were held in high esteem because of their theological competence. Was there anything wrong with them? Why were they associated with the Pharisees as critics and enemies of Jesus who eventually plotted with others to eliminate him? To this issue we will return below.

Finally, there were the *Pharisees*. Theirs was a lay movement, consisting largely of merchants and craftsmen, in contrast to the priestly class and the scribes, who were a mixed group composed of both priests and laypeople. This movement got started about the second half of the second century B.C. in the struggle to resist Hellenic influences that were believed to have a corrupting effect upon the Jewish faith. While the derivation of the word "Pharisee" is obscure, there is some measure of agreement among scholars that it comes from the Hebrew *parash*, which means "one who is separate." The word *parash* is also associated with the Hebrew word for "holy," *qadosh* (cf. Lev. 11:44-45). To be separate is to be holy. The root meaning has a double sense. On the one hand, there is the sense of being separate from what corrupts. While initially this meant resisting the Hellenization of the Jewish faith by keeping away from it at a safe distance, it eventually took on the meaning of separating from all that was regarded as "unclean" in the light of the Law, as for instance the *am-ha-arez,* "the people of the land" who were "impure" by race and religion, or the "sinners and tax collectors" with whom Jesus kept company, but of this behavior of Jesus the scribes and Pharisees strongly complained (Lk. 15:1-2).

On the other hand, there is the sense of sticking adhesively and rigorously to what makes for sanctity and purity, for holiness. This meant in practice a strict interpretation of the Law and scrupulous adherence to it, for it was the Law understood as God's will and therefore demanding strict and absolute obedience which made for separation unto holiness! This led to the development of an elaborate system of a legal and ritual tradition which the Pharisees observed with fanatical rigor. And so they were accused by their opponents of building a wall around the Law so that what became of paramount importance to them was the wall itself and not what it protected. This was partly reflected in the criticism of Jesus about neglect of the weightier matters of the Law in Matthew 23:23, to which we will return later. The Pharisees did not only pay the tithe, which was a lay obligation, but adhered closely to the regulations for purity, such as "the washing of hands before meals," which was a ritual duty laid only upon priests (Mk. 7:1-5). This together with the titles by which they designated themselves, such as "the pious," "the righteous," gave the impression that the Pharisees understood themselves to be "the holy ones," "the true Israel," "the priestly people of God."[1] The Pharisee was driven by the passion to be holy in terms of the standards of the Law as he understood them. So then what was wrong with the Pharisee and his movement?

From what has been said it now seems clear that the four groups of people we have just described were the cream of the crop in Jewish society, using the Law as the standard of measurement. We use them here also as a representative group to model the best of what a human being can be in the Mosaic dispensation. As such they represent a sharp contrast to the other group of people which was described earlier in the preceding chapter. We also use this group here to reflect the worst of what a human being can become in Jewish society, namely, to become lost, sick, and poor.

Both groups of people, the "worst" and the "best," can provide models of what people can be in any given society that is ordered by law. Law need not be written or surrounded with the aura of divine majesty, so long as it provides a basis and a framework for the ordering of human life-together in small or large communities. We have seen how salvation in the form of the coming near of the kingdom of God affected the lives of the victims of Mosaic society through the ministry of Jesus. We must now see how the other group of people was affected by the same saving event that had broken through in Jewish society through the ministry of Jesus Christ! If we succeed in portraying the way Jesus handled this other group we would then have a total picture of the way salvation in the Kingdom of God through the ministry of Jesus affected the representative groups of people in Jewish society. How did Jesus minister in a saving way to the rich and righteous of Jewish society?

Exposing What Is Lacking and Wrong with the Elite

Jesus' strategy of ministering to the rich and the righteous initially sought to build on their desire to realize the best that was available to them in the Law. They wanted to become perfect by the standards of the Law. Moreover, they sincerely believed that they were on the way towards fulfilling this purpose in terms of the way they were carrying on. The precepts and practices which they observed in becoming perfect by the Law were themselves understood by them as part and parcel of the Law. If they were to be judged in their understanding and performance the only fair rod of measurement would be the Law itself. It would seem that Jesus had no trouble with this. He would only be fulfilling a policy he had laid down at the beginning of his ministry, namely, to fulfill the Law completely and to encourage others to do so (Mt. 5:17-19).

But Jesus went beyond this. He also judged the Law in terms of something higher than it, namely, the coming kingdom of God which has drawn near in and through him. It was the searchlight of the Kingdom and its righteousness that Jesus used in evaluating the righteousness of the Law and of those who sought to fulfill it (Mt. 5:20). This had the effect of exposing what is still lacking in the best of a society and its elites, as well as revealing what is distorted and wrong in it.

The shape of Jesus' ministry to the rich and righteous of Israel included the following elements: (a) he affirmed or appreciated what they sought; (b) he pointed out what was lacking in them; (c) he exposed what they were in effect truly after, namely, their idolatry; (d) he pronounced "woes" upon them; (e) and finally, all this constituted virtually a call to repentance and faith in response to the Kingdom that had drawn near in and through him. We have already dealt with the first. We will deal with (b) and (c) together in what follows, and with (d) and (e) in the final section.

We have already noted Jesus' appreciation for the rich young ruler who came to him (see p. 54). Seeing his desire to be perfect, Jesus pointed out to him the "lack" that he had asked Jesus about (Mt. 19:20-21). What he "lacked" was not apparent in the light of the Law. In fact, from the perspective of the Law he did not seem to lack anything, for all that the Law had required of him he had observed from his youth. The lack could only be seen and specified in the light of the coming near of the Kingdom. Jesus said to the young man: "If you would be perfect, go, sell what you possess and give it to the poor, and you will have treasure in heaven; and come, follow me" (Mt. 19:21 RSV). The "perfection" that is enjoined here is that of the Kingdom, not of the Law. What the rich young ruler was asked to do follows exactly the movement of the Kingdom, which is to reverse the present order and direction of his life, namely, to go, sell what he had and give it to the poor and then to come after Jesus and follow him. Jesus likened the movement of the coming of the Kingdom to a "treasure hidden in a field, which a man found and covered up; then in his joy he goes and sells all that he has and buys that field" (Mt. 13:44 RSV). The rich young ruler was shown what he lacked and given concrete advice as to how to fulfill it. He was given a definite choice between following the righteousness of the Law or the righteousness of the Kingdom.

He made a choice, but it was not to move with the Kingdom and follow Jesus. Instead the young man "went away sorrowful; *for he had great possessions*" (Mt. 19:22 RSV; Mk. 10:22; Lk. 18:23). The final choice of the rich young ruler was not for eternal life; it also was not for the righteousness of the Law; and it definitely was not for the kingdom of God and discipleship in Jesus. What he valued most, the one thing he clung to and would not let go because it was proof of his achievement and merit, the source of his security and the promise of his destiny, was his wealth. This was his idol (cf. Mt. 5:24). It was not wealth as such, but the *idolizing* of wealth which blinded the rich young ruler and prevented him from seeing what really counts in God's eyes. It is not wealth as treasure in itself but *treasuring it for ourselves on earth* which hinders us from laying up treasures for *ourselves in heaven* (Mt. 5:19). This young man preferred to be rich "for himself" rather than "rich toward God" (Lk. 12:21). His fatal sin was the idolatry of wealth, not the mere possession of wealth. One can be rich without idolizing wealth. An advice from Paul to Timothy is worth heeding: "But those who *desire to be rich* fall into temptation, into a snare, into many senseless and hurtful desires that plunge men into ruin and destruction. *For the love of money* is the root of all evils; it is through *this craving* that some have wandered away from the faith and pierced their hearts with many pangs. . . . As for the rich in this world, charge them not to be haughty, *nor to set their hopes on uncertain riches but on God* who richly furnishes us with everything to enjoy. *They are to do good, to be rich in good deeds,* liberal and generous, thus *laying up for themselves a good foundation for the future,* so that they may *take hold of the life which is life indeed"* (1 Tim. 6:9-10; 17-19 RSV).

What was wrong with the *priesthood* and the Temple worship, especially those who ministered in the Temple in Jerusalem? We have already noted that the priests had a tradition of doing some measure and form of fiscal administration in the Temple. Moreover, sacrificial worship at the Temple required certain services, such as the following: the supply and sale of suitable animals and birds (doves) for sacrifice; their inspection to safeguard their purity and their fitness for sacrifice, a service which necessarily entailed a fee; the exchange of the pilgrims' foreign money into Jewish currency that did not bear the image of a foreign king or emperor and was acceptable to the Temple authorities, and this also entailed a fee; buying and selling, which were necessary not only to maintain Temple worship but also to provide convenient service to pilgrims who came from many countries (Mk. 11:15-16).

It seems safe to conclude that all this necessary activity was authorized by the Temple authorities and that some of the priests were involved in it. That means the Temple priesthood engaged in, and profited from, this complex of business activity that went on in the Temple. But now Jesus charged that this Temple trade although authorized was carried out in dishonesty. Those who sold animals for sacrifice and those who charged fees for services were "robbing" their customers.

Furthermore, to avoid exposure they took refuge in the protection afforded them by their sacred duties and the sanctuary of the Temple. All this made of the Temple a "den of robbers." One could not resist the conclusion that the Temple priesthood called to serve God in sacred duties was now engaged in trade in a dishonest way for its own profit! This was a prostitution of the priestly calling! And worst of all, it "put God at the service of sin."[2] *This was what was terribly wrong with the priesthood. It worshiped at the altar of mammon. Called to sanctity, it became a sacrilege! Judged by the Law, it was found wanting!*

But was clergy involvement in the Temple trade all that Jesus attacked? The record speaks of Jesus *driving out* those who bought and sold and *overturning* the tables of the money changers and the seats of those who sold doves (Mk. 11:15-16). But the services of trade, money-changing, and inspection of animals for sacrifice were absolutely necessary for the institution of the Temple and the sacrificial system of worship that it enshrined. This complex of activity was the mechanism for securing its basic material support. Remove it and the whole Temple institution would be placed in grave crisis. In driving out the traders and overturning their tables, was not Jesus thereby undermining the whole Temple institution, including the sacrificial system of worship and the priesthood that went along with it? Was Jesus merely reforming the system of worship, or seeking its "destruction" and its possible "restoration" in a new form which would make God's house truly a "house of prayer"?

Other texts in the record indicate that Jesus seems to have meant something more than merely "cleansing the Temple" in driving out the traders and overturning their tables. Mark 13:1 speaks of Jesus as *predicting* the *destruction* of the Temple. Mark 14:57ff. speaks of someone reporting that he heard Jesus say, "I will destroy this temple that is made with hands and in three days I will build another, not made with hands" (RSV; cf. Mt. 26:60f.). This text reports that Jesus *threatened* the Temple with its destruction. Whether as prediction or threat, Jesus must have said something publicly or in the hearing of some people to the effect that the days of the Temple were already numbered! While it involves complex considerations that we cannot deal with here, I subscribe to the scholarly view that Jesus saw the replacement of the Temple as an institution of the Mosaic dispensation with another form of worship in which he would play a decisive part and in which the Gentiles would be included (Mk. 1:17; cf. Jn. 3:19-24). From this perspective, his action of ridding the Temple of its channel of support and his condemnation of priestly involvement in it are to be understood properly not as an act of reform but as an act of prophetic symbolism that signaled and dramatized and anticipated the abolition of the Temple.[3]

The reaction of the Temple authorities to the action of Jesus was swift and determined. Realizing the impact of the threat of destruction in what Jesus did, they "sought a way to destroy him" (Mk. 11:18 RSV). In the end they succeeded. Ironically enough, the Temple, too, was destroyed in A.D. 70 by the Romans, and it has never been restored until now. Instead a new form of worship has come into being, one that memorializes the sacrificial death of Jesus Christ and celebrates his resurrection into glory and anticipates the consummation of the kingdom of God, when God shall be all in all and through all and above all!

If it is true that Jesus saw the imminent abolition of the Temple and acted dramatically to symbolize it, what could have been the basis of his perception and judgment? When Jesus looked at what was going on in the Temple in the light of God's purpose in establishing it, his judgment was that it was found wanting. It failed in spite of the fact that it still played a central role in the life of Israel (Mk. 11:11, 17; cf. Isa. 56:7; Jer. 7:11). To continue it in its present form, even with some reforms in it, would only perpetuate a useless institution that had not fulfilled its primary purpose. It would mean foisting a grand deception upon the trusting. This would be immoral and in the end disastrous. And for the trusting to continue to place their security and hope in a grand deception would be crash idolatry! Jeremiah had warned, "Do not trust in these deceptive words: 'This is the temple of the LORD, the temple of the LORD, the temple of the LORD'" (7:4). While the Temple was sacrosanct, it was not eternal. God's purpose for it, however, is both sacred and eternal. A reassertion of God's sovereign purpose in the coming of His reign through the abolition of the Temple would seem to be highly in order. And so judged in the light of the kingdom of God as reigning in Jesus Christ, the Temple failed and was to be abolished and replaced by a form of worship that atones for the sins not just of one people but of all peoples and celebrates the glorious destiny of all humankind in the kingdom of God.

What was wrong with the *scribes?* We have already noted the importance of their profession as authorized interpreters of the Law ("they sit on Moses' seat"), their great theological learning, and their high social position (Mt. 23:2-3). Yet Jesus directed against them some of his most stinging reproaches (Lk. 11:45-52; 20:46; Mt. 23:1-22, 29-36). From the record, it appears that Jesus faulted them on a number of points.

First, Jesus accused them of *not practicing what they teach:* "they do not practice what they teach" (Mt. 23:3). They were to be obeyed in what they taught but not emulated in what they did (Mt. 23:2), and they themselves did not obey what they enjoined. *They fell short of being good teachers of the Law because they lacked the integrity expected of teachers.* Moreover, they interpreted the Law so strictly that it became a heavy burden imposed upon the people, while they themselves would not lift a finger to do what they demanded of others, or lend a helping hand to those who sought to obey what they imposed (Mt. 23:4; Lk. 11:46; cf. Acts 15:10). And so they became not only bad teachers but *hard taskmasters!*

Second, Jesus reproached the scribes for *silencing prophecy.* The scribes sought to play the role of the prophets in their self-understanding and professional activity as interpreters of the will of God (the Torah). To dramatize this claim publicly, they honored and memorialized the prophets who were killed by their "fathers" by "building their tombs" (Lk. 11:47). In doing this, they little knew that they were actually corroborating and consenting to the killing of the prophets by their fathers (Lk. 11:48). This had the implication that when God raised a new prophet who spoke the will of God in contemporary terms (as Jesus was doing in proclaiming the message of the kingdom of God), these "curators of tradition" would like nothing better than to silence him by persecution and murder (Lk. 11:48-51; Mt. 23:29-30). The scribes celebrated prophecy by entombing it as a thing of the past. Their efforts to make it come alive through their casuistry actually killed it by making it impossible to obey. So in addition to being bad teachers and hard taskmasters, they were *embalmers of prophecy!*

Third, Jesus accused the scribes of actually *preventing people from entering the kingdom of God* (Lk. 11:52). As teachers of the Law it was their professional duty to make known the will of God for obedience unto salvation! Instead of revealing all that they knew about the Law and the way to salvation, they actually held much of it as a secret and so withheld it from being publicly known. So much of scribal learning was *esoteric.*[4] It was meant only for the initiated, and this was practically limited to their fellow scribes. If this was saving knowledge, and there was no doubt that it was so regarded, then the people were deprived of the knowledge of the way to salvation. They were thus prevented from being "saved." And yet even with their own esoteric knowledge the scribes themselves did not enter the way to salvation (Lk. 11:52). They taught "salvation" but were not themselves saved, and worse they hindered those who would be saved! They were not only embalmers of prophecy, they were also *undertakers of salvation.*

Finally, Jesus exposed the *self-idolatry of the scribes* (Mt. 23:5-7; Lk. 20:45-47). As it was the vocation of the priest to represent the sanctity of God, so it was the calling of the scribe to represent the majesty of the will of God. It was his duty to pay homage to that majesty both in teaching and doing. His life was to be a mirror of that majesty so that people will see it and acknowledge it and honor it in worship and obedience and faithfulness. What the scribe actually did was to promote deliberately his own self-importance publicly and to enjoy the adulation that people publicly accorded him. Jesus reproached the scribes for doing their deeds to be "seen by men." "They love the place of honor at feasts and the best seats in the synagogues" (RSV). They liked to be recognized and saluted in the marketplaces and enjoyed being called rabbi (Mt. 23:5-7). They wore the sort of clothes that readily and unmistakably identified them and so promoted their social standing! (Mt. 23:5; Lk. 20:46). Self-idolatry was the sin of the scribe. It was worse than the sin of the priest and the rich who worshiped wealth; at least these people did not worship themselves! So in addition to being a bad teacher, a hard taskmaster, an embalmer of prophecy, an undertaker of salvation, the scribe was also a *self-idolater!* Judged in terms of the Law he taught, he was found wanting. And the Law itself did not have the resources for preventing the sins of the scribe, let alone healing them and repairing the damage they inflicted! And so judged in the light of the kingdom of God, the Law itself was found wanting!

Now we come to the *Pharisees.* The strictures of Jesus against them were quite different from those which he leveled against the scribes. Although scribe and Pharisee often appeared together in the record, they were two different groups. One reason for their appearance together was the fact that the leaders and influential members of the Pharisaic movement were scribes. This did not, however, diminish the distinction between the two communities. The scribe sought *to know* the Law and interpret it. The Pharisee sought *to practice* the Law and be made perfect by doing it. This distinction accounted for their different sins.

The cardinal sin of which the Pharisee was accused by Jesus was *hypocrisy* (Mt. 23:23-28; 6:1-18; Lk. 11:3-44). The root meaning of this word in Greek is "to play a part." The word has meant pretending to be what one is not. A hypocrite is one who pretends to be what he is not. The Pharisee wanted to be holy and perfect by fully obeying all the duties imposed by the Law. Thus in addition to the duties laid upon laypeople, the Pharisee took upon himself to obey even those duties laid upon the priest. The Torah specified rules governing purity and diet when the priests were doing their duties as priests. But the Pharisaic community wanted these rules to be practiced by all its members who were laypeople. It wanted these rules to be observed not only in the everyday life of priests but also in the daily life of all the people.[5] It wanted its members to be as clean as the priest when he was officiating as priest. In this way Israel was to become the "priestly people" of God. For this reason, the Pharisaic movement opposed the Sadducees, who wanted the rules for the priest to apply only to the priest and not also to the laypeople. For laypeople to assume duties and standards that belong only to priests is clearly a form of pretension. It is to be what one is not! In this sense, the Pharisee was a hypocrite.

Moreover, in his effort to fulfill all obligations imposed by the Law on priest and lay alike, the Pharisee succeeded only in observing the peripheral and external details of the Law, and not the main substance of the Law. Jesus' accusation on this point was sharp: "You tithe mint, dill, and cumin, and have neglected the weightier matters of the law: justice and mercy and faith. It is these you ought to have practiced without neglecting the others" (Mt. 23:23). And yet the Pharisee wanted to appear before himself and before the public that he succeeded in observing the whole of the Law. So Jesus accused the Pharisee of appearing clean and beautiful on the outside, but unclean and iniquitous on the inside (Mt. 23:25-27). This was undoubtedly rank hypocrisy. Jesus minced no words in driving home this point: "So you also outwardly appear righteous to men, but within you are full of hypocrisy and iniquity" (Mt. 23:28 RSV).

Moreover, Jesus doubted the sincerity of the Pharisee's desire to obey the will of God. Since it was God's Law which was being obeyed, then it must be God who must judge whether one has fully observed the Law or not. He alone is the appropriate audience before whom one performs; he alone is the proper judge of the performance. The Pharisee should have behaved in such a way as to make this truth obvious and unmistakable. Instead, he behaved in a way that made it obscure and ambiguous. The Pharisee pretended to obey God when in fact he was only playing up to the people and desired only to be seen by them. While he ostensibly sought God's approval, he was actually only seeking the praise of men (Mt. 6:2, 5, 16). What was absolutely important to him was to be seen and be praised by the public for his virtuoso performance and not by the God whose will he pretended to be doing! In this sense, the Pharisee was a hypocrite! While pretending to worship God, he was actually worshiping himself. Ultimately, the Pharisee, like the scribe, was a self-idolater! Judged by the Law, he too was found wanting. What needed to be done by him would also appear clear from the Law, namely, to acknowledge one's failure and sin and so to repent! But can a "righteous" person repent when he is not aware that he has fallen short of his obligation? Only the appearance of the reign of God in the light of which even the Law must be judged can provide the ground for repentance and faith.

Pronouncement of "Woe" as a Call to Repentance

While Jesus showed compassion to the lost, the sick, and the poor, he pronounced a stinging "woe" upon the elite righteous. What does it mean to pronounce "woe" upon someone? We find examples of pronouncing "woe" in Isaiah 5 and in Amos 6. A cursory analysis of these prophetic examples reveals some essential elements. They include the following:

a) It is *Yahweh* Himself who makes the pronouncement. The "woe" is weighted with His initiative and authority. It is therefore to be taken seriously.

b) The pronouncement is made in connection with some form of wrongdoing or sin (Isa. 5:8, 11, 18, 20, etc.; Amos 6:7). The "woe" is a divine judgment upon such sin. As such, it is both an *exposure* and a *censure*. The sin is exposed by God Himself in His light so that it is truly revealed as sin. The sin is also censured by God Himself by the standard of His will so that it is truly judged as sinful!

c) The pronouncement anticipates a dreadful doom that is impending or is sure to happen if the wrongdoer continues to persist in his present course. There is a strong sense of foreboding. The disaster that is to come is connected with the sin that is condemned. It is presented as an inevitable consequence of it. The prophetic "woe" is followed by a "therefore" which introduces the dire consequence. In Isaiah 5 the woes in verses 8 and 11 are followed by "therefore" in verses 13 and 14; the woes in verses 18-22 are followed by "therefore" in verses 24-25. In Amos 6 the woes in verses 1 and 4 are followed by "therefore" in verse 7.

d) The pronouncement of woe is to be understood as a *warning signal* that God will no longer tolerate the wrongdoing and His judgment will surely be rendered in all its severity. Therefore, there is sure danger ahead!

e) The pronouncement of woe *creates a critical moment of choice* for the one to whom the warning is given! He must act accordingly. It is not yet too late to change course and so avoid the danger that lies ahead! If, on the other hand, he does not heed the warning, he puts himself in grave danger.

It is my opinion that the same framework formed the background for the pronouncements of "woe" by Jesus upon the scribes and Pharisees. It is safe also to assume that they were understood in their prophetic significance. In Luke 6 the four beatitudes that Jesus spoke (verses 20-22) were followed by four "woes" (verses 24-25). The "woes" were directed to the rich and the righteous. In Matthew 23 and Luke 11 the "woes" that Jesus pronounced were directly related to specific sins which he exposed and censured. The point is to show a clear contrast between being "blessed" and being "woed."

There are, however, several new elements in the "woe" pronouncement of Jesus that need to be underscored. These new elements heightened the seriousness of the pronouncement and intensified the urgency of heeding it. One new element is the fact that it was *Jesus himself* who pronounced the "woe" upon the scribes and Pharisees. He represented the initiative, authority, and judgment of God. It was not the "Thus says the Lord" of the prophet who spoke here, and certainly not the "you have heard that it was said to the men of old." It was the Jesus of "But I say unto you" who spoke the "woe."

Another new factor is the fact that the opportunity to change course and avoid the danger is now connected with the reign of God that has drawn nigh in Jesus Christ, and its intention is to save, not to condemn. The Kingdom of God is now in the midst of Israel and so the time of salvation is now! It is not yet too late for the rich and the righteous to change course. While the consequence of not heeding the warning was not explicitly stated, it is nonetheless clearly implied. The likely consequence, however, is to be seen by reference to the reign of God which has drawn nigh in Jesus Christ. Failure to enter the Kingdom would inevitably mean excluding oneself from it. This is the dreadful doom that awaited those who refused to enter. In the Gospel of Matthew the pronouncements of the woe are followed by the lament of Jesus over Jerusalem, who killed prophets and stoned those who are sent to her (23:37). With a deep sense of foreboding, Jesus said: "How often would I have gathered your children together as a hen gathers her brood under her wings, *and you would not! Behold, your house is forsaken and desolate"* (23:37-38 RSV).

Did Jesus not really call "the righteous" to repentance? If one were to take into account only what he was reported to have said in Mark 2:17 and Luke 15:7, 10, then the conclusion is inescapable: he did not. But it seems clear from what has been said above that Jesus did and said other things which could be rightly construed as a call to repentance to "the righteous." He exposed the failure, the hypocrisy, and the idolatry behind their facade of righteousness. At the risk of being hated and endangering his life, he took pains to show that the so-called "righteous" were in fact worse sinners than "the lost sheep" of the house of Israel. The sharp "woe" that he pronounced upon them was both an exposure and a censure of their unacknowledged sins. It was a warning to them that danger loomed ahead and they must act accordingly if they were to avoid it. The coming of the reign of God in Jesus Christ was the precise opportunity for salvation. It therefore constituted for them a critical moment of decision fraught with the weight of destiny! Did not all this mean a clarion call to repentance to "the rich" and "the righteous"? Was not all this a demand that they acknowledge their guilt, turn away from their sin and change the course of their lives, recognize and confess Jesus Christ as their new master and so make of themselves his disciples, and finally trust only in God and in no other, including their own righteousness, for their salvation?

How did the rich and righteous of Israel respond to the call to repentance? The rich young ruler who sought eternal life *left Jesus and went on his own way, sad,* "for he had great possessions"! Following Jesus' pronouncement of woe upon the scribes and Pharisees as recorded in the Gospel of Luke (11:42-52), the scribes and Pharisees responded by seeking "to press him hard, and to provoke him to speak of many things, lying in wait for him, to catch at something he might say" (Lk. 11:53-54 RSV; cf. Mk. 12:13). The response of the chief priests and scribes to the cleansing of the Temple was to find a way "to destroy" Jesus (Mk. 11:18; cf. 14:1-2). None of these responses could be construed as repentance and faith!

We have been dealing with Jesus' strategy for social transformation as an aspect of our effort to locate a basis and a rationale for mission evangelism that includes a witness to social salvation in our time and context. So far we have considered two aspects of Jesus' strategy. We find this outlined by Matthew in the Sermon on the Mount. The first has to do with the surpassing and replacement of the Law of Moses with the kingdom of God as *the basis for life-together.* Then we went on to consider lengthily how the kingdom of God through the ministry of Jesus deals with people in Jewish society. The reign of God in Jesus saves both the worst and the best people in this society. Mission evangelism finds a basis in the social experience of salvation both at the level of *a new foundation for social life and in the way people—both good and bad—are radically changed in terms of repentance and faith by the reign of God!*

We now come to a third component in the strategy of Jesus for social salvation, namely, the change he sought to effect in the structures of society. In what follows we try to do two things: (a) to show the scope of the Kingdom of God as covering the essential structures of society; and (b) to indicate the kind of change Jesus called for in those structures.

Notes

1. See Joachim Jeremias, *New Testament Theology,* Vol. 1 (London: SCM Press, 1971), p. 144.

2. Ibid.

3. E. P. Sanders, *Jesus and Judaism* (London: SCM Press, 1985), pp. 61-76; Herman C. Waetjan, *A Reordering of Power* (Minneapolis: Fortress Press, 1989), pp. 179-84.

4. See Joachim Jeremias, *Jerusalem in the Time of Jesus* (Philadelphia: Fortress Press, 1967), pp. 237-40.

5. Ibid., pp. 265-66.

CHAPTER 4

THE KINGDOM AND THE STRUCTURE OF SOCIETY

The Scope of the Kingdom

A society includes not only its basis and its people, but also its structure. The Mosaic dispensation supplied a basis and a sense of belonging for life-together among its people. It also provided a social framework for regulating the interaction of its people and so gave it a sense of order. The elements of this social framework, together with the values, norms, and behavior that they entailed, are what is meant by the term "social structure." Each form of social structure specifies certain patterns of human behavior and interaction, provides their parameters, and requires norms or standards for regulating them. All these are generated, and formed, and passed on by culture. The kingdom of God in the vision of Jesus certainly meant far more than providing a new basis for society. If it is to have social relevance it must cover also the fundamental structure of society. If the kingdom of God is to supplant the Mosaic vision in ordering life-together, then its significance for the structure of society must also be clearly seen. Jesus introduces his "But I say unto you" with reference to a specific element of social structure that is covered by the Mosaic dispensation. The significance of this is quite simply that the kingdom of God as it dawned in Jesus intends to cover the whole range of social structure in Jewish society. It could do nothing less. It would be well to trace what might be the thought of Jesus on this matter in the Sermon on the Mount in the Gospel of Matthew (chaps. 5–7).

Let us first note the structure of the formula of antithesis as used in Matthew 5. It includes (a) a statement of the giving of the commandment, which showed its source and authority (Moses); (b) then it names the particular law addressed to a specific social structure, as, for example, the law against killing, which addressed the social structure of human life (Mt. 5:21); (c) followed by Jesus' "But I say unto you," which addressed the same social structure; and finally (d) it formulates the kind of change Jesus called for. Our concern in this section is with (b) and (c) in this formula. We have already taken up (a) in a previous section. We shall take up (d) in the section following this one.

Three further introductory considerations are in order before proceeding. We note first that the *element* of social structure is the same in both the Mosaic dispensation and in Jesus' "But I say unto you." This is because it is an essential element of society as such. It is rooted both in nature and in human nature and so is a "given" in, or a potentiality of, creation as such. Furthermore, it necessarily gives rise to some form of human interaction and behavior, which can become disorderly and destructive of society if not regulated.

We note secondly that the form for shaping human behavior in a particular form of social structure is the Law. Human behavior in society is regulated by Law in its various forms (divine, natural, customary, positive, apoditic, casuistic, etc.).

Finally, we note that Jesus called for change in the forms and norms and dynamics of human behavior *within* a specific form of social structure, not for a change *of* the element of social structure. For example: Jesus did not call for a change of human life but for a change in the laws and patterns of behavior relating to human life. He did call for a change *of* the primal *basis* of social structure, which we considered earlier, and the call for change in human behavior is in accordance with this more fundamental change. We shall now consider the *elements* of social structure in what follows. We will take up the kind of change Jesus called for in the following section.

1. In Matthew 5:21 the law that is invoked is about killing. The issue about killing is the element of *human life as such*. We are dealing here with the elemental fact of human life and the way a society values it. The fact of human life is a fundamental element of society. Without human beings, who are alive and who interact with each other, there is no society. And the attitudes, values, norms, and behavior that deal with this fact are behavioral aspects of social structure. The law on murder is an example of such a norm dealing with a form of behavior with respect to human life. No society is without forms and norms of behavior relating to human life.

2. In verse 27 the law against adultery, which is a form of behavior,

is mentioned. Adultery is a sexual sin. It can be committed only by sexual beings. And so the *element* of social structure that is addressed here is *human sexuality*. Next to human life in importance in society is human sexuality. The creation of the human being as male and female (i.e., as sexual) is of the same level and significance as his creation in the image of God (Gen. 2:27). The interaction in its various forms of male and female is fundamental in society. It can even be claimed that this is an aspect of the foundation of human sociality.

3. In verse 31 the law on divorce, which is again a form of human behavior, is considered. Divorce is the dissolution of a marriage. Therefore the primary issue addressed here is that of *human marriage*. This again is a fundamental *element* of social structure. It arises directly out of human sexuality and is the primary social institutional vehicle for the reproduction of human life and the perpetuation of society! The practices and behavior surrounding marriage and family are basic aspects of social structure in any society. No society is without some form of marriage and the behavior it entails.

4. In verse 33 the law against swearing falsely is taken up. Swearing falsely, which is a form of human behavior, has to do with the use of language. Therefore, the primary issue that is addressed here is *human language*. Again this is an *elemental* dimension of social structure. It is a potentiality unique to being human. Only human beings require, and have the potentiality for, language as an essential condition for community life. It is through language that reality is grasped and symbolized. Language tells the truth about the way things are. In telling, it communicates; in communicating, it builds up community and community must be based on reality and truth and meaning. Language makes society possible!

5. In verse 38 the law on retaliation, which again is a form of human behavior, is invoked. The issue that is addressed here is that of retributive justice. This entails the whole question of justice in human behavior and society. The *element* of social structure that is involved here is that of *human justice*. Again this is fundamental in society, as no society is without some form of justice. Without some acceptable measure of justice, a society collapses into anarchy, which could pave the way for tyranny, which in turn inevitably suppresses justice!

6. In verse 43 the law about the right treatment of the neighbor and the enemy is discussed. The issue here is *the right way of relating and*

interacting among human beings. Should one love only the neighbor and hate the enemy? Who is the "neighbor" and who is the "enemy"? The *element* of social structure that is being addressed here is *human relating, which is fundamental to being human, and it gives rise to forms of relationships and ways of interaction.* All societies have forms of human relationships, and human interaction takes place within and through those relationships.

The material in chapters 6 and 7 in Matthew is no longer covered textually by the formula we mentioned above. But there are elements of social structure that are discussed, and they are no less important than those already considered. Moreover, they are considered within the aegis of the Mosaic dispensation, and Jesus has much to say about them. They state what Jesus proscribes or condemns, and what he advocates or recommends. It would seem proper, therefore, to extend our attempt to identify the forms of social structure covered by the kingdom of God to include this material.

7. In Matthew 6:1-8 the *practice of piety* (again a form of human behavior) is taken up for consideration. Since Matthew 7:7-12 also deals with the theme of prayer, we shall include it here. The forms of piety that are considered include almsgiving, prayer, and fasting. These have to do with the practice of religion in Jewish society. They necessarily entail the beliefs and rituals connected with them. The *element* of social structure that is addressed here is that of *human piety,* the human relation to deity, which gives rise to the practice of religion in society. Again this is a basic element of social structure. No society seems to be without some form of religion that is practiced by its people.

8. In Matthew 6:19-33 we find considerations having to do with "treasures on earth" and the value and distribution of material goods essential to human life such as food, clothing, and shelter. Here we are dealing with the issues of property and material goods and their value. The element at issue here is the need for economic goods which are absolutely necessary for survival. And there are, of course, a variety of economic activities and systems. Again this is basic to society, for no society is without some way of producing and distributing and valuing the goods and services necessary to maintain life!

9. Matthew 7:1-7 has to do with the activity of making judgments, which is a distinctively human characteristic and seems to be unavoidable in social relationship. This raises the issue of the standards or

frames of reference in terms of which judgments are made. These are not mere private ideals but are socially shared norms. As verse 2 makes clear: the measure by which one judges is the same measure by which one is judged. We are here dealing with *social norms and community standards*. We know of no society that is without them. Social norms are essential to society.

10. The rest of the Sermon (Mt. 7:13-27) deals with the themes of the two ways of knowing a tree by its fruits, of true discipleship as doing the will of the Father, of hearing and doing the word that Jesus speaks. The "words" of Jesus here obviously refer to the whole discourse in the Sermon on the Mount. One who hears and does them is likened to a wise man who builds his house upon a solid rock. The words of Jesus are the solid foundation for a life that walks the narrow way but "leads to life," that bears good fruits, that "does the will of my Father," and thus shall enter the kingdom of heaven. The storms and stresses of earthly existence will beat upon that life and it shall stand! One might say that all this has to do with the general stability, order, direction, quality of life, and the commitment and discipline of a people that are character-istic of a society. No society seems to be without some general *form of order and sense of direction*. While this may not be as visible and con-crete as are the others considered thus far, still the sense of order and direction of a society is a fundamental form of social structure.

We have now identified ten forms of social structure in a society: human life, sexuality, marriage, language, justice, human relations, the relation to deity and the practice of piety, economic goods, social norms and standards, and finally the sense of order and direction of a society. Needless to say, these are all basic to society. Anyone who says that the gospel of the Kingdom has nothing to do with social structure and insti-tutions must reckon with this obvious fact. While these forms of social structure have all been gleaned from Mosaic society, they are not meant to be exhaustive but illustrative of the range of social structure. For exam-ple, nothing is mentioned here about politics and government, educa-tion, and technology, which are very important forms of social structure. In view of this, one must not limit the forms of social structure covered by the kingdom only to those described above. Moreover, what Jesus says of the relevance of the kingdom of God to these structures must not be confined only to them, or that this was all that Jesus had to say. This will become clearer when we deal with the ethos of love.

Changes in the Social Structure

As mentioned earlier, Jesus did not change the basic elements of social structure of Jewish society, as these are essential and necessary components of life-together. But he did call for a radical change of their primal basis. Or better still, he made it clear that even the Torah—which is the basis of Jewish society and its structure—is grounded in, and so must become indeed a genuine expression of, the reign of God, which has now drawn nigh in Jesus. *The more primal reality is the reign of God and thus it relativizes and supersedes the Torah as the basis of life-together, because even the Torah is based on the reign of God.*

The elemental dimensions of the structure of society insofar as they are a given of creation or a potentiality of creation are also to be understood as expressing the will or coming reign of God. This being the case, Jesus now calls for change in the human behavior which they generate that is obedient to, and consistent with, not just the Law, but the reign of God, which is the primal basis of the Law. *The crucial point to grasp is the claim of Jesus that the reign of God must come to expression in human behavior within and through the structure of society.* We attempt to make this clear as we look briefly at the changes Jesus demanded in the structure of society.

1. To show that it is the reign of God which is active in the command against murder, Jesus not only reaffirms but radicalizes the Law at two points (Mt. 5:21-26; Ex. 20:13; Deut. 5:17; 16:18). First, murder in the view of Jesus is not merely the actual deed of taking the life of a fellow Jew (the word "brother" here refers to a fellow Jew), but in fact includes its root or source in the inner feelings and thoughts that seek the harm of a brother, or tend to belittle his person, and thus to disvalue the gift of life and dishonor the God who gave it.

The Law looks only at the overt deed. It is activated only when it appears to have been violated by an actual deed. If it looks into the sources or roots of the deed at all, it is only after the deed has been committed, but not before. The purpose of the inquiry is not to prevent but to understand the deed. Because of this character of the Law, it cannot prevent the deed that violates it from taking place.

In the view of Jesus, however, the root of murder is anger, which is a strong inner feeling that seeks to harm or belittle another person, and may culminate in treating the other person as "a fool," that is, one who does not acknowledge God and so is not one of His people (cf. 7:26;

23:17; 25:2, 3, 8). A fool is one who says in his heart there is no God and behaves accordingly (Ps. 14:1; 53:1). To treat someone as "a fool" in this sense is to banish him/her from the presence of God and exclude him/her from the community of His people. He is regarded as an outcast. This provides an excuse for taking his/her life.

From the perspective of Jesus, the way to deal with murder is to prevent it from being done, rather than to judge it after it has been done. The best way to do this is to prevent it from arising in its source, in the inner being of a person where it erupts as feeling and thought in the form of anger, insult, and utter disregard for the life, person, and dignity of another. The Law cannot do this because it cannot penetrate to this level of the wellsprings of action. But only God in His reign can do this. Of course, God cannot and does not ignore murder when it is already done as an overt act, and in this way He affirms the Law. But He looks at murder already as an inner act arising from its source. In this way He transcends the Law because He is able to penetrate to the heart of a person and can judge what is taking place there even before it issues forth into an overt deed. If murder is to be prevented at all, it has to be judged and condemned in its inward form as God in His reign sees it, rather than in its overt form as deed as the Law sees it.

If murder is seen in the light of God's reign, how does one behave to prevent it? Jesus recommends an action with two steps. First, if murder is to be prevented one must deal with it in the context of worship rather than in a court of law. It is in worship that the heart is exposed to God, and so it is in worship that God reveals what He sees in the heart. Second, if in worship one sees or realizes that a brother or sister has something against "you" (i.e., as the one "sinned against"), then it is you as the one offended, who has a reason to be angry with your brother or sister, who must offer reconciliation to him/her as part of your worship! With this offer of reconciliation initiated by the one "sinned against" as an expression of true worship, anger is prevented from arising both in the offended and in the offending party. And if reconciliation takes place, which is a sign of God's forgiveness, then murder is nipped at the bud. It is in worship that God is glorified, the gift of life is valued, the dignity of a person is honored, and the fellowship of God's people is celebrated. When all these are appreciated as they must be in worship—for that is what worship is—then the conditioning source of murder is removed.

Jesus also radicalizes the judgment against murder. When murder is allowed to become a deed and seen in its overt form as a deed in the light of the Law, then it is a court of Law that renders the judgment. Courts of Law are hierarchical; there is a lower and a higher court which provides for the right and process of appeal in order to ensure that the right judgment is rendered. This whole arrangement testifies to the fact that judgments rendered by courts are fallible. They are fallible both in deciding guilt and in passing sentence. And the reason they are fallible is the fact that they are *human* judgments rendered according to the Law as humanly understood. And yet it is this fallible judgment that finally can put a person in prison, take away his freedom, and curtail his life. But if murder were seen in the light of God's reign, then the one qualified to render judgment is God Himself in His reign. However, the reign of God as expressed in Jesus is one that seeks to save rather than to condemn. God's judgment to save is more primal than the Law's judgment to condemn. And the context in which this is rendered is the service of worship rather than the court of Law. Therefore, it is best to avail in worship of God's judgment to save and reconcile rather than be placed under the judgment of Law which condemns and punishes. Because the judgment of God is saving, there is no need to appeal it. Only judgments that condemn and punish are appealable! One who has been judged not guilty correctly and justly does not appeal the verdict. The judgment to save—which only God can render—is therefore final and executory. The more radical, ultimate, and final judgment is God's judgment to save!

2. Jesus' word on adultery argues somewhat along the same lines as his word on murder. In the light of God's coming reign which has drawn near, he exposes adultery in its inner roots before it becomes an overt deed. Adultery includes not merely the act itself but the root from which it springs, namely, lust. Jesus does not condemn the natural desire of a man for a woman, and vice versa. But he recognizes that natural desire can easily escalate into lust, which is an intense, excessive, and unrestrained sexual appetite seeking gratification at all cost, even by means of coveting another man's wife. A classic biblical example is David's lust for Bathsheba (2 Sam. 11–12).

In Jesus' mind, lust is already adultery. One "who looks at a woman lustfully has already committed adultery with her in his heart." Adultery, therefore, is not just a deed; it is at root a feeling and a thought, which becomes a will and then escalates into a passionate, uncontrollable deed. One who lusts does not regard the opposite sex as a sacred partner in the fellowship of life but merely as a means for self-gratification. Lust does not respect the sanctity of marriage and does not mind if it leads to its dissolution. One who lusts after a woman makes an adulteress of the woman by regarding her as capable of being unfaithful to her husband. And so adultery becomes the condition for the breakup of marriage. It is ironic that sexuality, which is God's gift as a prime condition for making life-together possible, now becomes a means for causing alienation and destroying life-together in marriage. The reign of God comes to expression precisely in exposing adultery as originally lust, which is ultimately unfaithfulness to God and self-idolatry.

What the reign of God requires is to regard sexuality as a condition for human sociality. And that means to acknowledge human interdependence, to appreciate human otherness, to respect the other as a person in his/her own right and not as an object of lustful desire or manipulation, and to promote the other's good and welfare. The judgment of the reign of God upon lust is equally primal: it is the whole man who is to be made whole by the Kingdom. It is not merely one's deeds that are judged, but the agent of the deed, the doer, the person himself (Mt. 5:29-30). The concern of Jesus is: condemn the deed, but save the agent by forgiveness. God makes him whole so that out of his wholeness he will act wholly, with integrity and perfection.

3. The discussion on adultery naturally leads into the consideration of divorce which breaks up marriage. We have to look at Matthew 5:31-32 in relation to Matthew 19:3-9, which it anticipates. Perhaps it would help if one were to notice a pattern that seems to be emerging in the way Jesus has been handling the issues so far. First, there is the *overt deed* that is covered by a particular commandment of the Law. Second, Jesus goes behind the overt deed to its *inner source in the heart of the human being*. There the Law cannot penetrate and its commandment does not apply. For the Law is activated and begins to apply only when a deed is overtly committed and public evidence or witness is therefore available. But the reign of God can pierce to the inner self, for God looks directly into the heart, and He reigns from the heart over the whole person and not just over the person's activities! And so in the light of God's reign, Jesus calls for change not just of behavior but of heart and of the inner person, which are the primal sources of action! Third, in the case

about divorce, he moves past behind the overt deed and the inner self *right back into the beginning of things, that is to say, in creation* (Mt. 19:4, 8). The radicalization of deed and agent goes into the primal beginning of things! The reign of God must be seen as operating not only in the heart of the person where action begins but in the beginning of creation where God's primal intentions are revealed.

What then can be said about marriage from this perspective of the reign of God. We note several things. For one thing, being male and female—human sexuality—is God's creation and so is "from the beginning." For another thing, marriage has its basis in human sexuality, in being male and female (Mt. 19:5). Furthermore, God's intention in marriage is to make one flesh out of the two. Moreover, it is God who joins man and woman together in marriage. What God has therefore joined together, no human being can put asunder (Mt. 19:6). The obvious conclusion from all this is that from the beginning God intended that *there is to be no divorce, no dissolution of marriage.*

In view of this, the logical question for a Jew to ask is: "Why then did Moses command one to give a certificate of divorce, and to put her away?" (Mt. 19:7 RSV). The answer of Jesus has the following components. First, divorce is not a part of God's intention in marriage "from the beginning." Second, divorce was *"allowed"* by Moses: it was permitted and not commanded. Third, it was allowed "by *Moses*" and so was part of the human legal tradition that originated from him. The allowance for divorce cannot be traced back to the will of God. Fourth, it was allowed by Moses because of the "hardness of heart" of the Jews. This has several important implications. Hardness of heart *presupposes* already the presence and activity of sin, which was not part of creation and of the beginning of things. Sin came "later"! The "hardening of the heart" is already a *consequence* of sin. It connotes the refusal to acknowledge sin and to repent and so to persist in it. In order to bring about knowledge of sin and repentance of it and hopefully to put a stop to it, the Law was given (cf. Gal. 3:19; Rom. 7:7). The Law and its operation presuppose the "reality" and power of sin, and its purpose is to bring about knowledge of sin with the view to repentance and desistance!

The allowance for divorce was shaped in relation to the condition of sin. The one factor that makes it legally permissible is that of "unchastity" or immorality on the part of the wife. Therefore, the more appropriate behavior is not to create the situation where the allowance for divorce is activated and becomes a likely option. The reign of God is best accomplished when those whom God has joined together truly become one flesh and no human law or legal permission is authorized to put them asunder!

But if the situation that permits divorce takes place, what then? The next best possible option is not to exercise it, but to be compassionate and redemptive and forgiving! The condition that makes divorce permissible is also the opportunity to practice redeeming love and reconciliation, which in essence is the reign of God! Finally, when divorce is exercised as an option, it only increases the incidence of adultery, for "whoever marries a divorced woman commits adultery" and thereby provides the reason and the opportunity of dissolving a marriage! (Mt. 5:32). How does one put a break to this vicious cycle? Only by forgiveness, which condemns the deed but saves the doer!

4. From human life to sexuality to marriage, we come to the next important factor that makes for human sociality, namely, language. It is here considered in the form of swearing falsely (Mt. 5:33-37). How does the reign of God come to bear in power and immediacy upon this aspect of society?

An essential function of language is to tell the truth, for it is through language that reality is grasped and symbolized for communication. It is also by language that one binds oneself to a vow or pledge that one makes, and when one does this one must keep his or her word. This is the Law (Lev.19:12; Num. 30:2; Deut. 23:21-22). The word by which we make a vow tells the truth that we are the kind of person who keeps a promise and therefore we will not break our word.

The fact of the matter, however, is that we do not always tell the truth or fulfill the vows that we make. There is the evil of lying and of bad faith and unfaithfulness in us and in our world (cf. Mt. 5:37). We can and do misuse language by telling a lie or swearing falsely or breaking a promise. Because this situation gives rise to suspicion about our sincerity or doubt about the truth of what we say, we feel the need to guarantee our sincerity and the truth of what we say. Our merely saying so is not enough. And so we swear or take an oath. We do this by invoking a higher power—usually the power of deity—to guarantee the truth of what we say and whose retribution is besought in case the vow is not kept. This seems to have been a practice throughout the world. The

Jews did it, too (Lev. 6:1ff.; Ezek. 16:59; Zech. 8:17). And it has contin-ued to be practiced to this day. Because it has become some sort of a universal habit that is taken for granted, we are careless about the oaths that we take or the swearing that we make.

Thus, oath-taking or swearing testifies to four deplorable elements in the human condition. First, it reflects our untruthfulness. Our need to swear is precisely a sign that we stand in untruth! Second, it shows our misuse of language. We have used language to tell a lie, to exaggerate, to make propaganda, to manipulate people. In prostituting language we break community and promote conflict. Third, by swearing to God we bind Him to our linguistic transactions to guarantee their truth. We put Him at our disposal in a situation of untruth and discord. We blaspheme His Name. And finally, what is guaranteed as true is only what is cov-ered by the oath. What is not covered by the oath may be regarded as falsehood or a lie and is declared outside of God's provenance. This lim-its the sovereignty of truth, and permits language to tell a lie!

The change that Jesus demanded in the behavior related to this form of social structure is to forbid swearing absolutely: *"But I say to you, Do not swear at all"* (Mt. 5:34, emphasis added; cf. James 5:12). Jesus is thus putting an end to a universal human practice! He is reversing the status quo by restoring the primal use of language, namely, to tell the truth by either a Yes or a No! He appeals to the near presence of the kingdom of God as his reason for prohibiting swearing absolutely. In swearing by God one has to name Him. But by the force of custom, a Jew cannot name God, so he swears by using some metaphor that intends the real-ity of God, such as "heaven" or "earth" or "Jerusalem." Thus, heaven stands for "the throne of God." Earth is God's "footstool." And Jerusalem is "the city of the great King" (Mt. 5:34-35). By swearing by any of these signs of His presence, one actually intends the fullness of His deity and the sovereignty of His presence. In short, one invokes the reign of God, which is precisely the one thing that one cannot bind, not even as a condition for speaking the truth. God is in no way at our disposal!

Since the reign of God has drawn near in Jesus Christ, one can sim-ply and freely tell the truth. He need not lie anymore. In God's King-dom untruth is banished. Truth can be told because it can now stand in the light by which it is affirmed and seen as truth. There is no need to swear as a means of guaranteeing the truth of one's language! Swear-ing, therefore, has no place in the community of the Kingdom. More-

over, swearing assumes that God can be put at our disposal. This is bla-
tantly presumptuous, for God is never at our disposal. We cannot and
should not even swear by our head because we cannot "make one hair
white or black" (Mt. 5:36). It is God who has the power to determine
the color of the hair on our head. In short, it is we human beings who
are at the disposal of God and not the other way around! Since we cannot bind Him to what we say, we must not swear by Him at all! It is
enough to tell the truth in the presence of the reign of God!

5. The law on retributive justice and the question as to how one
should treat the neighbor and the enemy raise in a basic way the issue
of the ethos of the kingdom of God. We intend to deal with this in terms
of the ethic of love in chapter 7.

6. We come to the practice of religion and the good works that it
entails (Mt. 6:1-18). The practice of religion has to do with one's relationship to God who is called "our Father" in the texts we are considering (Mt. 6:1, 4, 6, 8, 9, 14, 15, 18). In the Jewish faith, there were three
types of activity which were considered standard ways of practicing religion. These were almsgiving, praying, and fasting. Jesus assumed their
standard character. Although they were done by human agents, they
were by definition directed towards God, for they were activities within
the structure of relationship with God. This was true even in the case of
almsgiving, which was done to the poor. To give alms was to show char-
ity to the poor in obedience to God. The issue that was being addressed
was: What would be the right way of doing these religious activities? Put
in this way, the issue implied the question of the righteousness that
should "exceed" the righteousness of the scribes and Pharisees, who
were the official practitioners of Judaism (Mt. 5:20). In short, what was
being raised here is nothing less than "the righteousness of the kingdom
of God" (cf. Mt. 6:33). Stated in terms of our interest, how does the reign
of God in Jesus Christ come to bear upon the practice of religion?

Jesus named the one thing that is terribly wrong about the practice of
religion in his day, and this is *hypocrisy* (Mt. 23:1-36). While we have
already dealt with this issue in an earlier section (see pp. 59-62), there
are still some aspects of the problem that need to be brought out.
Because the scribes and the Pharisees were regarded by the Jewish public as the official representatives of Judaism, their practice of piety was
seen as the right way. For this reason, their way of almsgiving, praying,
and fasting was to be emulated by the rank and file among the Jews.

But Jesus was not deceived. He saw through their practice, and he decided that there was much in it that needed to be straightened out or "rightwised." To do this, he not only had to expose what was wrong in the Pharisaic practice of piety but also had to show the right way as demanded by the kingdom of God, especially with respect to the standard activities through which piety was lived out.

According to the text under consideration, there were three major features of the hypocrisy that characterized the practice of piety by those who were its standard-bearers in Jesus' time. These were the following: (a) it was practiced before men; (b) it was practiced for the purpose of being seen and praised by them; and (c) it had no further reward than what it had sought and already received, namely, for its practitioners to be seen and be praised by the public and to bask in the glory of being appreciated as a doer of good works (Mt. 6:1). These were criticisms that applied to the three standard ways of practicing piety. It applied to those who gave alms (Mt. 6:2). It applied to those who prayed (Mt. 6:5). And it was true also of those who fasted (6:16).

But why would this way of practicing piety be considered faulty? This will be seen more clearly when viewed in the light of what Jesus considered to be the right way of practicing righteousness! Jesus introduced his position on the right way of practicing piety by the phrase "But when . . ." (Mt. 6:3, with respect to almsgiving; 6:6 with respect to prayer; and 6:17 with respect to fasting). The point underscored the contrast between the way of the hypocrites and the way of Jesus and laid down the judgment that the former was wrong and the latter right.

Jesus contrasted his way from each of the three faults he had seen in the way of the hypocrites. First, *the only right audience for the practice of piety is not the human public but only God and none other.* Therefore, the practice of righteousness must be directed to God alone and done in His presence. The human public is the wrong audience. To direct the practice of piety deliberately to the human public while knowing it to be the wrong audience is patently a form of idolatry.

Those who give alms in the Pharisaic way "sound the trumpet" to call the attention of the public to what they do. But those who give alms in the way of Jesus do not publicize before the public what they do. This is the sense of, "Do not let your left hand know what your right hand is doing" (Mt. 6:3). The giving of alms must be "in secret," that is, away from the public's eye.

Those who pray in the way of the hypocrites "love to stand and pray in the synagogues and at the street corners, so that they may be seen by others." But those who pray in the way of Jesus go into a room; they shut the door and pray in secret to God the Father who is in secret (Mt. 6:5-6).

Those who fast, emulating the way of the hypocrites, "look dismal" and "disfigure their faces" so that "their fasting may be seen by others." But those who fast following the way of Jesus oil their hair and comb it, wash their faces, and direct their fasting only to God (Mt. 6:16-17).

Second, *the right motive for the practice of piety is to please God and not to bask in the praise of others*. Since God is the sole audience of piety, it is absolutely important that He alone should "see" what is done and so be pleased by what He sees (Mt. 6:4, 6, 18). Piety is only for the eyes of God and not for the sight of the human public! Only God can decide this! Consequently, it is what is good and acceptable in God's sight that piety aims to do, not what is good and acceptable in the eyes of the human public! The aim of piety is to please God and glorify Him; any other motive would be wrong.

It is ironic, however, that the standard activities for the practice of piety easily lend themselves to the wrong motives. A person may ostensibly help the poor by sharing his goods, not with the purpose of really helping, but to demonstrate his generosity and bask in the praise and gratitude of those who receive his alms! A person may pray for the purpose of publicizing his exceptional piety and enjoy the adulation of the people who appreciate his religious devotion! A person may fast for the purpose of showing that he is in control of himself and lives a disciplined life—which moralists value—and not really to humble oneself in the presence of God and to practice the way of self-offering and self-giving on behalf and for the sake of the good of others! To covet the praise of the public to boost one's egocentric trip to the heights of piety is nothing less than self-idolatry. Self-abasement for the glory of God is the true motive of piety!

Third, *the right reward for the practice of piety is what God determines and gives, not what the pious want and the public gives*. The practice of piety is premised on the assumption that it will be rewarded. Jesus did not question this assumption. He presupposed it. God the Father rewards the piety that expresses itself in almsgiving, praying, and fasting (Mt. 6:1, 4, 6, 18; cf. 5:46; 19:27-30). This view is in direct contrast to the view which holds that doing good to be really good is for its own sake, and not for the sake of any profit or reward that may accrue from it. Jesus believed that the doing of good that is directed to God and for His glory is to be rewarded.

But it matters a great deal what the reward is, and who determines and gives it. In the case of those who practice piety in the hypocritical way, it is they who decide what the reward is to be, and from whom they are to receive it. Jesus said of these people: "Truly I say to you, they have received their reward" (Mt. 6:2, 5, 16 NASB). The word "received" here means in Greek, "received payment in full." The reward that was sought and received by those who practiced piety in the Pharisaic way is the praise and adulation of the human public. Since they have already received this in full, there is nothing more for them to expect. They got what they wanted in full and so nothing more is coming to them. In the case of those who practice piety in the way of Jesus, it is God the Father who "sees" and is pleased who determines the reward and gives it. The attitude of the one who practices piety in the way of Jesus is one of complete trust in God. He leaves the matter of reward entirely to Him. As the classical Calvinist would say, he is even prepared to be damned for the glory of God!

The kingdom of God reigns in the practice of piety when it is directed to God alone, when the only motive is to glorify Him, and when He is completely trusted for any reward at all.

Jesus in the text in Matthew added a note on prayer which further showed how the reign of God should impact the practice of piety. He indicated not only the *right way* to pray but also the *right prayer,* namely, his prayer. In the text in Matthew, the right prayer is given to correct the way the Gentiles prayed, which was to "heap up empty phrases . . . for they think that they will be heard for their many words" (Mt. 6:7 RSV). Babbling in prayer is a sign of lack of trust; it is a frantic effort at manipulation, and so it borders on magic. Jesus said to his hearers: Do not be like the heathen in their babbling prayers (Mt. 6:8). He then introduced the right prayer with the words, "Pray then like this . . ." (Mt. 6:8 RSV; cf. Lk. 11:1-4). This prayer has come to be known as the Lord's Prayer.

We cannot here analyze in detail the Lord's Prayer. It is sufficient to note that its structure clearly indicates how the reign of God shapes prayer into its right attitude, its true form, and its correct content. *The attitude proper to prayer is the trust that "your Father knows what you need before you ask him"* (Mt. 6:8). Prayer rests upon the sure confidence that God is our Father and we are His children (cf. Rom. 8:15; Gal. 4:5-6). God may be many other things, but for prayer He cannot be less or other than "Our Father." Our Father *knows* our need. Trust is rightly placed upon one who knows us, who is not a stranger to us, who is not hostile in His knowledge of us. God knows *better* than we do because He created us and so knows our frame (Ps. 139:13-16). And what He knows of our need is indeed what is truly needed by us. He knows what is good for us more than we ever can! Because he already knows, He anticipates our need and is ready to give it to us even before we ask! That is because *he cares deeply.* His care is responsive to our need and generous in meeting it. This kind of caring evokes the trusting that issues forth in prayer.

The form that is appropriate to prayer is that of petition. The Lord's Prayer is petitionary throughout. It is not primarily a prayer of praise and adoration, nor only of confession and penitence, nor merely of thanksgiving and celebration. Even when prayer is cast in any of these forms, it is still essentially petitionary. We beseech God *to hear* our prayer in any of its forms. Why is prayer properly petitionary?

Prayer that is elementally shaped by trust rises forth in the form of petition. Because we trust, we ask and seek and knock (Mt. 7:7-8; cf. Mk. 11:24). Prayer as petition expresses truly our status before God. We are God's creatures whom He graciously created out of nothing through His Spirit. Human existence is a standing out of nothing by being made to look up to God for being and life and the abundance of life. The posture of creation before God is expressed by the psalmist.

> These [i.e., the creatures] all look to thee,
>   to give them their food in due season.
> When thou givest to them, they gather it up;
>   when thou openest thy hand, they are filled
>   with good things.
> When thou hidest thy face, they are dismayed;
>   when thou takest away their breath, they die,
>   and return to their dust.
> When thou sendest forth thy Spirit, they are created;
>   and thou renewest the face of the ground.
>   (Ps. 104:27-30 RSV)

Prayer as petition expresses our inescapable dependence upon God for everything. Before God we can only approach in prayer with empty hands waiting to be filled. Petition is the form of the Lord's Prayer.

In prayer as petition we lay before God our most profound concerns and aspirations. Nothing orders our values and priorities as prayer does! In the Lord's Prayer Jesus lays bare before his Father the dominant concerns of his life and ministry. His prayer contains two sets of petitions. The first set contains three petitions that express *his concern about God.* They include (a) the hallowing of God's name, (b) the coming of His Kingdom, and (c) the doing of His will on earth as it is in heaven! This means that *Jesus is concerned that God be God in His reign and that He be truly acknowledged as such on earth as it is in heaven.* The act of prayer as petition is precisely the expression of the primordial concern that God be God in all the fullness of His name, His reign, and His will on earth as in heaven! If God, as it were, cops out from being God, the universe collapses! If the center cannot hold, all things fall apart![1] And so the first concern of Jesus in his prayer—as in his life and ministry and death—is that God reign in the fullness of His deity!

The next set of petitions expresses the concern of Jesus about the *human being.* They include (a) the provision of daily bread, (b) the cancellation of debts and the forgiveness of sins, (c) the avoidance of temptation, and (d) the deliverance from evil. The fact that this set of petitions follows from the first means that it depends upon the first, and that the effect upon earth of God's reign is precisely the fulfillment of this second set of petitions. In short, when God's name is hallowed, and His reign comes, and His will is done on earth, then humanity is given its daily bread, its debts are canceled and its sins forgiven, it is enabled to stand up against temptation, and is delivered from evil! *When God reigns humanity benefits!* Therefore, it is only fitting that from earliest times, the church responded gratefully to the Lord's Prayer by ascribing eternal power and glory to God: "Thine is the power and the glory forever!" This doxological ascription prevents the logic of the petition from being twisted around. One cannot say, because humanity stands to benefit, therefore God must reign! The psalmist expresses the right petitionary perspective: "The LORD reigns; let the earth rejoice" (Ps. 97:1 RSV).

7. We come to the form of social structure dealing with property and material goods (Mt. 6:19-34; cf. Lk. 12:13-32). Like the word on the practice of piety, the remarks of Jesus on this issue were not introduced by

the antithesis formula. They were, nevertheless, constructed in a similar way. This is clearly apparent in the text. Jesus spoke of both what he forbade and what he advocated: "*Do not lay up* for yourselves treasures on earth . . . *but lay up* for yourselves treasures in heaven" (Mt. 6:19-20 RSV, emphasis added). Moreover, both Matthew and Luke deal with material possessions and being anxious about life. Not only does this suggest the probability that this material was found by both of them in this original form, but that they seem to indicate that there is an inner relationship between wealth and anxiety.

In my view, there is such a relationship. Both rest upon a phenomenon that is peculiarly human, namely, *the capacity to treasure or to value.* Not only do people distinguish between good and evil, right and wrong, true and false, but they appreciate and value what is good and right and true, and depreciate and deplore what is evil, wrong, and false. Moreover, they can discern between good, better, and best and prefer the higher over the lower! The inordinate desire for material goods and the profound anxiety about life both arise from the capacity to value. The coming reign of God which has drawn nigh in Jesus must be seen as having a critical impact upon this unique human capacity which has far-reaching consequences in the ordering of human life and society!

The laying up of treasures is an exercise in valuing. People value: they desire goods, and so they lay up treasures. Jesus simply assumed this phenomenon. In fact the acknowledgment of the kingdom of God as a "treasure hidden in a field" for which one must be prepared to sell all that one has in order to buy that field (Mt. 13:44) rests upon this fact of human nature. But Jesus implied that there are some basic questions about this human phenomenon that must be raised. What should people value? How are they affected by their valuing? Is there an order of importance among values? What is the right order of priority in valuing?

The answer to these questions depends upon the soundness of the eyes and the light in which one sees (Mt. 6:22-23). This is, of course, figurative language for moral perception. If the eyes are bad and can only admit little light, sight is impaired and the world appears dark! That is to say, moral discernment is impaired. If the eyes are sound and they can take in much light so that sight is clear and far-reaching, then moral insight is sharp and penetrating and the world and its goods are seen in their true proportions and value. One can then develop a proper scale of values, act according to moral priorities, and live by the truth! One cannot doubt that the value system of a society is a basic structure of its order.

Jesus rightly observed that there are two types of valuing. One type is treasuring on earth, and the other is treasuring in heaven. Treasuring on earth is the valuing of goods that can fade, erode, or be stolen. In short, any good that can be lost is not worth valuing and accumulating. Under this criterion, most of what people regard as truly valuable and so worth pursuing and accumulating would be viewed as "treasures on earth." This would include such goods as material wealth, power, rank and prestige, beauty and comfort, and so forth. A society that is ordered around these values and shapes its people to pursue and live by them is actually hewing out cisterns, "broken cisterns, that can hold no water" (Jer. 2:13 RSV).

Jesus did not deny the relative importance of these goods. There is some measure of worth in them that attracts people to value them. What he proscribed strongly is the kind of valuing that orients life dominantly in their direction and so makes idols out of them. The wisdom of the word of Jesus on treasuring comes from the insight that one's valuing determines one's life-orientation and ultimately one's destiny: "Where your treasure is, there will your heart be also" (Mt. 6:21). What ultimately shapes and orients life is actually one's master or idol. And "no one can serve two masters; for either he will hate the one and love the other, or he will be devoted to the one and despise the other. You cannot serve God and mammon" (Mt. 6:24). Treasuring on earth is serving mammon!

But what does treasuring in heaven entail? Negatively and in contrast to treasuring on earth, it would mean the pursuit of goods that last and cannot be lost! Jesus specified later in the text what these goods were, namely, the kingdom of God and its righteousness (Mt. 6:33). But this answer is connected with goods about which people are anxious. The inner connection between valuing and worrying must be seen in order to appreciate the point of Jesus. What we value we do not want to lose. And if what we value fades or erodes or can be stolen so that it can be lost, then we worry about losing it! This is most vividly illustrated by our anxiety about our life (Mt. 6:25). We value our life. But life fades, erodes, and is lost in death. It is threatened with loss all the time. And so we are profoundly anxious about it! Our anxiety drives us to pursue and obtain those goods that would ensure life: food, drink, clothing, shelter and by extension, wealth, power, comfort. Can one imagine the massive industries that have been painstakingly built to secure these goods, the amount of time, energy, and skill to acquire them, the conflict and violence they have caused in fighting over them?

The tragic irony in all this is that in pursuing the goods that support life, we use, expend, exhaust, and eventually lose our life. The end becomes the means, while the means become the end. The means for life becomes more important than life itself. There is here a tragic inversion of values! And so Jesus asks: Is not life more than food and the body more than clothing? (Mt. 6:25). This question should devastate our scale of values and force a reordering of our priorities!

Moreover, we do not only work tirelessly to avoid the loss of life; we also want to prolong it! We are deeply worried about its aging. We sorely want to add at least a cubit to our span of life and to cover the deepening lines and wrinkles on its face (Mt. 6:27). We worry about becoming naked, and so we put on some clothing. But we want to clothe ourselves also with fashionable clothes, with a good name, a fine reputation, a beautiful image, a high social position! And while we are engrossed in protecting our vulnerability to hunger, aging, and nakedness, which in the end is an exercise in futility, God in his providence feeds the birds of the air and clothes the lilies of the fields. And so Jesus asks: "Are you not of more value than they? . . . Will he not much more clothe you—you of little faith?" (Mt. 6:26, 30).

Jesus sought to drive home the point that human valuing takes place within the providence of God. Treasuring in heaven is reckoning with the logic of God's providential ordering. In that ordering, there are at least two ways of scaling values. One way follows the logic that if that which is higher is present, then the lower is presupposed to be already there also. If God has created human life and the human body, then it goes without saying that all the means that will sustain human life, such as food, clothing, and shelter, will also be given. The other way is the opposite of this, and it is equally valid: if the lesser is adequately provided for then how much more will the greater be taken care of? If God feeds the birds and clothes the lilies even though they make no provision for securing their own existence, will He not much more take care of the human being who is of greater value than the birds and the lilies? In other words, God has His own way of valuing and to reckon with His valuing means to treasure those things that He deeply cares about!

If this is what treasuring in heaven means, and if one's treasure is what shapes and directs the heart, what then must the human heart value if it is to reckon with the providential order of God? In short, what is human life for? If food is for life, and life is for the achievement of human selfhood, then what is the human self for? The answer of Jesus: *the human self is for seeking the reign of God and for living in its righteousness!* This is first in the order of Jesus' values! And if it is sought and realized, then all the other things that human beings value—the treasures of earth—will also be given and appreciated in terms of the measure of value that is appropriate to them! In Luke this seeking first of God's kingdom is matched by the assurance: "It is your Father's good pleasure to give you the kingdom" (Lk. 12:32).

8. We now come to the form of social structure dealing with social norms and community standards. As indicated earlier, this issue is raised by the phenomenon of *judging*. Making a judgment is usually done on the basis of law, or custom, or social norms and community standards. And these are usually shared norms (Mt. 7:2). But Jesus seems to prohibit making any judgment at all: "Judge not, that you be not judged" (Mt. 7:1-6 RSV; cf. Lk. 6:32-42). The antithetical force of this prohibition becomes clear and sharp when seen against what precedes it and what follows it.

It has just been shown that treasuring is an exercise in valuing. One cannot avoid making a judgment in valuing, for one must (a) distinguish between good and evil, between true and false, and between grades of good—between good, better, and best; and (b) together with this act of discrimination goes the sense of appreciation for what is perceived as valuable! Both discrimination and appreciation are dimensions of "judging."

Moreover, the issues that Jesus discussed following his word against judging imply the inescapability of judging. Jesus spoke of removing the speck out of a brother's eye, of not giving to the dogs what is holy, of knowing what to pray for, of doing to others what one would like others to do to oneself (Mt. 7:3-12). All these imply the necessity of judging. And so while taking seriously the antithetical character of the prohibition, one must still have to grasp the sense and thrust of the prohibition against judging in terms of the impact of the coming of the kingdom of God!

The "judging" that seems to have been in the mind of Jesus and which he prohibits is the sort that includes three dimensions. First, in everyday life the act of judging has an evaluational character. Any evaluation already contains the beginnings of criticism and condemnation.

Second, condemnation necessarily has a future orientation. It consigns a person to a fate that is yet to take place as a result of a deed that was evaluated according to standards current at the time that it was done or judged. Thus, to condemn a person is to declare him without hope in a future that has been determined by the past! This is a future determined by the past. Does anyone have control over someone's future? Does anyone have the right and the sufficient knowledge to declare anyone as hopeless?

Third, in view of the future orientation of judgment, and because of the element of condemnation contained in it, should it not be understood as a prerogative that rightfully belongs to God? Only God may rightly pass judgment on anyone because only He can truly discriminate between good and evil, and only He holds and knows the future of anyone! This being the case, one must not judge at all, unless one is prepared to be judged by the same judgment with which one has judged; that is to say, by the norms that are socially shared!

It seems, however, that there is a more important reason for the prohibition against judging besides what has been said so far. This has to do with the fact that the coming kingdom of God has already drawn near in Jesus Christ. The antithetical feature of the prohibition derives from this event. The coming near of the reign of God has a threefold radical impact upon the activity of judging. First, *it invalidates the social norms of the Mosaic community as a standard for judging*. It puts them out of operation and so one must not use them anymore. Second, *the coming of the Kingdom replaces the Mosaic social norms by putting itself in their place*. Therefore, the reign of God in Jesus is now to be the measure by which judging is to be done. But its norms are not the same as the old ones. It has certain characteristics that must be reckoned with as a standard of judgment.

For one thing, the future orientation of judging has now been brought to bear immediately upon the present with the coming near of the kingdom of God in Jesus. As a result, it is now the future which shapes the past and the present, instead of the other way around, as in the old style of judging. To judge now under conditions of the Kingdom is to provide a future for the past; it is to open up the possibility of a new beginning where there was none before. To judge now is to make hope possible! Moreover, the purpose of the coming of the Kingdom is to save, not to condemn. Therefore, any judging that is made on it as a basis or measure must have the same intention: to save and heal, not to condemn and destroy!

The third impact of the reign of God upon judging is that *since a new measure has been put in place, a new style of judging must now come into operation.* It should be the sort that takes into account the characteristic features of this new standard. That new style is exemplified in the instructions of Jesus that followed the prohibition against judging. For one thing, judging must no longer be made from a self-righteous perspective. One realizes that he has a "log in his own eye" which he must himself remove first, before he can even begin "to see the speck in his brother's eye," let alone presume to remove it (Mt. 7:3-4). The condemnatory sting in judging must be removed and replaced with compassion and forgiveness out of a common need for God's mercy!

For another thing, judging discerns and protects what is truly and essentially important. It identifies what is really "holy" and appreciates it in its full value, and it will not allow it to be defaced, deformed, or trampled upon by those who do not appreciate it (Mt. 7:6). It will not confuse the minutiae for the substance, the Law for the Kingdom! And if it is necessary to make a stand for what truly counts, it will not be found wanting, even in the face of persecution!

Furthermore, judging rests upon the sure confidence that it is God who judges and that He judges mercifully. Therefore, judging need no longer be self-justifying; it need not prove itself right at all by its own standard! For it is God who in grace justifies and makes right and saves! The judging that is entailed in asking, seeking, and knocking is prompted not by our need but by the readiness of God to give "good things to those who ask him" (Mt. 7:7-11). Prayer is evoked by God's giving, not by our needing! And so what we pray for is judged by what God gives and not by what we ask! Judging becomes petition; it is prayer!

Finally, the new style of judging makes the good we want others to do to us to be the basis and measure of what we are to do or give to others (Mt. 7:12). In the old style, what we dish out is what we get in return; it is a self-oriented ethic. In the new style, what we expect from others is what we should give or do to them; it is an other-determined and therefore an other-directed ethic! What is truly good is what comes to us as a gift from the other. And since this comes to us only upon the initiative of the other, the only way to make it happen is for us to take the initiative in doing it to them. And so we do the good that is truly good for them, even as they do the good that is truly good for us! The good that is done is a shared good, and it is out of such a shared good that the full measure for judging the good evolves! Jesus says that this is the essence of the Law and the Prophets! It becomes the rule of thumb, as it were, for the new style of judging that fulfills the Law and the Prophets precisely by transcending them.

9. We come to the concluding section of the Sermon on the Mount (Mt. 7:13-27). In our reading of this section, the issues that are discussed point to an aspect of social structure that is crucial to life-together. This has to do with the *sense of order, stability, and direction of a society*. These are secured by (a) the strength of the basis of a society, (b) its sense of purpose, (c) the commitment of its people to its goals, and (d) its ability to overcome its enemies, whether in the form of crises, threats, or detractors! We are not here dealing with the politico-economic or ideological framework of a society, but rather with its animating power, its inner sense of order, and the thrust of its movement. Put in another way, we are probing into the "soul" of a society. It is my opinion that the concluding section of the Sermon on the Mount addresses this particular dimension of social structure. As we explore this claim in what follows, we shall discover that we are doing nothing more than summarize what we have covered in this section.

Jesus claimed that a personal and social life built upon the reign of God has a rock-like foundation. The phrase "these words of mine" in Matthew 7:24 obviously refers to the whole discourse of Jesus on the Mount as summarized and presented by Matthew. The words of Jesus represent and reveal "the will of (his) Father" (7:21). The substance and thrust of God's will as proclaimed by Jesus is that the coming reign of God is now "at hand" in Jesus Christ. Jesus quite obviously intended *his words* to provide a new foundation for social life, covering all essential elements of social structure, and calling for changes consistent with that new basis. He wanted *his words* to be a foundation-rock for the "house" of personal and social life (7:24-25). He was doing this radical action on his own initiative, substituting *his words* for the Torah and his authority for the authority of Moses (cf. Mt. 5:2, 27, 33, etc.). Jesus was confident that if life-together were built upon the foundation of his words, it would stand and last. It will overcome the threats, crises, and detractors that will beat upon it as it lives through time and history. In the end it will be affirmed by God and so will be made to stand through eternity! The reason for all this is that it rests upon the foundation of the reign of God in Jesus Christ! Whereas, if it were built on some other foundation besides the words of Jesus it would be established upon "sand" and it would collapse under the beatings of history!

Jesus claimed that society is built upon its rock foundation in the reign of God by both "hearing" and "doing" (Mt. 7:24). God's reign is His business. It is His right to reign. He reigns by His own initiative and power. He determines the ways and means of His reign. The effects of His reign are completely within His control. He has determined that He will reign in Jesus Christ through human agency. And so He reveals His will for human hearing and doing. He reigns through human hearing and doing. It is by human hearing and doing that His will and reign come to pass in human affairs! It is in the form of human hearing and doing that God's reign comes to be incarnate or embodied in human history. It is through human hearing and doing that His will becomes both formative and normative for the shaping and ordering of human society! Human hearing and doing constitute the essence of discipleship! To hear is to learn, know, and understand, and so to exercise the creative power of thought!

To do is to obey what one hears. It is to shape and alter reality according to the creative power of thought. Hearing and doing are the two most potent capacities of human agency! To be a disciple is to employ these potencies in the service of the reign of God! It will not do to enlist only one and not the other (Mt. 7:21-23). To hear only and not do, or do only and not hear, is to be a false disciple. Either way constitutes antinomianism or lawlessness. One who hears and does not do is a libertine. One who does but does not hear is an activist. And both are "lawless" in the sense that they do not hear and do the will of God, but only obey their own autonomous will. And so a society of "lawless" people will not stand and last. It will collapse into anarchy and chaos. Only a society that hears and does the will of God in His reign will surely stand and last!

Jesus claimed that personal and social life has to make a choice as to which way and direction it should go. There is a narrow gate that enters into a way that is hard to travel, but in the end it leads to life, although only a few find it. There is a wide gate which enters into a road that is easy to travel, but in the end it leads to destruction, and many find their way into it. Jesus is here invoking the age-old doctrine of the two ways (Mt. 7:13-14; cf. Deut. 11:26-28; 30:15-20; Ps. 1:6; 119:29-30; 139:24; Jer. 21:8). Each way represents a life-possibility and a way of ordering life-together. A point of entry, a road to travel, a final destination: such is the inescapable course of human life. And anyone who runs this course must enter by a gate, travel the road headed in a certain direction, and end up somewhere.

It makes all the difference, however, which gate one enters, which road one travels, and which destination one finally ends up in! For one leads into life, the other leads into death! Jesus, therefore, *recommends* a choice: it is to "enter through the narrow gate" (Mt. 7:13). Those who enter through the narrow gate are prepared to walk the way of com-mitment, faithfulness, and discipline by both hearing and doing the will of God. This way of discipleship is hard. It will demand the denial of self, the taking up of a cross, and the following after Jesus along his way. It will be required to bear fruit—good fruit—and it may need pruning from time to time to make this possible. But in the end it will lead to life.

On the other hand, Jesus *warns* that the other gate is wide and the road is easy, but it ends in destruction and those who enter and go by it are many. It does not require a life of discipleship, and no commit-ment and discipline are asked of it. But it ends in destruction! A rec-ommendation and a warning together make up the word of Jesus on this point. He thus creates a critical moment of decision fraught with the burden of life and death! This is evangelism in action!

We have been seeking to determine the elements of Jesus' strategy of social transformation in his ministry. So far we have dealt with three major elements of this social strategy. The first had to do with the ful-fillment and virtual replacement of the Law by the approach of the com-ing reign of God as the new foundation of Jewish social existence. The second described the various ways through which salvation was expe-rienced by both the "sinners" and the "righteous" of Jewish society. The approach of the coming reign of God offered new possibilities of life to all types of people in Jewish society. The third element focused on the structure and institutions of society and the kind of radical changes in lifestyle and behavior demanded by the approach of the kingdom of God.

Seen from the perspective of social change, these are the sort of changes any movement of radical social reform would want to achieve. Any social change of real and lasting significance must at least alter the basis of society with a new or different one, make available new possibilities of a better life to its people, and effect redeeming or liberating changes in social structure and behavior.

From the perspective of Jesus, these were changes that were demanded directly, urgently, and necessarily by the approach of the coming reign of God that has drawn near. As changes that altered the status quo in terms of returning to God and the restructuring of social life, they constitute an essential element of the "repentance and faith" which are the right and proper response to the breaking-in of the coming reign of God in Jesus Christ. There is, therefore, an "evangelical" dimension in presentation, perception, and response in the core of the social experience of salvation.

For this reason we are justified in including social salvation as an elemental aspect of mission evangelism in its strategy for social change.

Note

1. William Butler Yeats, "The Second Coming," reprinted in *Understanding Poetry*, edited by Cleanth Brooks and Robert Penn Warren (New York: Henry Holt and Company, 1950), p. 506.

CHAPTER 5
THE CALL TO DISCIPLESHIP

There is a fourth essential component in the strategy of Jesus for social transformation. And like the three we have so far identified, it is elemental in his experience. This has to do with *the formation of a new community* that seeks to live out a new style of life which is consistent with, and expressive of, the fundamental changes that were sought to be achieved. This fourth element is as important as the others. The viability of the changes sought in the social vision and its strategy will depend upon some people who are ready to take them up, make them work effectively in concrete ways, and demonstrate publicly their capacity to make life better in all its dimensions. Moreover, these people must be gathered into a new form of life-together, into a new community, which deliberately anticipates the promises of the new social vision that called it forth in the first place; and in being so, it becomes a living and powerful example in the present of what can be hoped for in the future. Blazing a new way of life and pioneering a new form of community require the courage of adventure, the readiness to experiment, and the commitment to struggle and endure to the end. Such a significant venture would require a committed and cohesive group that sees the vision steadily, pursues it steadfastly, and leads the way fearlessly towards its realization against all odds. This is the impetus that motivates the formation of cause-oriented groups, political parties, and radical or revolutionary communities.

These considerations inevitably lead to the question, did Jesus *intend* to establish the church as the avant-garde community of his social vision? The issue was formulated in the form of a historical observation by Alfred Loisy, a leader of the modern Catholic reform movement, at the turn of the century: "Jesus foretold the kingdom, and it was the Church that came."[1] There is a great deal of scholarly controversy surrounding this issue, into which we shall not enter here. There cannot be any doubt, however, about the fact that Jesus formed a circle of disciples around him with whom he shared his deepest thoughts about his mission and destiny, forged them into a community with a new ethos, and sent them out on a mission to Israel. It was this circle of disciples which in fact constituted the nucleus of a new people of God—the church—that was to emerge later as a community distinct from Israel following the death and resurrection of Jesus. In what follows we shall deal with some elements that are at the core of this new community.

Faith, Repentance, and Discipleship

Jesus was an itinerant preacher. "He went about all Galilee" (Mt. 4:23 RSV) and of course he traveled to Jerusalem once or twice in his public career. He told Simon and those who sought him, "Let us go on to the next towns, that I may preach there also; for that is why I came out" (Mk. 1:38 RSV; cf. Lk. 4:43-44). He went about "all the cities and villages" (Mt. 9:35). And wherever he went, he taught, he preached, he healed, he cast out demons (Mt. 4:23-24; 9:35). He sat at table with sinners and tax collectors and precisely in this way he brought them into the sphere of the reign of God (Mk. 2:15; Mt. 9:10). His fame spread far and wide and "great crowds followed him from Galilee, the Decapolis, Jerusalem, Judea, and from beyond the Jordan" (Mt. 4:24-25). There were many who responded in repentance and faith to the presence of the reign of God in him. He "called to him the multitude with his disciples" and he issued to them a general call to discipleship: "If any man would come after me, let him deny himself and take up his cross and follow me" (Mk. 8:34 RSV).

This summons to discipleship is as genuinely historical to Jesus as his call to repentance and faith. In fact there is an inner essential relationship between them so that the occurrence of one necessarily entails the other. Those who respond in repentance do so out of faith in the God whose coming reign has drawn near through the forgiveness that Jesus offers, and those who repent and believe find themselves inevitably responding as well to the call to follow after Jesus and so to a life of discipleship in him. *It is this threefold response of faith, repentance, and discipleship that brings a person directly into the sphere of the reign of God in Jesus, which at the same time entails entering a new form of life-together or fellowship in which persons become, as Paul would put it later, "members one of another."*

Among the many who came under the saving power of the reign of God in and through Jesus and who followed him, there was a core group (Mk. 4:10; 8:34) which in the synoptic tradition was regularly referred to as "his disciples" or "the Twelve" (Mk. 2:15-16, 23; 3:7, 13; 4:10; 6:1-7, 45; 8:27, 34; etc.). It seems that if we are to understand the nature and purpose of discipleship, it is to the calling of the disciples of Jesus that we must turn for guidance and understanding. The essence of discipleship is summarized in somewhat stylized form in texts such as the following: Mark 3:13-19; 6:7-12; 8:31–9:1; Matthew 10:1–11:1; Luke 9:1-6; 10:1-12; cf. 9:57-62. There are also other texts that describe the way some of the individual disciples were called: Mark 1:16-20; 2:13-14; Matthew 4:18-22; 9:9; Mark 5:27-28; John 1:35-42. A close analysis of these texts would yield a pattern that clearly portrays the essential structure and content of discipleship.

The Call

The first element to note is that *it is Jesus who calls.* He is absolutely sovereign in this whole act of calling and making disciples. He takes the initiative. It is as Jesus passes by that he sees Simon and Andrew and James and John and he *decides* to call them and he in fact *calls* them (Mk. 1:16-20). Levi, the tax collector, was called by the same sovereign initiative (Mk. 2:14). Other texts underline the same emphasis: it is Jesus who *"called to him those whom he desired."* He *"appointed them* to be with him"; *he sent* them out to preach; *he gave* them authority to cast out demons and *he even renamed* some of them (Mk. 3:13-19). The Johannine Jesus underlines his sovereign initiative in the whole process of disciple-making: "You did not choose me, but I chose you. And I appointed you . . ." (Jn. 15:16).

The first part of this Johannine remark of Jesus underscores the fact that one does not become a disciple through one's own initiative. Luke reports a man who came up to Jesus and voluntarily offered to follow him wherever he would go (Lk. 9:57). Jesus threw cold water on his enthusiasm by describing himself as a poor itinerant preacher with no fixed residence, and so this man would have no security for his future with him at all! (Lk. 9:58). The man named Legion whom Jesus liberated from demon-possession voluntarily "begged" to follow after Jesus and be with him. But Jesus refused him, and sent him instead on a preaching mission to his hometown (Mk. 5:18-20).

Jesus' method of calling his own disciples is in contrast to the traditional way by which a person becomes a disciple in the ancient world. In rabbinic Judaism, a would-be disciple chose the teacher in whose school he wanted to train. Of course, the teacher would have to agree to take in the pupil. But the initiative lay with the pupil, not with the teacher. The same pattern held for those who wished to study philosophy in the Hellenistic world. The pupil initially chose the school of philosophy and the teacher whose teaching had attracted him. In contrast to this, Jesus called, chose, and appointed his own disciples. This style is unique to Jesus in the ancient world. Is there an explanation for this? We shall deal with this issue below.

The second point to notice is that the call of Jesus is "Follow me" (Mk. 2:14; cf. 1:17; Lk. 5:27; Mt. 9:9). These two words encompass the whole range of what it means to be a disciple of Jesus. Each word carries a load of meaning which one must understand and appreciate. The word "me" points to the reality of Jesus as a concrete person. The summons to follow him is to enter as the person one is into a personal relationship with him as the person he is. Normally, a disciple relates as a pupil, a learner, a student, to his master as a teacher. The relationship is a learning-teaching one. What is important here is the knowledge factor—its teaching and learning. The whole relation between student and teacher is precisely just that—nothing more! What the teacher has to offer is not himself, but his teaching. What the student is about is not to appreciate the teacher as a person but to understand his teaching! In contrast to this, in Jesus' call to discipleship, one's whole person is drawn into engagement with the full reality of Jesus as the person he is. The engagement is not simply one of mind, but also of heart and will and strength, indeed, of the total self. The character of the engagement is one of "love," that is, of mutual, total self-giving. The aim of the engagement is not simply the enlightening of the mind but the saving of the whole person!

Moreover, the "me" of Jesus entails what is most significant about his person. What that is, there cannot be any doubt at all. The be-all and end-all of Jesus' person and existence is nothing more nor less than the reality of the coming reign of God breaking in through him upon the world in a decisively saving way! The "me" of Jesus is the sphere of the rule of God! To enter into personal relationship with Jesus is to come under the saving power of this rule. But this rule has its own way, its own order, its own style of doing things and relating to people and living life and facing death. To enter into its sphere is to live according to its way, and so to follow, to follow after Jesus who is the sphere of God's rule and is, therefore, the way of God's rule. But the way of God's rule is precisely to save, to heal, to liberate, to forgive, to love the enemy, to reach out in fellowship with the outcast, to serve the good of the other. It is the way of self-denial, of losing oneself, of bearing one's cross daily and following after Jesus!

The root sense of the Greek word *(akolouthein)* translated "to follow" is "to go or come after" or "to follow after." It brings forth the image of someone walking determinedly along a road leading to somewhere and followed from behind by someone who is equally resolved. The one who is being followed is always ahead; he leads the way, and he never falls behind. The one who is following comes after. He is a few steps behind, and he walks the same way as the leader.

This image in some respects portrays the relationship between Jesus and his disciples. To follow Jesus is "to follow after" him. However, it gives the impression that there is already a way, a road, leading to somewhere, and all that Jesus has to do is walk ahead on this way, on this road that is already there and lead his disciples on it. This is absolutely not the case. The fact of the matter is that there is no way at all yet, until the Lord himself hacks out a trail in the wilderness. There is as yet no way in the wilderness, and only as the Lord himself blazes out a way does there come to be a way at all for both the Lord and the disciple! And the way he makes is the only right way; there is no other!

The Lord leads not so much by walking ahead on a road already there, but precisely by making and paving a way that only he alone, and nobody else, can provide. In and through him alone has the reign of God broken from the future into the wilderness of the present, and so he becomes the way into that future, which alone is the right and only future for humankind! As the maker and paver of *this way*, which is he as the way, he must always be ahead and lead, otherwise there is no way and there is no one to follow. And it is by making a way which he himself is that he leads. Leadership is making a way and paving it for others to follow. It is being *the* way for others! It is in this sense that Jesus is Lord and he must be followed! But it is also exactly the same sense in which he is servant! For Jesus, the leader is one who serves (Lk. 22:26). He serves by leading, by making and paving and being the way—the only right way—for others! To lead is to be the way for others (Lk. 22:26; Jn. 13:8-9, 12-15; 14:6). Because Jesus is servant, he must be followed for the simple reason that he does not lead where he has not already gone. As Lord and servant, Jesus is always ahead; the disciples only come or follow after him. But what specifically does it mean to "follow after" Jesus? We shall return to this issue below.

A third elemental point to note is that the call of Jesus to follow him includes a promise: "I will make you become fishers of men" (Mk. 1:17 RSV; Mt. 4:19; Lk. 5:10). The language of Jesus here is, of course, figurative. He promises a new way of making a living somewhat similar to what the fishermen whom he had called were already doing. While they were now catching fish, they would eventually be "catching people" (Lk. 5:10). It would be a gross mistake, however, to understand this as merely a new form of livelihood or another way of earning a living, and so identify it with becoming a *professional* minister of the gospel. Jesus sent out his disciples with his own authority *to participate in the work he was doing* (Mk. 3:14-15; 6:7-12). Later as the risen Lord, he would commission them to become his "witnesses in Jerusalem, and in all Judea and Samaria, and to the ends of the earth" (Acts 1:8; cf. Lk. 24:44-49; Mt. 28:16-20). He exhorted his disciples to be "the light of the world" and make their "light so shine before men" so that their good works may be seen by men and "give glory to your Father who is in heaven" (Mt. 5:14-16 RSV). What lies at the heart of discipleship is living the life of witness to the reign of God by participating in the work of Jesus so that the world at large may see his good works and give glory to the God who is his Father! It is to a life that witnesses to God before men that becoming "fishers of men" points.

It would equally be a mistake of enormous proportions if this form of life were limited to the twelve disciples who eventually became apostles of the risen Lord. The life of witness to God who is the Father of the Lord Jesus Christ is the destiny to which every human being is called. It is everyone's destiny in the sense that it is the purpose for which the human being is created. In Genesis 1:27 it is written that "God created humankind in his image, in the image of God he created them; male and female he created them." God created the human being in his image so that the human being may image God, that is, reflect the reality and character and activity of God. The nature and life of the human being are meant to light up and point to and reflect clearly and unmistakably, the reality and character and activity of God. To be an image of God is to be a mirror for God in the world! To be made in the image of God is precisely to be a witness to Him, to speak His truth, to point to His reality, to light up His nature, to do His will, to fulfill His purpose, to reflect His glory!

No human being, however, has seen God, and so no one knows for certain what God looks like. One cannot, therefore, draw an image of God which one can then reflect in and through his life! One cannot witness to something one has not seen or heard! And if he does, his witness is false! So how then can the human being fulfill his life-calling and realize the purpose of his creation? How can one *live in truth,* that is, *be* in the image of God, which is the truth of our creation? How can one *bear witness to the truth,* that is, *reflect* the image of God, which is the destiny of our creation?

The answer to this profound problem of human life is to be found in discipleship. A unique feature of discipleship in Jesus is being *shown by him as to who the Father is.* At a time when Jesus was being repudiated by almost all of Israel (Mt. 11:11-24), Jesus rejoices in the Holy Spirit and privately prays: "I thank thee, Father, Lord of heaven and earth, that thou hast hidden these things from the wise and understanding and revealed them to babes; yea, Father, for such was thy gracious will. All things have been delivered to me by my Father; and no one knows the Son except the Father, and no one knows the Father except the Son and any one to whom the Son chooses to reveal him" (Mt. 11:25-27 RSV; cf. Lk. 10:21-22). The "babes" referred to here are the disciples of Jesus. They come to know the Father through the Father Himself disclosing or revealing Himself to them. The Father does this through the Son, who alone knows the Father and therefore can truly reveal Him. And the Son has chosen to reveal the Father to his disciples. This knowledge of the Father has been hidden from the rest of humanity, even from the wise and understanding! The call to discipleship is to share in the knowledge of God what nobody else has known and which only Jesus reveals. To be a disciple of Jesus is to be in the truth of this knowledge and so become a bearer of its truth.

The claim that Jesus is the revealer of the God who is his Father is connected in the New Testament with the claim that *Jesus himself is the very "image of God"* (2 Cor. 4:4, emphasis added). "He is the image of the invisible God" (Col. 1:15). The glory of God has shown on the face of Jesus Christ (2 Cor. 4:6). He is the image of God precisely because he "is in the bosom of the Father," that is, he shares in the being and nature and activity of God (Jn. 1:18 RSV). "In him all the fullness of God was pleased to dwell" (Col. 1:19; 2:9). He is the image of God also because as a human being he truly fulfills his vocation of being a true witness to God. For in all that he said and did, in the manner he related to people, and in the way he lived his life and died his death, he was nothing more and nothing less than quite simply a witness to the reality of God his Father! Jesus was truly human precisely in being quite simply a witness of God! The simplest and profoundest word that can be said of Jesus is: "He has made him (the Father) known" (Jn. 1:18). He is the one man who fully fulfilled his destiny of being made in the image of God and thereby became the only image of God that humanly reflects truly and clearly and fully the reality of God!

If these considerations are anywhere near the truth, then we must be prepared to join the New Testament in the further claim that *being made in the image of God is precisely being created in Jesus Christ, who is the image of God.* We are made as human beings in Jesus Christ as the image of God. We are enabled to fulfill our destiny as human beings to reflect the reality of God, to be His image, His mirror, in the world, by being witnesses of Jesus Christ. *The call to discipleship is, therefore, nothing less than the call to fulfill the meaning and purpose of being created a human being, namely, to be in Jesus Christ by following after him and becoming his witnesses!* The call to discipleship is open to all human beings simply because they are created for this destiny. The call of the Twelve is meant to exemplify and represent this universal call.

A fourth elemental point to ponder is that the call to become "fishers of men" is issued in the form of a promise: *"I will make you fishers of men."* What is being promised to those whom he calls is in the future and it is their true future. What they were now—catchers of fish, or catchers of anything else for that matter—has no future to it and to continue in it is to persist in something that is not their real future. Luke records an incident in which Peter, responding to Jesus' word to him to "put out into the deep and let down your net for a catch" said: "Master, we toiled all night and took nothing!" (Lk. 5:4-5 RSV). This is exactly a true commentary on human life and vocation outside of the discipleship of Jesus. It is a life that "toils all night" for nothing!

But when Peter obeyed Jesus' word and let down the nets, and caught "a great shoal of fish" so that their nets were breaking, Peter was astonished at the enormous catch and then he suddenly realized who he was: "I am a sinful man" (Lk. 5:6-9). *A life that toils all night for nothing by a human being who has missed the mark and has fallen short of his destiny is the characteristic of human existence outside of the discipleship of Jesus.* It is revealed for what it is in its futility and worthlessness precisely by the call of Jesus to discipleship. The call exposes life outside of discipleship to be without a future. In this sense, the call is at the same time a judgment on present life and on the status quo. Implicitly it is a call for repentance.

The new future that the call of Jesus makes available is not possible, however, apart from him. It is he who makes it possible and available. The "I" of Jesus in the promise "I will make you" assumes the power to create a new future which he makes available to human beings. The creation of possibility which is availed of and actualized by human beings in their freedom and decision is precisely the meaning of God as creator. Jesus assumes precisely this power and fulfills exactly this role in his call to discipleship.

At the same time, actualizing a possibility concretely entails a remaking of self, a change of loyalty and commitment, and a redirection of life. It calls for a *metanoia,* a decisive return to the Lord and a radical change of life: from catching fish to catching human beings by following Jesus. Such a total remaking of self is precisely the meaning of God as Savior. Jesus assumes fully this power and effectively fulfills this role in his call to discipleship. It is, nevertheless, the case that the realizing of the possibility of a new mode of life and the remaking of self are not arbitrarily imposed upon the human being as determination from without but through inner empowerment and self-enabling. They happen to the human being *as* he actively follows after Jesus. To come after Jesus is itself a self-transforming activity or process: it makes one *become* fishers of people!

The Response

A fifth essential point that must be taken into account is that the call of Jesus to follow him and become what God intends human beings to be *demands a specific response.* If the texts that record the response are to be trusted, they undoubtedly indicate an obedient response that was decisive, unconditional, total, and final. Upon hearing the call, those who were called "immediately left" whatever they were doing and any connection they had and "followed him" (Mk. 1:18, 20; 2:14). To appreciate this kind of response, we need to see it within the crisis into which the call of Jesus unexpectedly plunged the disciples.

We may note first of all that the call of Jesus came unexpectedly to people whose patterns of life and activity had already been established. Simon and his brother, Andrew, were already fishermen. *They already had a living.* At the time the call of Jesus came, they were busy fishing at sea. The same was true with the Zebedee brothers, James and John. They were making a living as fishermen, and at the time Jesus called them "they were in their boat mending the nets." *They had properties—* boat and nets—in connection with their occupation as fishermen. *They had hired servants* who were dependent upon them for their living as well. There was *a market for their "product." They had families* whom they loved and for whose support they were responsible. They must have had plans about the future for themselves and their families based on their present situation. They must have had family roots and friends in their village. These were not mere unrelated and useless items under their disposal at will. They represented deeply held values and life-support relationships that shaped and settled their lives. They formed their mode of being in the world and shaped their identity in it: *they were and were known to be fishermen.*

Moreover, the social milieu of the time did not encourage "social change" and mobility. Family life in a rural village was cohesive. Individual life was rooted firmly in the community by custom and tradition which were not hospitable to sudden change. Finding gainful employment in an economy of endemic poverty was not easy. Hazarding an uncertain future could stir up fears that could not be reasonably allayed even by the adventurous in spirit.

Given these factors, would the people whom Jesus called have easily abandoned their mode of life in exchange for something so unpromising and uncertain as following a poor and itinerant preacher?

Jesus would have expected them to consider the alternatives and "to sit down and count the cost." This is a practice embedded in the wisdom of common sense, and Jesus urged it as a prudential measure especially to those whom he was calling to discipleship (Lk. 14:25-33). For his part, Jesus made the terms of his invitation rather clear and uncompromising. Following him meant self-denial, participation in his suffering, being totally committed to him, and readiness to sacrifice one's life for him and for the gospel (Mk. 8:34-35; Lk. 14:27; Mt. 10:38-39). To follow him entailed loving him more than family (Mt. 10:37). If this meant "hating" one's family or being "against" one's family, one must not hesitate to do so (Lk. 14:25-26; Mt. 10:35-36; cf. Mk. 3:31-35). It could happen that in following Jesus a person's "foes will be those of his own household" (Mt. 10:36 RSV). Indeed, in the light of discipleship all that human beings normally value, such as life, family, vocation, property, and friendship, pale into insignificance and they must by no means stand in the way of following Jesus!

It is clear that the call to discipleship literally entails a reversal of values: only Jesus and he alone becomes the master-value and everything else must become as nothing (Mt. 6:24; cf. 7:33). Jesus graphically portrays this dramatic reversal of values in terms of the parable of the Hidden Treasure: "The kingdom of heaven is like treasure hidden in a field, which a man found and covered up; then in his joy he goes and sells all that he has and buys that field" (Mt. 13:44 RSV; cf. 13:45). Is one prepared to sell all that one has and buy the field with the hidden treasure? In Luke 14:33 Jesus gives a solemn warning: "Whoever of you does not renounce all that he has cannot be my disciple" (RSV). Are there any who will not readily "renounce" all that they have or value and will not become disciples of Jesus? They must be many! And those who will must be very few!

Considering alternatives and counting the cost imply the possibility of a negative response. Jesus was no sanguine optimist. He was realistic enough to expect that some people would not say *yes* to his call and would give excuses which in their view would be justifiable. In the parable of the Great Banquet (Lk. 14:15-24) the reasons for refusing Jesus are given. We are here assuming that the invitation to the banquet of the Kingdom is similar to the call to discipleship. In this parable a first invitation had already been made. When everything was ready for the banquet, those who were invited were called a second time to come, thus definitely implying that the host really wanted to have his guests come and enjoy the great feast that he so generously prepared for them. Thus, they would have no reason to doubt the sincerity of the host.

But ironically none of those who were originally invited came. They all gave excuses for their refusal to come. One excused himself by saying that he had bought a field and he must go and see it (Lk. 14:18). Another said he had bought five yoke of oxen and he had to go and examine them (Lk. 14:19). And a third said he had just married a wife and he could not come (Lk. 14:20). The first two excuses had to do with economic values: property, livelihood, commerce, business commitments, management concerns. The third excuse had to do with family life values: marriage ties, family responsibilities, home life. Clearly the values of the world have a greater attraction and a more forceful hold on people than the promises of the Kingdom and its call to enter it in discipleship.

Luke also records another incident that typifies a reason for refusing Jesus which is not covered by those already mentioned. Jesus said to a man, "Follow me." But the man said to him, "Lord, first let me go and bury my father." But he said to him, "Let the dead bury their own dead" (Lk. 9:59-60). Here we have the case of one who was called by Jesus. He wanted to follow, but he felt he had to do something *first* before he could follow Jesus, namely, to bury his dead father! Now, in Jewish culture as in most cultures, custom, filial obligation, and piety dictate that one should attend to the burial of one's father. And this must come first before anything else, for obvious reasons! The son who wanted to bury his dead father first had a good reason sanctioned by culture and religion for refusing Jesus at the instance of his call! Surely, he cannot be forbidden to do a filial duty!

But for Jesus this was not a good enough reason for refusing his call; indeed, no reason for refusal is good enough. And no refusal could deter him either. He said to the man who wanted to bury his father first, "Let the dead bury their own dead; but as for you, go and proclaim the kingdom of God" (Lk. 9:60). Did this not imply that the person who refused the call of Jesus by attending to something else first is as good as dead since he refused a life with a new future? The dead cannot in any way deter Jesus from carrying on his mission! And in the parable of the Great Banquet, the refusal of the invited guests was no reason at all to cancel the feast. It was held as scheduled, and with a different set of guests who came by invitation from the city streets—the poor and maimed and blind and lame; and from the highways and hedges—the Gentiles (Lk. 14:21-24).

Why is it that no human refusal could deter Jesus? And why is it that no reason for refusal is ever good enough? This does not in any way mean that one cannot refuse Jesus, or that one has no choice on the matter. In fact, the opposite is the case. The call of Jesus puts one in a crisis of decision in which one has to make a choice. The call of Jesus to discipleship plunges one into radical freedom in the immediacy of God's presence and the choice that one makes is either of life or of death! Either/or before God—that is the situation of radical freedom into which Jesus' call puts a person inescapably!

The reason for this is the fact that the call of Jesus is no ordinary invitation. It does not come from a human source pointing to a natural human possibility. Rather, it is a call that comes *to* the human scene from a transcendent source and opens up a life possibility in it that is not latent in any given potentiality that can naturally unfold or develop. We have already seen that the call is in fact a judgment on the human situation that already engages anyone. What we are now anywhere and at any time—fishermen or otherwise—is not our proper destiny and it has no future. To persist in it is to proceed inexorably in a course that will fatefully end in our destruction because it will make us fall short, and so miss the mark, of the glory that God has prepared for us from the foundation of the world! The call of Jesus surprisingly in sheer grace offers us a way out of this fate by opening up a new life possibility that comes directly from the sphere of God's rule; it is one of repentance and faith and discipleship. His offer is given to us in the form of promise: it has a future to it, which is our future; and it can be fulfilled by precisely following after him! To refuse him is to reject what is properly *ours* from God! To follow him is to become what we are in God's sight!

What then is the right response to this kind of a call? The response of the disciples has been stylized to exemplify for all how the call of Jesus to discipleship is to be answered properly. "And immediately they left their nets and followed him" (Mk. 1:18). And again in Mark 1:20: "And they left their father Zebedee in the boat with the hired men, and followed him." The word "immediately" must not be taken to imply that those whom Jesus called did not take enough time to ponder the call and deliberate carefully on how they should respond to it. Their decision was not hurriedly or rashly made. If it were, Jesus would have readily noticed it and would most likely have exposed its hastiness and insincerity. Rather, the word "immediately" is meant to convey *unhesitating obedience*. Once the disciples made up their mind, they acted right away. They decided deliberately, freely, and responsibly. Their obedience was an *act of radical freedom,* and so it was genuine obedience. Alternatively, because the disciples obeyed in freedom, their freedom was authentic. Only the free really obey, and only those who obey freely remain truly free. Obedient freedom is a mark of discipleship!

The phrase "left . . . and followed him" is profoundly significant. It is another way of dramatically portraying radical *repentance,* which consists of a two-sided movement of the self. One side is giving up something and abandoning it completely. The other side is embracing something else that is new and different and pursuing it determinedly. The word translated "left" (leaving) literally means "to abandon." This suggests that the disciples without hesitation cut themselves loose completely from whatever it was that engaged them and any values and commitments they entailed and abandoned them. No matter how good or enjoyable their mode of life had been, they now see it to be without any future (cf. Phil. 3:4-11). They were ready to give it up and never return to it again. *Repentance is not only the abandoning of sin but the giving up of the life connected with it, including its values and its joys and its hopes!* The obedience of genuine discipleship entails this radical repentance.

At the same time as the disciples were abandoning their old mode of life and leaving it behind completely, they were exchanging it for something else which they considered to be so much better and were ready to go after it, namely, to follow Jesus! It is the fact that they now can follow Jesus that they could abandon and leave behind whatever they were and had before. A new and better alternative mode of life rendered meaningless and hopeless whatever they had been before. And because Jesus represented an alternative vision which has appeared in their horizon, they decided to follow after him! In following after him, they were literally entering the sphere of God's rule which has made its decisive appearance in Jesus. This means that Jesus did not come from the past; he comes from the future, from the future of God's reign and is therefore the bearer of the future in God! And so to follow Jesus entailed following him into the future from whence he came, namely, the future of God's reign. *Repentance is not simply a return to God, but a turning to God who has turned to us in Jesus Christ and so has given us a future in him.* Jesus is worth following precisely because of our future in him which has been made available to us by God's turning to us in him! The obedience of radical repentance entails embracing our future in the sphere of God's reign which has drawn near to us in the call of Jesus to discipleship.

To radical freedom and radical repentance we add a third, namely, radical responsibility, as the essential components of the response of the disciples to the call of Jesus. Freedom entails obedience to the call and obedience brings about the changes that constitute genuine repentance. The pursuit of both obedience and repentance in following Jesus gives rise to new responsibilities that have to be borne radically and perseveringly. The self that follows Jesus becomes an active subject; it will not be allowed to slouch in sloth. It will be severely challenged to respond fittingly to the obligations and responsibilities of its new mode of life in the context of its new horizon, namely, the sphere of God's rule.

Its *new vision for itself* in the sphere of God's rule as a potential child of God must be realized against all odds and trials. It must become self-creative of what it can be, not in itself, but *in* Jesus Christ, and it must become self-actualizing not in its power, but in the power inspired by the spirit of Jesus. But can this be done only in self-denial? How can one be self-creative by being self-denying? One can follow Jesus only by denying himself, and yet it is precisely by following Jesus that one becomes what he truly should be!

Moreover, *its new understanding of the other person* in the sphere of God's rule will demand new relationships and obligations that must be satisfied. The outcast becomes a guest at table fellowship. Who should host him? The despised Samaritan must become more neighborly to a stricken Jew than the paragons of legal virtue. Who should this be? The enemy must be loved and his good must be sought. Who must practice this? And one must forgive seventy times seven! Who can be as reconciling as to do this? The self that follows Jesus must be all these and more. He must become redemptive by being a redeeming servant of others. Is this not what it means to bear one's cross daily and so participate in the suffering of Christ which redeems?

Its *perception of the world* in the sphere of God's rule transforms the world into a theater of God's glory. But right now it is not! It is an arena of combat between good and evil and all the odds seem to be in favor of the villain. Can the self that follows Jesus afford to be a gallery spectator in this earthly and cosmic drama whose outcome makes no difference to him/her at all? Must he/she not become rather a steward of God's grace in creation and salvation and so join Him as a fellow worker in Jesus Christ in making the "earth as it is in heaven"? Does not the prayer that Jesus taught his disciples express his deepest aspirations? And must not the disciple that follows Jesus pray the same prayer and so aspire to the same vision and thus participate actively in realizing the mission of Jesus? What else does following Jesus mean except participating in his work and thereby assuming the radical responsibility of becoming a fellow worker with God in Jesus Christ?

So far we have dealt with one aspect of the nucleus of the new community brought into being through Jesus. It has to do with the call of Jesus to discipleship and the proper human response to it as exemplified by the first disciples. In concluding this section, we may note that the *sense of community that underlies discipleship has a covenant structure.* On the one hand, it is initiated by a gracious call from a transcendent source that makes a response possible and so demands it. On the other hand, it is sealed by a fitting response that pledges absolute obedience to it.

In its bare essential structure, it is obvious that discipleship bears a similarity to the covenant community between Yahweh and Israel. In this relationship Yahweh in a gracious act of deliverance which liberated Israel from bondage to Egypt becomes the Lord and God of Israel, and Israel through an act of gratitude and ratification becomes "a kingdom of priests and a holy nation" unto Yahweh and pledges that "all that the LORD has spoken we will do" (Ex. 19:1-9 RSV). This fact attests to the truth that the biblical vision of community is covenantal in essence: God alone is our God for He has decided to be so, and our vocation is to be His people.

However, the community generated by discipleship establishes a relationship in which a new reality is at the center, namely, Jesus Christ as the bearer of the kingdom of God. He is the sovereign subject of the call and is the sole object of the response. To be a disciple is to be bound to a covenantal relationship in which Jesus Christ is the object of absolute commitment, unswerving loyalty, and faithful obedience. Discipleship has the character of following after him all the way, even to the point of being martyred for him and for his cause.

This fact may bear resemblance to the absolute loyalty of social or ideological revolutionaries to their cause and their apparent readiness to become martyrs for their social vision. It differs radically from them, however, in that discipleship is a personal relationship to a *personal and historic reality,* namely, Jesus of Nazareth! Its ground, furthermore, is an initiative from a transcendent source that has come to the human scene. Its essence is genuinely *religious;* it is not a religious surrogate! Moreover, its covenantal or dialogic "partner" is not an abstract idea or utopian dream or an elusive vision but the radically and genuinely "other," namely, God incarnate with us, God Immanuel! This means that its sense of community is thoroughly *social.* It is interaction with a real "thou"; it is being with a genuine "other"! Reciprocally, the "I" in this interaction becomes an authentic "I," a self who is free to relate fittingly to the really other! Discipleship is genuine community!

Note

1. Alfred Loisy, *The Gospel and the Church,* 1912, p. 166.

CHAPTER 6

BEING WITH JESUS

We now come to a second essential element in what constitutes community or life-together among those whom Jesus called to be his disciples. It is clear from the record that they were not only called to follow him, *but also to be with him* (Mk. 3:14). There are two aspects in being with Jesus that will be taken into account here. One has to do with fellowship with Jesus, and the other is the fellowship among those who are with Jesus. We shall deal first with fellowship with Jesus.

There is no doubt that following after Jesus brings one into direct touch with him as Lord and Master. But the relationship here is asymmetrical: Jesus is seen as primarily Lord and Master, while the disciple is a servant and a pupil. The community between disciple and lord is framed by the covenantal framework of Lord and servant, of Master and pupil. The disciple follows after, he does not walk beside, the master.

In the second aspect of community we are dealing with here, the accent, however, is not on the teacher being above the pupil, or the servant under the master, but on the *disciple becoming like his teacher, the servant becoming like his master* (Mt. 10:24-25). For when the disciple is fully taught he will be like his teacher, although he may not rise above or be greater than his teacher (Lk. 6:40; Jn. 13:16; 15:20). The fellowship between Jesus and his disciples here is one of equality, intimacy, and friendship. In this dimension of fellowship Jesus no longer calls disciples as servants, but rather treats them as his friends. Indeed, what distinguishes a servant from a friend is that the servant "does not know what his master is doing," while a friend is one to whom Jesus has revealed all that he has heard of his Father (Jn. 15:15). And as will be shown below, it is within the framework of intimate friendship that the disciples learn of Jesus and are trained in his ways.

Being with Jesus on His Journeys

In addition to following after, the disciples *walked beside Jesus. They lived their lives by being with Jesus.* This was done in a variety of ways. *They literally accompanied Jesus on his many journeys* within and out of Galilee: through grainfields (Mk. 2:23), crisscrossing the sea of Galilee (Mk. 3:7; 6:45, etc.), to the country of the Gerasenes, which is non-kosher territory (Mk. 5:1), to places where they could be by themselves with Jesus (Mk. 6:32; 9:2), through the villages of Caesarea Philippi (Mk. 8:29), and of course to Jerusalem (Mk. 10:32; 11:11), and so forth. These journeys afforded the disciples the opportunity to appreciate Jesus' commitment to carry out indefatigably his mission of preaching the gospel of the Kingdom to all of Israel. He said to his disciples: "Let us go on to the next towns, that I may preach there also; for that is why I came out" (Mk. 1:38 RSV; Lk. 4:43).

Being with Jesus in His Mighty Works

Some or all of the twelve disciples were present at those many occasions when Jesus was performing "mighty works" of various sorts. A sampling of these instances in Mark's Gospel would include the following: the healing of Simon's mother-in-law (1:29-31), the stilling of the storm at sea (4:37-41), the healing of the man whose name was Legion (5:1-20), the healing of the woman with an issue of blood (5:25-34), the raising of Jairus's daughter (5:35-43), the feeding of the five thousand (6:47-52; cf. 8:1-10), Jesus' walking on the sea at night (6:47-52), the curing of the demoniac boy (8:14-29), the healing of Bartimaeus, the blind beggar (10:46-52), the cursing of the fig tree (11:12-14, 20-21), and many other similar incidents.

These were no doubt revealing occasions when the disciples had the opportunity to see Jesus in action in this particular aspect of his mission and thus to come to know him better. They would have seen his compassion for people who suffered, how crowds of people trusted him and came to him to be taught and healed and comforted. They must have marveled at the power at work mightily through him in a variety of healing and liberating ways. And while all these illuminating incidents afforded the disciples learning opportunities for knowing Jesus better, these incidents at the same time deepened the mystery of his identity and intensified the disciples' wonder as to who he really was!

Being with Jesus in the Intimacy of His Prayer Life

Jesus had a vital personal prayer life. In the morning he would rise up early—"a great while before day"—and go to "a lonely place" to pray (Mk. 1:35 RSV). At the end of the day, he would seek a quiet place where he could be alone with his Father in prayer (Mk. 6:46). Many of his mighty works were done through prayer; some of them were possible only through prayer (Mk. 9:28-29). Luke reports that the Lord's Prayer was taught to the disciples at the request of one of them who apparently had observed Jesus praying (Lk. 11:1-4). Jesus was "transfigured" while in the act of prayer in the presence of some of his disciples (Mk. 9:2-8). In moments of profound crisis, Jesus would pray to know his Father's will and ask for strength to do it, as he did in Gethsemane (Mk. 14:32-42). On that fateful occasion, he invited three of his disciples to join him and to watch with him. In the intimacy of their company he bared the state of his soul to them at that critical time and said: "My soul is very sorrowful, even unto death; remain here, and watch" (Mk. 14:34 RSV). Then going a little farther, he fell on the ground and prayed that, if it were possible, the hour might pass from him. And he said, "Abba, Father, all things are possible to thee; remove this cup from me; yet not what I will, but what thou wilt" (Mk. 14:35-36 RSV). After this he went to see the three disciples and to his disappointment he found them asleep. He said to Peter: "Simon, are you asleep? Could you not watch one hour?" (Mk. 14:37 RSV). Three times Jesus prayed, and each time afterward he returned and found the three disciples he had invited sound asleep. And all this happened on the night of his betrayal and arrest! (Mk. 14:43-50).

What is to be made out of this? One's prayer life is a very personal and private affair. Only God is the rightful audience of personal prayer. To pray to Him one must be in a private place and come to Him secretly (Mt. 6:6). And yet Jesus invited his disciples to be in prayer with him on several occasions! *This was not merely an invitation to friendship but to an intimate sharing in what is most personal and private about a person's religious life, namely, his relation to God as expressed in private prayer!* Jesus allowed his disciples to see how it was privately between him and his Father when presumably nobody else was looking. They could not have missed the reverent familiarity and solemn ease with which he approached God, calling Him *Abba,* Father, which was unusual in Jewish religious practice! He taught them a prayer which apparently expressed in a nutshell the substance of what he prayed for.

He shared with them what he bared before God, namely, the agony of his soul as he faced the cup of suffering and the hour of his death! He invited them to watch with him—*to be with him*—at the hour of his deepest need! If the disciples fell asleep and failed miserably in being with Jesus at a most critical moment, it was not because Jesus did not desire their intimate company!

Being with Jesus in His Preaching and Teaching

Besides the disciples' being with Jesus on his journeys, in his works of healing, and in his prayer life, *they were with him also in his preaching and teaching activities*. We may note some of the occasions that indicate this.

1. There were times when Jesus was teaching "the crowds" and the disciples were also there as part of the audience. Mark 4:11 shows Jesus teaching a crowd by the lake. Verse 10 implies that the Twelve and other disciples were in the audience and heard what Jesus taught, which had to do with the parable of the sower (Mk. 4:3-8). In Mark 7:14-15 Jesus called the crowd to listen to his teaching about what truly defiles human beings which he gave in the form of a parable. In verse 17 the disciples asked about the parable. This obviously implies that the disciples were in the audience with the crowd. Again in Mark 8:34 Jesus is reported as calling the crowd, together with his disciples, so that he might teach them about the requirements of discipleship. No doubt these instances afforded the disciples opportunity to hear and learn what Jesus proclaimed or taught openly to the general public.

2. There were also occasions when Jesus had private teaching sessions with the disciples. These were occasions in which either the disciples asked questions of Jesus, or it was Jesus asking questions of the disciples. The former became opportunities for Jesus to further explain his teaching for the enlightenment and benefit of his disciples. Two examples may be cited from Mark's Gospel. In Mark 4:10 the Twelve asked Jesus "when he was alone" about the meaning of the parable of the sower and Jesus gave a detailed answer (4:13-20). In Mark 7:17 after Jesus "had left the crowd and entered the house" he was asked by his disciples about what renders a person "unclean." Jesus gave a profound if elaborate answer (7:20-23). In both instances Jesus complained about the dull-headedness and lack of understanding of the disciples (Mk. 4:13; 7:18).

In some of these private sessions, it was Jesus who asked the questions. This time the disciples did not have to listen but were forced to reflect on what they had seen and heard and make their own judgment accordingly. Several examples in Mark's Gospel may be mentioned. On one occasion the disciples had forgotten to bring bread with them on one of their journeys of crossing the lake with Jesus. Afraid that they would go hungry, they were worried about where to get some bread. Perceiving their worried discussion, Jesus said to them: "Why do you discuss the fact that you have no bread? Do you not yet perceive or understand? Are your hearts hardened? Having eyes do you not see, and having ears do you not hear? And do you not remember? When I broke the five loaves for the five thousand, how many baskets full of broken pieces did you take up?" The disciples replied, "Twelve." Then Jesus pressed them for their own judgment: "Do you not yet understand?" (8:14-21 RSV).

Another example are the questions that Jesus put to the disciples at Caesarea Philippi concerning who he was. The occasion was a critical point in the ministry of Jesus. His popular public ministry was about to end, and he was about to begin his last and fateful journey to Jerusalem. The disciples had enough opportunity to observe Jesus in action and they now had a basis for forming their own judgment about him. And so he asked them two questions about his identity: "Who do men say that I am?" followed by, "But who do you say that I am?" (Mk. 8:27-30 RSV). Peter's reply to the latter question was correct, but still incomplete and he didn't understand at all what it meant for Jesus (8:31-33).

From what has been said above, it can be seen that these private teaching sessions were an opportunity for mutual learning between Jesus and his disciples. On the one hand, the disciples were greatly enriched in their understanding of the teaching of Jesus by the answers that he gave to their questions. Moreover, they were also made to reflect by the searching questions that Jesus put to them on what they had observed and experienced in being with him and use this as a basis for making their own considered judgment about Jesus.

On the other hand, Jesus came to know from their questions and from the answers they gave to his own questions the extent of their knowledge and the limit of their understanding and what was still lacking in their knowledge and training in preparing them for the challenge and task of discipleship! Jesus must have realized that what was most crucial about himself and his mission had not been taught yet, let alone understood, among his inner circle of disciples. And he proceeded to use the little remaining time in the course of his final journey to Jerusalem to teach them what was still lacking.

3. It appears that the remaining time in the journey from Caesarea Philippi to Jerusalem was spent by Jesus with his disciples mostly to teach them the one thing that was unique and most significant about his mission. When he passed by his hometown in Galilee, he would not let anyone know he was around as he didn't want to be distracted from the one thing he was then doing, namely, "teaching his disciples" (Mk. 9:30-31). What was he teaching them at this time?

On one occasion Jesus told his disciples that one privilege they had as disciples which others did not enjoy was the fact that to them "has been given the secret of the kingdom of God" (Mk. 4:11). Although he had spoken publicly to many about the kingdom of God, he did so in parables, that is, in "riddles" (Mk. 4:33). The effect of this manner of speaking is that although people heard what was said, they, nevertheless, did not understand (Mk. 4:12). Therefore, they could not have known and understood "the secret of the kingdom of God." But he had private sessions with his disciples, and on these occasions "he explained everything" to them (Mk. 4:34). What was the "secret of the kingdom of God"?

A great deal of scholarly controversy attends this issue, and we shall not get involved in this debate here. It seems clear, however, that the one theme that dominates the teaching of Jesus to his disciples from Caesarea Philippi on and which did not figure in any direct sense in what he had taught them earlier has to do with his suffering, death, and resurrection (Mk. 8:31-33; 9:30-32; 10:32-34; 12:1-12). The text in Mark states that Jesus had emphasized this "plainly" (8:32 RSV). It was no longer said in parable so that there could not be any ambiguity about its meaning. But when Peter first heard it from Jesus' lips, he could not accept it; and he rebuked Jesus even for the thought of it (Mk. 8:32). Clearly rejection and suffering and death were not part of the destiny of the Messiah or the Son of Man in the mind of Peter, as indeed in the thinking of Peter's contemporaries, for that matter. But Jesus thought otherwise, and he rebuked Peter in return, saying: "Out of my sight, Satan! You think as men think, not as God thinks" (Mk. 8:32 REB).

This sharp remark of Jesus could only mean that rejection, suffering, and death constitute the destiny of the Son of Man, whereas a nonsuffering Messiah would have no redeeming significance and would be plainly of the devil. The advent of the reign of God in Jesus could only happen decisively through the crucifixion, death, and resurrection of Jesus. Moreover, suffering and death were definitely a matter of necessity for the Son of Man in carrying out his mission: "The Son of Man *must* suffer . . ." (Mk. 8:31). This strong sense of destiny could only come from God's thinking and willing it. Jesus was convinced that a suffering messiah was indeed in the mind and will of God: it is what God has determined. And what God determines, happens! To think otherwise is to think as a human being, and so to misunderstand God. And sure enough, the disciples did not understand this teaching of Jesus about himself, although he had plainly talked about it with them (Mk. 9:32).

To be sure, there are considerations that caution against faulting the disciples for their lack of understanding at this stage of their relationship to Jesus. For one thing, in itself the idea that the Messiah will be rejected and will suffer and die and that this horrible fate is willed by God and made to happen by Him to an innocent man was very hard to accept. The notion of vicarious suffering was not completely unknown in the faith-traditions of Israel, as indicated by the figure of the Suffering Servant in Deutero-Isaiah (Isa. 53:1-12) and in being presupposed by the system of Temple worship. Still it would have been helpful to the disciples had Jesus justified and explained his premonitions about his destiny and its possible significance. It does not appear in the records that Jesus did this. He did not give his disciples anything firm to hang on with his claim, as it were. Moreover, what Jesus taught about his "fate" had to happen first, and its "necessity" seen in its historical inevitability, before it could be understood and appreciated by the disciples. Furthermore, its saving significance and the vicarious involvement of God in it as the centerpiece of God's plan for the salvation of humankind could only be discerned, valued, and affirmed in the light of the vindication of Jesus through his resurrection from the dead (cf. Rom. 16:25; Eph. 3:3-4, 9).

In fairness to the disciples, we must say that they did eventually come to understand "the mystery of the Kingdom" after the events that Jesus foretold about himself took place (Acts 2:22-36). But the basis for the possibility of that understanding is to be sought in the fact that Jesus was indeed *with* his disciples, took time to teach them, never gave up on them despite their dull-headedness, and finally forgave them for their desertion (Mk. 14:50), denial, and betrayal (Mk. 14:43-46; 66:72) and reconciled them to himself and sent them out as his apostles (Mk. 16:7, 14-15). *Being with Jesus* is the ground and milieu for understanding who Jesus is and his teaching. One does not first know and understand Jesus and then come to join him and be with him. Rather, one comes to join him and be with him upon his call and within this fellowship, one may then come to know him and appreciate him and understand his teaching, especially what is unique and fundamental about him and his teaching.

Being with Jesus in His Controversies

To the four ways of being with Jesus that have already been considered, a fifth may be added, namely, *being with him in his controversies.* This aspect of the story of Jesus is quite different from the others we have dealt with so far. His journeys spread his fame far and wide. His "mighty works" attracted not only those who needed his help but great crowds of people from near and far. His prayer life brought him private solitude away from the maddening crowds and quiet rest from the tensions of controversy. His preaching and teaching activity boldly displayed the authority and content of his message in open public, and people were constrained to listen by the sheer power of his message and the captivating style in which it was presented. The public response to all this was generally favorable. It took note of the "newness" of Jesus' message and the force of his "authority" and it reacted in "amazement" (Mk. 1:27-28). If there was any "questioning" at all that was prompted by this "amazement," it was expressed only "among themselves" (Mk. 1:27 RSV). It did not break out into open criticism of Jesus; at least, not yet!

There were, however, other activities of Jesus and aspects of his teaching that did not sit well with other groups with whom he came into contact. This provoked criticism. At first the critical response was subdued and muted; the "questioning (was) in their hearts" or "within themselves" (Mk. 2:6, 8). It did not take long, however, before it broke out into the open and was brought to his attention, although indirectly at first (Mk. 2:16, 18). Soon the criticism escalated into open confrontation and hostility (Mk. 3:6; 11:18). The hostility eventually erupted into violence when Jesus was arrested, tried, and finally crucified (Mk. 12:12; 14:1, 46; 15:21-32). In many of the incidents of controversy, his disciples were there with him. Thus, the situation of conflict afforded the disciples another way of being with Jesus. This mode of being with him gave them an opportunity to see Jesus in action in the face of opposition and hostility, a condition quite different from adulation and popularity. How Jesus handled himself and his "enemies" in the situation of conflict was another window opened to the disciples through which they could see and understand what was at stake in the mission and identity of Jesus! In what follows we will take note of some of these incidents of controversy and seek to discern what is at issue in them!

Controversy About the Disciples

There were occasions when the bone of contention had to do with something that the disciples did, and the matter was brought to the attention of Jesus for his response. For example, there was the question why the disciples of Jesus did not fast in contrast to the disciples of John and to the Pharisees, both of whom fasted (Mk. 2:18). This was an obvious violation of religious tradition, for fasting was then regarded as an expression of contrition for sin and so it was valued as one of the cardinal forms of piety. This apparent misbehavior of the disciples was brought to the attention of their Master by "people" representing the practitioners of this custom of piety, notably the Pharisees. In doing this, the Pharisees were actually criticizing Jesus. He was the real target of their attack. The disciples were most likely not aware of the critical significance of their failure to observe the custom of fasting. Jesus had to explain what it meant from his point of view. His reply compared the relationship between him and his disciples to that of the bridegroom and the wedding guests (Mk. 2:19). The relationship is one of joy and feasting and celebration for as long as the Lord is with them. But the time will come "when the bridegroom is taken away from them," and then the disciples will fast appropriately in sorrow for the absence of the Lord (Mk. 2:19-20).

The answer of Jesus is continued in the form of analogies that underscore the utter incompatibility of the old and the new. "No one puts new wine into old wineskins; otherwise, the wine will burst the skins, and the wine is lost, and so are the skins; but one puts new wine into fresh wineskins" (Mk. 2:22). This means that the breakthrough of the kingdom of God in Jesus is something utterly new and is incompatible with the old order. It calls for joy and celebration in which fasting—as a religious custom of the old dispensation—has no place. *Being with Jesus is life in the sphere of the new and its festive spirit.*

Another example is an incident in which while going their way through the grainfields on a Sabbath, the disciples plucked heads of grain (Mk. 2:23). The Pharisees rightly pointed out to Jesus that what the disciples were doing "is not lawful on the sabbath" (Mk. 2:24). At issue now is not just a violation of pious custom but of Mosaic Law (Ex. 34:21; Deut. 5:12-15). In pointing this out, the Pharisees were indirectly attacking Jesus by exposing what the disciples were doing as sacrilegious! In allowing them to violate the Sabbath Jesus as the Master was held directly "culpable" for the behavior of his disciples! Could the disciples have known ahead how Jesus would interpret their behavior in a favorable light and show it to be right after all?

The reply of Jesus consisted in three parts. The first cites a precedent in the Old Testament which allows exception to the general rule (1 Sam. 21:1-6). Because of hunger and there being no bread except the "bread of the Presence," which only the priest may eat, Ahimelech, the priest, gave to David and his companions the only bread there was to eat (1 Sam. 21:4, 6; Mk. 2:26). Jesus, in effect, is saying that extreme human need in an emergency situation is a basis for breaking a general rule. In short, *basic human need takes priority over law and its rules.*

But Jesus was not satisfied in stating this apparently cardinal truth merely in the form of an exception. That would still leave law as taking precedence over human welfare as a general principle. This would justify all forms of legalism, which runs the danger of reducing the "weightier matters of the law" to the minutiae of rules which are rigidly observed at the expense of human welfare. To avoid this ever-present danger and to state the truth fully, he would now elevate the exception to a universal principle. He now makes the sovereign claim that "The sabbath was made for man, not man for the sabbath" (Mk. 2:27 RSV). In this formulation, *it is not merely basic human need, but the human being as such, which takes priority over the Sabbath,* and by extension over all human institutions and laws. The institution of the Sabbath and all the laws governing it were designed to secure and sustain human reality and promote the human good. The rationale and purpose of all human institutions is to serve humanity and its welfare.

Still Jesus did not appear to be contented with this principle as now formulated by him to stand by itself. To let the principle stand alone by itself is to risk the danger of leaving to human judgment and decision what constitutes human reality and human good! Why would such a risk be dangerous? Is not the measure of the human being and his good the human being as such? And if so, has he not then the inalienable right to decide by himself what is good for himself? This, of course, is *humanism* in its basic form and substance. But the operating assumptions of Jesus go far deeper than those of humanism, and his vision of human good far transcends the reach of human aspiration.

While it is true that the Sabbath was made for man, it is not true that the human being ordained this. Jesus assumes in his formulation that it is God who has determined this. Therefore, the principle that human reality and its good take precedence over law and institutions *is divinely ordained;* it is not a human principle! This has the effect of affirming the concern of humanism, which is human reality and its good, but goes beyond it by grounding it in the will of God and making it the concern of God Himself! Thus, the human being's concern for himself must be rooted in, and be an expression of, God's concern for human reality and its good! God Himself is concerned about the human being's concern for itself.

To establish this truth on more solid foundation, Jesus makes a further astounding claim as part of his three-pronged answer to the criticism of the Pharisees: "So the Son of Man is lord even of the sabbath" (Mk. 2:28). Before proceeding to unpack what we think is contained in this claim of Jesus, we must mention two possible misunderstandings we must avoid by all means. One is that the word "so" might lead to the understanding that this claim of Jesus—that the Son of Man is Lord of even the Sabbath—is a direct implication or extension of the humanistic element in the principle that the Sabbath was made for man. This would be a wrong reading. Rather, it is to be understood as the extension of the divine subject or ground of that principle. Thus, it is to be read as follows: since *it is God* who ordained the Sabbath for man, and not man for the Sabbath, so the Son of man is Lord even of the Sabbath. It is God who made the Son of Man Lord of the Sabbath.

The other possible misunderstanding is that the term "Son of Man" might be taken to mean as referring to the human being as such. If understood in this way, then the reading would be: So the human being himself (Son of Man) is Lord even of the Sabbath. This would again reduce the claim of Jesus to a mere humanistic principle. Rather, the term "Son of Man" must be understood *messianically,* that is, as referring to a divine agent anointed and sent by God to carry out His will.

If we read the claim of Jesus as suggested above, then several important truths can be affirmed in their proper relationship. First, the subject of both claims—that the Sabbath was made for man and that the Son of Man is Lord of the Sabbath—is none other than God alone! Not only did God ordain the Sabbath for the human being, He also anointed and sent someone to carry out this decision. Second, the humanistic element receives both a divine and a missiological grounding. Since God has ordained the Sabbath *for the good of the human being,* so it has become His mission to see to it that it is done. Third, if we identify the Son of Man with Jesus—as indeed we must if we are to avoid a humanistic reduction as well as a divine abstraction—then it is precisely the mission of Jesus as the historical agent of God to secure and promote the well-being of humanity. Fourth, the Son of Man as Lord of the Sabbath decides the good that is to be done on the Sabbath. A forceful demonstration of this is in Mark 3:1-6 where Jesus is reported to have asked the Pharisees who lay in watch for him: "Is it lawful to do good or to do harm on the sabbath, to save life or to kill?" and then without further ado he proceeded to heal the man with a withered hand, thus infuriating the Pharisees and further intensifying their desire to do away with him! What the disciples did on a Sabbath to satisfy their hunger is therefore in line with doing good and saving a life.

If all this is anywhere near the truth, then we must not shirk the conclusion that God's concern for the human being is to be sought in what Jesus Christ says and does about him/her. It is Jesus Christ who determines who the human being is and what is his or her good. The measure of being human is not in the human being as such but in Jesus Christ! He has become this measure precisely by being *the* true human being who does what is truly good for the human being! *Thus, to be with Jesus is to exist in what makes a person truly and fully human!*

In concluding this section, it is well to note that a community can sustain its sense of unity if it is able to defend itself successfully against criticism and opposition. If it cannot, it is likely to disintegrate! Moreover, the defense against opposition is the responsibility primarily of the leadership. Failure on the part of the leadership to carry out this responsibility successfully would result in a loss of confidence in the leadership and this would have the effect of weakening and eventually dissolving the cohesion that binds the community together. We have seen that Jesus did not fail in this task. He regarded the criticisms against his disciples as attacks on himself and his leadership. He took up the cudgels on their behalf and proved them to be on the right track. He was able to assure them that they were indeed part of a new order that he represented and for which they should rejoice and celebrate. Moreover, he strengthened their conviction that in being with him they were in fact existing in the truth that makes them truly and fully human! *Controversy only served to cement their community with Jesus!*

Opposition to Jesus and the Issue of Authority

If Jesus succeeded in overcoming criticism against his disciples, did he do as well in handling the opposition and hostility that were directly leveled against him? We will now consider this rather interesting question. After looking at the record, we may discover that the answer is not as straightforward as we may want it to be, one way or the other. The reason for this ambiguity is due partly to the fact that the issues in the controversy are many and complex, and partly because they require a resolution at many different levels. Some of those levels are not accessible to human probing. In the end we may find ourselves at the threshold of a genuine mystery!

In any serious controversy there is a bone of contention. It is very important that this is identified as precisely as possible. Accurate diagnosis is half the cure, if the illness is curable! What exactly was the point at issue between Jesus and his adversaries? Answering this question would be easy if the issue were the same for both Jesus and his critics, and the only difference between them is their way of looking at it and the variety of arguments, or answers they give to defend their viewpoint. But this does not appear to be the case. In some conflicts the contenders raise their own issues about their opponents and bring them into the fray and they may not even be joined at all! Jesus raised his own issues with his opponents and they did the same with Jesus, and there is hard evidence that suggests that the issues mutually raised between them were never joined at all (Mk. 11:27-33; 12:35-37).

We have already made an effort to identify the issues that Jesus himself raised with his various opponents. But now we have to look at the controversy from the side of his opponents and seek to find out what were the issues they raised with Jesus. A look at the record, for example in Mark's Gospel, will show that a great many issues were raised with Jesus by his opponents. We shall detail some of these, selecting those at which it is reasonable to assume the disciples were present with

Jesus. But on further analysis and reflection there appears to be one substantial issue that runs through them all, and this seems to be the one essential point that was being raised with Jesus. This has to do with *the question of authority!* We will look at some of the incidents of controversy with this hypothesis in mind and see if it holds true.

In the very first public teaching appearance of Jesus in a synagogue in Capernaum as presented by Mark (1:21-22; cf. Lk. 4:31-32), the people who heard Jesus readily took note of a major unmistakable difference between Jesus and the scribes who were the official teachers of the Law: Jesus "taught them as one having authority, and not as the scribes" (1:22; cf. Lk. 4:32). Here the "authority" that "astonished" the people was *connected with his teaching,* the substance of which is summarized in Mark 1:14-15 as the drawing nigh of the coming reign of God and the response of repentance and faith that was demanded. Shortly thereafter, Jesus healed in the synagogue a man with an unclean spirit. This also amazed those who saw it, and it elicited the comment, "With authority he commands even the unclean spirits, and they obey him" (Mk. 1:23-27 RSV; cf. Lk. 4:33-36). The authority that Jesus possessed is *connected this time with his power to exorcise unclean spirits.* In the next episode in Mark's Gospel, Jesus heals Simon Peter's mother-in-law of fever by taking her by the hand and lifting her up (Mk. 1:29-31). Although here there is no specific word connecting the authority of Jesus *with his healing activity,* Mark clearly intends such a connection by his editorial comment which describes the response of the people: "That evening, at sundown, they brought to him all who were sick or possessed with demons. And the whole city was gathered together around the door. And he cured many who were sick with various diseases, and cast out many demons . . ." (Mk. 1:32-34; cf. Mt. 8:16-17; Lk. 4:40-41).

Three obvious things must be noted in all this: (a) Jesus had unusual authority; (b) he exercised it to help people through his teaching, healing, and exorcising activities; and (c) Jesus stood out sharply as being different from the scribes! Now, the remark that Jesus taught with authority and not as the scribes was not merely descriptive; it was also evaluative. And the evaluation was double-edged. On the one hand, it was complimentary of Jesus. On the other hand, it was derogatory of the scribes. This remark captured the sense of tension provoked by the public appearance of Jesus. Thus, at the very beginning of his ministry an ominous cloud of tension already appeared. This would thicken and darken and intensify into a full-blown storm in the course of the public career of Jesus.

But this was at the beginning of that ministry. Towards the end of his career what was first noticed as a cause for astonishment by the people became a weapon for attack by the official leaders of Israel—the chief priests, the scribes, and the elders, the same people who sit in the Sanhedrin. They did not come to Jesus as individuals representing only themselves but as official representatives of the people. This time the confrontation took place not in the village synagogue but in the city Temple, the official seat of power and authority in Israel in all matters religious, judicial, and financial. This means that the entire official Jewish establishment with all the power at its command was ranged against Jesus! The audacious challenge they hurled against Jesus was in terms of authority: "By what authority are you doing these things? Who gave you this authority to do them?" (Mk. 11:27-28; Mt. 21:23; Lk. 20:1-2). In Luke the gauntlet was thrown at Jesus while he was "teaching the people . . . and preaching the gospel" (Lk. 20:1 RSV).

But all three Gospels have the words "these things" that point to what Jesus was doing. This could mean that what is included in this reference is not only the teaching and preaching activity of Jesus and the cleansing of the Temple which immediately preceded this confrontation and provoked it (Mk. 11:15-18; cf. Mt. 21:12-17; Lk. 19:45-48; Jn. 2:13-22), but all the activities that comprised the public ministry of Jesus through which his authority was exercised. By calling into question the authority by which all "these things" are done, the whole ministry of Jesus is being undermined in its legitimacy and validity. Discrediting his authority would also fatally weaken the trust and confidence of his followers in him and this would certainly lead to the breakup of the community that he forged with them. In other words, the attack struck at the very foundation of Jesus' life and career. The avowed aim of Jewish officialdom in confronting Jesus is not merely to discredit what Jesus lived for, but to destroy and kill him (Mk. 11:18). Why?

To appreciate the gravity of the dramatic attack on Jesus, it would be helpful to unpack what is contained in the question of authority, trace it as the main issue in the various episodes of controversy, point out the major implications, and finally consider the resolution of the issue at several levels. What follows is a consideration of these issues.

The Bearing of Authority on Action

The question asked of Jesus by the chief priests, scribes, and elders of Israel relates "authority" to "doing things." This seems to be appropriate because authority has to do with doing or action. Some things are done when they are "authorized," and if they are not authorized, then they should not be done. From this one can see that authority lies at the base of action. Authority is a ground or basis for doing or not doing some things. *The question of the chief priests is a question of the basis or ground of the actions of Jesus.*

Moreover, as a basis for action, authority has the effect of legitimizing and validating an action. A deed is not legitimate or valid just because it is done, just as a thing is not legitimate or valid just because it exists. There are many actions that are done which are not legitimately or validly done, just as there are things that exist illegitimately or invalidly, that is, they should not exist at all. That an event happened is not in itself a sufficient reason for its having happened. One may ask for its ground, for what gives rise to it, for its justifying and validating reason. *The question of the chief priests has to do with the sufficient reason for what Jesus was doing.*

It seems that it is also proper for the chief priests to ask the issue of authority since nothing in what they know as guardians of the Jewish people and custodians of their law and culture seems to justify or validate what Jesus was doing. If something has the effect of undoing radically what is already there existing and cannot be explained or justified in terms of what is already known, then one cannot prevent reason from asking the question of the "authority" that lies behind, or is the basis of, what is being done or is happening! It appears that what Jesus was doing and what it represents are a radical threat to what the chief priests, the scribes, and the elders represent. One cannot fault them *for asking Jesus "the authority" of what in effect threatens them to the very roots of their existence and their reason for being!*

Why does "authority" lie at the base of action? The answer is to be found in the nature of authority as it bears upon action. As far as one can see, there are five elements of authority that relate to action. For one thing, authority refers to the *ability* or capacity of an agent to carry out a particular action. One cannot do something if one does not have the ability or capacity to do it. This implies also that the ability in question must be the sort that can do the action. One may have ability but it may not be the kind that enables someone to do what one wants to do. Ability, therefore, is basic to an act. Authority as including ability lies at the base of an act.

For another thing, authority denotes the *right* of an agent to do certain things. An agent may have the ability to do certain things, but he may not have been "authorized," that is, conferred the right to do them and so he should not do them. *Might is no right at all.* A "right" necessarily emerges as a direct implication of certain given factors. If someone is a human being, he has certain rights by the sole fact that he is a human being. If someone is a woman, she has a right to behave as a woman does. If a person is married, he has conjugal rights. If a person holds a certain rank, he/she has a right to exercise the responsibility of his/her position. If one holds a certain office, he/she has a right to exercise the obligations of the office. If a person owns something, that person has a right to dispose of it.

Because "rights" directly and necessarily derive from certain given premises, they function as legitimating and validating factors. Because one owns a pair of shoes and has the right of disposal, one can wear them or sell them. If anyone should ask why he wears them, all he needs to say is that they are his shoes; and if asked why he sells them, all he needs to say is that they are his shoes and he can sell them. The right of ownership would justify what he does with his shoes. The question of the chief priests is a question of the right of Jesus to do the things he was doing. His right to do them would justify or validate his doing them. If he were trained and ordained a rabbi or scribe in the "regular" or legal way, he would have the right to teach or interpret the Law. He could not have replied by saying he did what he was doing because he could do them; ability alone does not give rise to right. The question "by what authority?" can also be transposed into the question "by what right?" without loss of meaning.

But "right" as has been shown above rests on given premises which necessarily give rise to them and from which they derive their legitimating or justifying function. It is, therefore, absolutely necessary to establish what these premises are and be certain about their givenness, that is, their factuality. The chief priests were not contented with asking Jesus "by what authority" did he do what he did; they followed this question with: "*Who* gave you this authority to do them?" (Mk. 11:28). They wanted to know who was the source of his authority! They wanted to be certain that the authority which gave Jesus his right is a proper one, that is, whether it is the sort of authority that *can and has the right* to give the kind of authority that Jesus had! Or put in another way, they wanted to determine whether the authority of Jesus was derived from or conferred by an appropriate source. This issue of *who* gave Jesus his authority is fundamental to all the elements of authority we are considering, and we shall return to it in due course.

Meanwhile, one must also note the fact that having the right to do an action does not necessarily mean that one *can* do it. An agent may not have the ability to do what he has a right to do. Right does not necessarily give rise to ability. *Right is no might at all!* For an action to be "authoritative," it must include both ability and right to act in a certain way. If an agent has only ability and no right, his action lacks "authority." By the same token, if he has a right to act in a certain way but cannot do the action because he has not the ability for it, then the agent also lacks "authority." *It is clear then that "authority" includes both ability and right and in this way it is absolutely basic to action.*

There is a third element of authority which is as equally important as ability and right, namely, power. This must be distinguished from ability, which has to do with capacity to act. *Power is the capacity of an agent to alter the way things are by his action.* Obviously ability is necessary to power, for it is through action which assumes the ability to act by which power alters reality. But ability to act is not necessarily power. One may do what he can. But one's action may not make any difference at all in reality. Obviously too, right is necessary to power insofar as it presupposes authorized action by which power makes a difference. But right does not necessarily lead into power because it may not be exercised and the action that it entails may not be done at all! But assuming that power is exercised properly through right action, its test as power is whether it makes any difference at all in reality. Does it make an impact upon the way things are and effect a change in their course or alter their relations or modify their structures? Does it originate a chain of events, or inaugurate a new historical era? Does it make a significant difference in someone's life? Does it heal disease and bring wholeness? Does it bring a change in point of view or in the order of values or in the style of life of a person? Does it overcome alienation and reconcile enemies and bring about peace? Can it create a new community or produce a "new creation"? These are the sort of things that power is supposed to achieve! When power succeeds in making a difference in reality it is without doubt "authoritative." *If action is intended to make an impact upon reality, then authority as power is basic to it.*

We must at this point take note of a possible change in the relation of power to ability and right and to the structure of authority because of the nature of power. Since power can alter reality it can change the sources of ability and the premises of rights. A government through its power to allocate resources may deprive its citizens of nutrients necessary for physical growth and development of capacities and severely limit opportunities for education and training so that eventually citizens and society at large are diminished in their abilities to act. Through the power of revolution the basis of rights may shift from an individual person to society as such. This may result in the abolition of rights derived from individuals as such and in rights that derive from society, or what its political arm is prepared to grant and protect.

A change in the derivations of ability and rights would have a chain effect in the character of authority and its legitimizing function. Monarchical authority may be replaced by consensus and participation. Charismatic authority may be bureaucratized and routinized (Max Weber). Understood in this sense power is more basic than authority as it can change the character of authority insofar as it is an element in any existing order. *Authority as power to alter reality is, therefore, a constant threat to the status quo. If Jesus had this sort of authority, would he not be a threat to the status quo represented by the leaders of Israel?* Would he not provoke the determined and organized effort to destroy and kill him? Can one fault the leaders of Israel in their desire to find out "who" gave Jesus the "authority" (read: power) to alter the way things are?

There is a fourth element of authority, namely, *freedom;* and this has to do with the *liberty to exercise a right to act in a way that alters reality*. Freedom appears to be a requirement of all the elements of authority that have been considered so far. One may have a *right,* but if he is not free to exercise it because of illness, or fear, or oppression, the right is only good on paper. One may have the *ability* to act in a certain way, but if he is not free to do so because he is in prison or in exile, his ability cannot issue in action. One may have *power* to change certain aspects of reality, but if he is deprived of the freedom or the opportunity to do so—as when a Mandela is imprisoned for twenty-seven years and cannot do anything to remove the evil of apartheid in South African society, although he has the capacity to do so in concert with others—then his power remains dormant and rendered useless. An agent may have all three elements of authority—ability, right, and power—but if he is not free to exercise his authority, he is virtually without authority!

An agent has to have the freedom to exercise his authority! If something prevents or limits his freedom to exercise his authority he will make no difference whatsoever in the way things are. He cannot rule, and ruling is the same as exercising authority. The best way, therefore, to render authority useless is to remove or curtail the freedom to exercise it, and in most instances, that is equivalent to destroying the agent. Does one wonder then why the authorities who opposed Jesus wanted him removed and "destroyed"? From this one can readily see that freedom is basic to authority. *In its proper sense authority includes freedom, the liberty to exercise it and in this way it is basic to action, especially the action of exercising authority itself!*

There is a fifth element of authority which has to do with the *purpose* or the aim for which authority is established or exercised. It seems that there are two possible ways in which purpose may relate to authority. One is to see purpose within the purview of authority. Seen in this way, the determination of purpose is part of the power of authority. An agent may claim that he is empowered by his authority to decide the purposes for which he exercises his authority. Here it is authority that establishes its own purposes. It would be reasonable, therefore, to ask the purpose of any action through which authority is exercised. The rationale for this is simply the fact that human agency is typically purposive. It is purpose that provides motivation and meaning to human action. If authority is exercised, which invariably entails taking action, it is reasonable to ask about the purpose for which it is being exercised! It does not seem to be the case, however, that this was what the authorities were asking when they questioned Jesus. Their question seems to be premised on another possibility of relating purpose to authority.

In this other option, purpose is seen as basic to, and regulative of, authority. Purpose here is related not to any specific action by which authority is exercised, but to the establishment or conferring of authority as such. For what purpose is an agent conferred or given authority as such? Or, what is his authority for? *Here it is purpose that establishes authority and regulates its exercise!* Seen in this way, authority is within the purview of the purpose that establishes it. It seems that it is this relationship of purpose to authority that is presupposed in the question of the chief priest! If this line of analysis is correct, then the answer to the question of the chief priest is to be found neither in the actions by which Jesus exercised his authority nor in the authority itself, but in the source of authority. Therefore, the question, "who gives you this authority?" is the correct question to ask!

Meanwhile, it seems obvious that the priestly authorities were threatened by Jesus. But the threat did not come from any one specific action of Jesus, although the cleansing of the Temple was for them, intolerably, a triggering act.

The threat came rather from the cumulative impact of the whole authority of Jesus. Their question implied that they wanted to know the purpose for which he had authority. It could be asked, however, that had they known the purpose of Jesus' authority, would they have judged it and its exercise in the light of that purpose? Would they have not known that purpose by examining the track record of Jesus' use of his authority in his public ministry? The record seems to indicate that they were strongly intimidated by their sense of Jesus as a dangerous threat to themselves and to what they represented so that the only proper action to take was to eliminate him.

We have now considered what seems to be the essential components of authority as it bears upon human action in the context of the question of the Jewish authorities in their confrontation with Jesus. They already knew the ability, power, and freedom of Jesus to do the things he did. What they asked has to do with the right, purpose, and source of his authority. With this understanding we shall now trace briefly how the authority which astonished the hearers of Jesus at the beginning of his career became an issue of life and death between him and the authorities towards the end of his public ministry. The significance of the analysis will become clear as we proceed.

The Issue of Authority in Its Various Forms

We begin with the editorial comment in Mark 1:22, which compares the authority of Jesus with the authority of the scribes. Although we cannot establish as a fact that the disciples were present at this initial incident, it is safe to assume that some of them were with Jesus as it would not be wide off the mark to presume that they went to the synagogue with him. Besides, the incident rightly understood sets out the parameters of the controversy about authority. We note that, of course, *the scribes had authority.* They had professional *training and ability* to teach the Law. They had a right to teach because they were ordained to this office of teaching. They had the *freedom* to interpret the Law within the framework of the traditions of interpretation, including the freedom to found schools of interpretation within the canons of tradition. The *purpose* of their teaching and their profession was to regulate the life of Israel according to the Law. The one thing the scribes did not have in their authority is the power to alter the Law and the canons of tradition that regulated its interpretation. But as a professional class officially charged with the task of educating the Jewish public with the Law and its interpretation, they were enormously influential in shaping Jewish consciousness and culture! In this sense there was power in their authority!

On the other hand, *Jesus also had authority.* But he did not teach as the scribes did. This means his authority did not come to him in the same way as the scribes obtained their authority. Jesus was not trained professionally as a scribe. He was not ordained to the office of a scribe. He did not teach by depending upon tradition, nor did he merely expound what previous authorities had already taught, as the scribes normally did when they taught. He claimed untrammeled freedom in interpreting the Law; something that no one dared to do before him. His aim in teaching was to reshape Jewish consciousness and way of life according to a new vision of life that was dawning, namely, the breakthrough into the present of the coming reign of God. His authority was not confined to his teaching. He had the power to alter the basis of Jewish life and consciousness and to redeem it from its afflictions and from the forces that sought to destroy it. In short, the authority of Jesus was not secured through the traditionally sanctioned way, and its power and effect far surpassed the impact of the traditional authority of the scribe. His teaching seemed to be "new" to those who initially heard it. The likes of his power had never been seen before (Mk. 2:12; cf. 4:41). From whence or from whom then did Jesus get this unusual authority? This question which was finally asked directly at the end of Jesus' career was already implicit from the very beginning of his public ministry!

At first his authority evoked mostly wonder, curiosity, and praise (Mk. 1:27; 2:12). But as the full implications of that authority began to unfold more fully in public, it began to provoke controversy. In making the paralytic walk Jesus did not merely exercise powers of healing but claimed *authority to forgive sin* (Mk. 2:1-12). Here Jesus was understood as claiming to do what only God alone can and has a right to do (Mk. 2:7). Jesus was seen as arrogating to himself a freedom and a power that belong only to God. No scribe or high priest would claim this authority for his office! For this reason his act of forgiving the paralytic was seen as blasphemy (Mk. 2:7). To be sure, the thought of blasphemy as a charge against Jesus was not expressed openly. But Jesus perceived it and responded to it openly. It was his response that brought into the open an unspoken charge of blasphemy against him. Later, following his betrayal and arrest, the high priest would charge Jesus formally and publicly of blasphemy (Mk. 14:63-64).

The issue about forgiveness, however, is not only with regard to who has authority to forgive; it has to do also with *whom* to forgive. In Jewish doctrine and piety based upon the Law, forgiveness—although always available—required prior repentance before it was granted. Only those who are sincerely penitent, who "bear fruit that befits repentance" (Mt. 3:8 RSV), *merit* the forgiveness of God. And penitence includes knowing one's sin, admitting one's guilt, reforming one's life, and "returning" to God and His ways. Forgiveness is therefore conditioned upon prior repentance, which is to be initiated by the sinner himself! Even the most wicked person may be saved if he repents at the end, but only *if* he repents. Repentance is always prior to and is a condition for forgiveness! It is the basis for the possibility of forgiveness. This view rests on an understanding of God as waiting for sinners to come to their senses in the light of His Law and turn to Him in sorrow and penitence for their sins and beg for His mercy and forgiveness (cf. Isa. 55:6-7; Jer. 29:12-14).

Jesus, however, has a different set of presuppositions. For him, God does not wait for sinners to turn first in penitence. Rather, God takes the initiative in turning to them by breaking through into their present with His coming reign. This initiative is an act of His grace; it is His characteristic way of reigning. As such He reigns in mercy and forgiveness. It is grace in the form of mercy and forgiveness which exposes sin and judges evil, not the Law and its penalty. It is this prior turning of God in mercy and forgiveness towards sinners—which by itself exposes them as sinners and judges them as evil—which is the basis for their turning to Him in repentance and trust in His mercy. It is the reign of God drawing nigh in Jesus which is the condition and possibility of repentance and faith! The logic of the gospel of Jesus is: The time is fulfilled (by God), the kingdom of God is at hand (God in His reign taking the initiative of turning to Israel in grace and mercy); repent and believe (the appropriate human response to and made possible by the breakthrough into the human present of the reign of God)!

This being the case, Jesus now dramatically enacts an implication and sign of the nearness of the reign of God by directly inviting sinners to enter the sphere of God's rule. He does this by forgiving a paralytic and so creates the condition for his repentance and his rising up to take up his pallet and walk as a child of God should (Mk. 2:1-12; cf. Mt. 9:1-8; Lk. 5:17-26). He sits at table in fellowship with tax collectors and sinners (all outcasts from the Law from the perspective of the Pharisees). His joining them in table fellowship is both an act of judgment as to who they were (as outcasts) and an act of forgiveness and reconciliation, and their joining him is an act of repentance that brings them into the sphere of God's reign and restores them into the community of His people (Mk. 2:15-17; Mt. 9:10-13; Lk. 5:29-32; cf. Mt. 8:11-18; Lk. 14:15-24). Jesus' authority included offering forgiveness and reconciliation to sinners and tax collectors precisely as the basis for their repentance and faith (Mk. 2:17). *It is forgiveness that makes for repentance,* and not the other way around! *His authority had the right and the liberty and the power to alter the conditions for coming into the sphere of God's rule! No one in Israel had claimed this authority for himself but him!*

But did the authority of Jesus give him the right to violate the Mosaic Law on the Sabbath, and by implication set aside the unquestioned authority of Moses? While the hostility against Jesus was beginning to build up, it was not until he was seen publicly violating the Sabbath law that the Pharisees became thoroughly infuriated with him and began openly to conspire with the Herodians against him and seek to destroy him (Mk. 3:1-6, cf. Mt. 12:9-14; Lk. 6:6-11). Apparently, openly violating the Sabbath laws was intolerable to the Pharisees. What is now at stake is *obedience* to the authority of Moses, which is expressed most unmistakably through observance of the Sabbath laws. The issue struck at the very raison d'être of Pharisaism, which prided itself in rigorous and meticulous obedience to the Law.

But Jesus mercilessly exposed the superficiality of Pharisaic piety by demonstrating that true obedience to the Law is not by strictly observing the letter of the Law but by achieving its purpose. He asked the Pharisees in the presence of a man with a withered hand: "Is it lawful to do good or to do harm on the sabbath, to save life or to kill?" (Mk. 3:4; cf. Mt. 9:9-

14; Lk. 6:6-11). The question is not rhetorical. It asked about *lawful* obedience, which may in fact put into question the strict obedience to the Law. *This means that strict obedience to the Law may not be lawful obedience to the Law! For Jesus, what constitutes lawful obedience to the Law is not necessarily strict obedience to the Law but achieving the purpose of the Law.* The Law as a whole intends good; it seeks to save! This is the purpose that established the Law and so of its authority. To accomplish this overall purpose, it may be necessary to break a particular expression of the Law. One may break the Law on the Sabbath in order to do good and save, which is the whole purpose of the Law. It is the intent of the Law that regulates its observance, and mere strict observance of the Law does not necessarily achieve its purpose! This is the same argument that Jesus used in criticizing the Pharisees for tithing "mint and rue and every herb, and neglect justice and the love of God" (Lk. 11:42 RSV). The point of Jesus is that it is the substance and purpose of the Law that must be fulfilled! When the letter of the Law or any particular expression of it stands in the way of achieving its purpose and substance, then it must give way!

Another aspect of the authority of Jesus which was quite unlike that of the scribes and came under their attack was his power to exorcise evil spirits or demons. The scribes were teachers of the Law, and their authority was confined to this activity. Jesus, however, not only taught and forgave, he also healed and exorcised. He had power to alter many aspects of the human condition and make an enormous difference for good in the lives of people. His power was so unusual that word had gone around that he was "beside himself," and that meant that he was "possessed" by some overwhelming power which took control of him (Mk. 3:21). He no longer could behave normally; he had lost his sanity. Naturally his family was concerned about his safety and sanity and they sought to take him home and care for him (Mk. 3:21-32).

But the scribes who came down to Capernaum from Jerusalem seized the rumor, built on it, and used it to attack Jesus, discredit his authority, and reject him in the presence of his family, his disciples, and the people of his hometown! They said of Jesus: "He is possessed by Beelzebub, and by the prince of demons he casts out demons" (Mk. 3:22 RSV). "Beelzebub" (Baalzebub in 2 Kgs. 1:2) literally means "the lord of the flies" and referred to the Canaanite deity which as the enemy of the God of Israel was regarded in Jewish belief as Satan himself. In short, Jesus was being accused as an agent of Satan. This meant that the *source* of Jesus' authority was Satan, the *nature* of his authority was satanic, the *purpose* of his authority was to achieve the aims of Satan, and the *exercise* of his authority was nothing less than demonic! If true, could there be a more devastating way of discrediting Jesus and his authority in the eyes of the public than by accusing him of being in league with the Evil One?

How did Jesus defend himself against this calumny? His reply is three-leveled; each level builds on the previous one so that there is a cumulative impact. The first part points to something that he and his enemies could agree on. The attack of the scribes implied that Satan was being cast out, that evil was being assaulted. Moreover, this attack against Satan and his kingdom of evil is connected with Jesus. Apparently the scribes had noticed the many exorcisms of Jesus so far reported and this formed the basis for their interpretation that it was "by the prince of demons that he [Jesus] casts out demons." And certainly Jesus could not agree more with his adversaries on this point. This is a critically significant agreement: both Jesus and his enemies agreed that evil is under assault by what Jesus was doing! Where they disagreed was in the power by which this was done! The scribes believed that this was being done through the power of Satan himself, and so Jesus was an agent of Satan!

So intense was their feeling of hostility against Jesus that his enemies could not think clearly and see the fallacy in the logic of their accusation. In the second point of his reply, Jesus points this out to them in the form of a rhetorical question: "How can Satan cast out Satan?" (Mk. 3:23). An entity cannot be for itself and at the same time be against itself if it is to survive! This would be self-contradiction that leads to self-division and finally results in self-dissolution, which could be fatal! Jesus illustrates this fateful process in "parable": "If a kingdom is divided against itself, that kingdom cannot stand. And if a house is divided against itself, that house will not be able to stand. And if Satan has risen up against himself and is divided, he cannot stand, but is coming to an end" (Mk. 3:24-26 RSV). Jesus points out that in the case of Satan, the root cause of his self-contradiction, self-division, and self-collapse is his "rising up against himself," that is, self-rebellion! Would Satan do this to himself? Certainly not! If Jesus were Satan, would he do this to himself? Certainly not! How then can Satan cast out Satan? Jesus could not be Satan, and Satan could not be Jesus!

And so Jesus moves on to the third and more devastating part of his reply! If indeed Satan is under assault and so "is coming to an end," this could only mean that someone stronger than Satan is overwhelming him and will cause his downfall! Jesus said: "But no one can enter a strong man's house and plunder his goods, unless he first binds the strong man; then indeed he may plunder his house" (Mk. 3:27 RSV). The "strong man" here obviously refers to Satan. But someone *stronger* than he has come. That the one who has come is stronger is shown in terms of a threefold activity. First, the stronger one can enter the house of the Evil One! That means he can overcome all the barriers and defenses that the Evil One can put up! Second, having entered the house, he now *captures* and *binds* the Evil One! That means the stronger one can render the Evil One inactive, powerless, and useless. Finally, the stronger one "plunders" the house and goods of the Evil One. That means the stronger one destroys the kingdom and cohorts and agents of the Evil One! Since both Jesus and his adversaries agree that Satan is under assault, and since Satan cannot do this to himself and since Jesus apparently is doing the casting out of Satan, then he, Jesus, is the Stronger One! The power of the authority of Jesus is bringing Satan to his downfall! In Luke, Jesus exaltingly voices this conviction: "I saw Satan fall like lightning from heaven" (Lk. 10:18 RSV).

The effect of Jesus' reply demolished the argument of his opponents and silenced them. But more important, it vindicated Jesus and his authority. One can only guess the impact of this vindication upon his disciples. Could it have strengthened their personal commitment to him and undergirded their sense of community with him?

Frustrated in their efforts to undermine the authority of Jesus and discredit his ministry by suspicion and calumny, the Pharisees came to Jesus again to argue with him and to seek a sign from him (Mk. 8:11-13; cf. Mt. 16:1-4). Their avowed purpose was "to test him" (Mk. 8:11). This "testing" implied that they were to judge Jesus by what they already knew about the ways of God with Israel, which, of course, was based on the Law and its traditions of interpretation. Moreover, they themselves specified the criteria by which the kind of sign they wanted may be identified and to which Jesus must conform. First, the sign must come from "heaven." That is to say, the *source* of the sign must be God Himself! Second, the sign itself must evidence *unusual power,* the sort that one would associate with God's power, if it is to be read as having God for its source! Nothing less than power coming from God would certify to the authenticity of Jesus' authority. Third, the sign must be "from Jesus." That is to say, it is to be *performed by Jesus himself.* This would test whether Jesus is indeed capable of doing what God alone can do! The sign must come from God in the form of what Jesus can do as demonstrating his power as of God! This was the kind of sign demanded of Jesus! If Jesus performed this sign according to specifications, it would confirm that his authority is from God and is of the nature of God's power! And who were to be the judges of all this? The Pharisees, of course. They already know what is of God, and they will apply it as a test on Jesus to find out whether Jesus is indeed of God as they think they know God!

Jesus refused to be drawn into argument with his adversaries and he flatly denied their request. His response was expressed with *feeling*, in *words*, and by an *action*. There was no way of misunderstanding it. The mood in which he expressed what he *felt* about the request is described by the Gospel writer in graphic language: "he sighed deeply in his spirit" (Mk. 8:12). Another way of putting this is to say: "he groaned inwardly." There can be no doubt that Jesus was expressing intense feelings of exasperation, frustration, sadness, and weariness over the persistent unbelief and hardness of heart of the religious leaders of his day! And these feelings welled up from the depths of his spirit! What Jesus *said* in response supplemented his feelings. It was also strong and very direct: "Truly, I say to you, no sign shall be given to this generation" (Mk. 8:12 RSV). The form, *"Truly, I say to you, no sign shall be given,"* expresses strong denial delivered emphatically! The denial is directed not merely to the Pharisees but also to those whom they represented, namely, their contemporaries who, like them, needed a "sign" to be persuaded as to the identity and power of Jesus. Finally, Jesus' refusal was carried out in the form of an *action:* he left them, got into a boat, and departed to the other side of the lake (Mk. 8:13). The sentence construction is terse; it describes the action as abrupt and brusque. The refusal was decisive!

It may be asked: Why did Jesus deny the request of the Pharisees for a sign that would authenticate his authority? In seeking an answer to this question, we dare not presume to know the mind of Jesus on the matter. We can only hazard a guess which seems warranted by some observations derived from reading the story of Jesus. For one thing, the purpose of the request "was to test" Jesus. This implies that the request was motivated by unbelief in Jesus and hostility against him. It arose out of bad faith. The Pharisees were convinced that they already knew who God is and what He thinks and does, and they merely wanted to test

Jesus on the basis of this bias or prejudgment. If Jesus honored their request, he would be submitting himself to this prejudice. Certainly, he would not pass the test! So what was the point?

For another thing, a sign points to something else. Its meaning is not straightforward. It has to be interpreted, and it can be understood in several different ways. The reading of its meaning will depend partly on the preunderstanding of the reader. If the preunderstanding is one of unbelief and hostility, it is very likely that the sign will be read in that light and it will do no more than confirm the preunderstanding. There is no guarantee that the sign will be read and understood as Jesus would have intended it. In the situation of Jesus, the odds were clearly stacked up against him. There seemed to be no way that any sign that Jesus would perform would be read in his favor!

Furthermore, the track record of Jesus indicates that he does not perform "mighty works" to persuade others to believe in him. He uses his power to perform miracles to help people in response to their need and their trust in him. The people who come to him for help do so out of faith in his compassion and power and readiness to serve. They do not come "to argue" with him or "to test him" in order to be convinced! In fact, the opposite is the case: they are already convinced of his power, and so they come to him! It is this trusting faith seeking help from him that Jesus unfailingly honors, not the arguing, testing, unbelieving approach of the Pharisees! Had he granted the request of the Pharisees, he would have honored unbelief! And so the question of this authority still hangs in the air!

Failing to settle the issue of authority indirectly through argument, calumny, and sign, the only way still open seems to be to ask Jesus directly in the hope that he will give a straightforward answer. And those who should ask Jesus directly must be the highest officials of the land, those who have the authority to compel Jesus for an answer. And so we come back full circle to the incident in the Temple in which there took place a direct confrontation between Jesus and the whole top Jewish official establishment. This time they asked Jesus directly: "By what authority are you doing these things? Who gave you this authority to do them?" (Mk. 11:28).

Jesus Extricates Himself from the Horns of a Dilemma

We have already considered the various implications of this question. We have only to be reminded that at this late stage in the career of Jesus the issue has become a matter of life or death for him. If he asserted explicitly that his authority came from God—which is what was implied by everything he has been doing—he would certainly be charged with blasphemy, which is a capital offense. If he denied unequivocally that his authority came from God he would be lying to himself and he would be deceiving all those who trusted and followed him. The rug would be pulled out from under his feet and his whole life's work and the community he formed would collapse in one fell swoop! Moreover, the people who can decide his fate on the basis of his answer were the very ones he was dealing with. They could use against him whatever he might say in answer to the question put to him. Furthermore, the decision to "destroy" him had already been made after the cleansing of the Temple. The only issue still to be decided was when and how (Mk. 11:18). And so Jesus was neatly trapped between the horns of a deadly dilemma! Is there a way out of this snare? Let us see how he answered the question.

The answer of Jesus was initially given in the form of a question. But before asking it, he stipulated one condition. If his interlocutors answered his question, he would also answer theirs. While there is nothing unusual about parrying a question with another one, the case of Jesus has a special significance which militates against understanding it as a form of evasion. In asking a counter question, Jesus was equalizing the odds; he was probing for a possible way out of the trap into which he was put by people who meant to do him harm! If they do not answer the question he was to put to them, it is only fair that he need not answer the question they put to him. The possibility of a standoff would be a fair deal for Jesus, under the circumstances! The record does not show that the authorities objected to the suggestion of Jesus, and so he proceeded to ask the question.

The question that Jesus asked was wisely chosen and shrewdly put: "Was the baptism of John from heaven or from men?" (Mk. 11:30 RSV). It is important to see the logical entailments of the question to appreciate its impact upon the interlocutors of Jesus.

First, the question had the effect of reminding his opponents of John the Baptist. The phenomenon of John the Baptist was still within easy recall, for it happened just in the recent past. Many important elements of John's career could still be remembered vividly and sharply.

Second, some details of John's public career would certainly be seen as strikingly similar to some aspects of the public career of Jesus. For example, John started a movement of religious revival which stood in the tradition of the prophets. He called for genuine repentance that included a reform of life and society, offered forgiveness to those who returned to the Lord, and pointed to a Coming One, "who is mightier than I, the thong of whose sandals I am not worthy to stoop down and untie" (Mk. 1:5-7 RSV; cf. Lk. 3:3-17). John was a charismatic, eccentric figure; his authority did not come through the regular institutional channels. Yet his preaching and baptism made a tremendous impact on people (Mk. 1:5; Lk. 3:10-14). He himself fearlessly issued the challenge of repentance to the religious and political establishment in terms they would not soon forget: "You brood of vipers! Who warned you to flee from the wrath to come? Bear fruit that befits repentance, and do not presume to say to yourselves, 'We have Abraham as our father'; for I tell you, God is able from these stones to raise up children to Abraham. Even now the ax is laid to the root of the trees; every tree therefore that does not bear good fruit is cut down and thrown into the fire" (Mt. 3:7-10 RSV). And certainly, the Pharisees—the paragons of religious obedience—would not fail to recall how on the whole they resisted John and his movement. These details would certainly appear to prefigure some of the broad lines of the career of Jesus. John the Baptist's ministry was rightly judged as a preparation for the ministry of Jesus (Mk. 1:2-3; Lk. 3:4-6; Mt. 3:2-3).

Third, with this reminder as a fresh background, Jesus now pressed his question: Was John's baptism from heaven or from men? Or put differently, was the authority of John from God or from men? Since the earlier response of the official religious establishment is now part of John the Baptist as an episode of recent Jewish history, the question of Jesus would have the effect of forcing his opponents to make an honest theological assessment, not only of John's movement, but also of the earlier response of religious officialdom to him. In answering the question of Jesus, they would not only be making a judgment on John's movement but also on the assessment of their immediate predecessors concerning John and so, in effect, of themselves as well since they agreed with that assessment!

Finally and more important, since the case of John was somewhat similar to that of Jesus, any answer they would give would in some sense constitute an answer to the very question they put to Jesus. Thus, by asking his opponents the question about John's baptism, Jesus was actually compelling them to answer their own question about himself (Mk. 11:30*b*).

So now, it was the opponents of Jesus who were in the quandary of a dilemma, placed there ironically by Jesus himself, no less! In starting out to argue with Jesus, they instead found themselves arguing with one another to decide how to answer Jesus. If they said that John's baptism was from heaven, they would be exposed in their own unbelief; if they denied it, they would lose their credibility among the people, "for all held that John was a real prophet" (Mk. 11:31-32 RSV). The only safe exit from the proverbial devil and the deep blue sea is the plea of ignorance! The opponents of Jesus opted for this way out: "We do not know" (Mk. 11:33). Did they really not know, or were they refusing to tell? It seems that the latter is the case, judging from the way Jesus read their reply. And so their refusal to tell provided Jesus with a sure way out of the dilemma into which he was originally placed by his opponents: "Neither will I tell you by what authority I am doing these things" (Mk. 11:33). Given the circumstances, Jesus' reply was unassailably fair!

And so the issue of Jesus' authority still remained unresolved! But why would not Jesus reveal the source of his authority and establish his right to exercise it? Was it because he himself did not know? Nothing, of course, was farther from the truth! Jesus knew without any doubt that his authority had come from God. His commissioning at his baptism by John was also his anointing with power through the descent of the Holy Spirit upon him (Mk. 1:9-11). He heard "the voice from heaven" declare who he was, namely, the beloved Son of God with whom God was well pleased to entrust a mission of salvation with full divine authority to accomplish it. At his transfiguration he was again reminded of who he was—God's beloved Son who had full authority to speak God's word and had the right to be listened to (Mk. 9:2-7). This occurred just before he undertook his final journey to Jerusalem where he was to contend with his enemies and reckon with his fate. It assured him of his Father's confirmation of what he was about to do and was encouraged to go ahead! Even the demons or unclean spirits recognized who he truly was, namely, the Son of God, and they readily acknowledged his authority over them (Mk. 1:24; 3:11-12). Except for the author of the earliest Gospel writing much later, and the Roman centurion making his confession later at the foot of the cross at the moment he saw Jesus die, no human being had ever identified Jesus as the Son of God in the story of Jesus as told by Mark (1:1; 15:39). And so in terms of direct and certain knowledge of who Jesus truly was and his authority, only God, the demons, and Jesus himself knew for sure.

Since there could not be any contemporary human witnesses to corroborate any testimony of Jesus about himself and his authority, would the authorities in Jerusalem have believed Jesus had he answered the question about his authority? There was every reason to doubt that they would. It seems clear that the situation of the authorities vis-à-vis Jesus on the question of his authority was exactly the same as that of the Pharisees asking Jesus for a sign to test him! *It was a situation of hostile unbelief!* Given this fact, the same reasons with which Jesus denied the request for a sign would explain why Jesus refused to answer the question about his authority!

Of course, Jesus' refusal only intensified the fury of his enemies against him and further strengthened their resolve to destroy him. Further debates with him only confirmed his ability to best them even on the trickiest of issues, such as paying taxes to Caesar (Mk. 12:13-17; cf. Mt. 22:15-22; Lk. 20:20-26), the question about the resurrection (Mk. 12:18-27; cf. Mt. 22:22-33; Lk. 20:27-38), and what is the great commandment (Mk. 12:28-34; Mt. 22:34-40). In the end, "no one dared to ask him any question" (Mk. 12:34). Jesus himself asked a question about his identity—and so of his authority—which his enemies could not answer. Their failure to answer it in the end served only to strengthen belief in him and his power (Mk. 12:35-37; cf. Mt. 22:41-46; Lk. 20:41-44). This had to do with the contention of the scribes that the Christ himself is the son of David. Jesus asked: "David himself calls him Lord; so how is he his son?" The episode ends with the words: "And the great throng heard him gladly" (RSV).

Having failed to discredit him by undermining his authority through argument, calumny, request for sign, and direct questioning, the only way left open to silence him was to get rid of him. And this the authorities finally succeeded in doing by crucifying him. But it could be asked whether the death of Jesus would settle at all the question concerning the truth about himself—the truth about his identity and authority. Would not executing a person without finally deciding beyond reasonable doubt the questions surrounding the charges against him be regarded anywhere as sheer miscarriage of justice? And suppose that the person concerned had found himself in a situation in which there was absolutely no way of clearing and vindicating himself and as a result voluntarily submitted himself to his own execution, would that not sanctify injustice into mystery? Who then would establish the truth about him and vindicate him? If reason could not decide by what authority he did what he did, if history in the end can only victimize him by the failure of justice, and if voluntary acceptance of a horrible death as an act of ultimate trust only sanctifies evil into a dark mystery, can faith in a loving almighty God be justified at all? Or put the other way around, would God be able to justify Himself at all in the face of such a death as that of Jesus of Nazareth?

Perhaps the latter way of stating the question of theodicy—the question of the justification of God—is the better one, for it puts the question right where it properly belongs—in God Himself. In the long run, there is no way human beings can justify before fellow human beings the ways of God. This enterprise is best left to God Himself. In a most profound way this was what Jesus did. In an act of absolute trust, he left the resolution of the question of his authority and of his identity entirely in the hands of God his Father. The authority of Jesus was from God and so was of God. Only God therefore may properly resolve any issue that may arise in connection with it, especially the issues of its origin and the right and purpose of its exercise. When it is questioned in its entirety as it was by the priestly authorities in Jerusalem, then only God may vindicate it beyond any question! And this it seems is exactly what God did in raising Jesus from the dead. It was in terms of the resurrection of Jesus—an act that only God alone can do—that God answered the question, "By what authority did Jesus do the things that he did?"

God's vindication of Jesus by raising him from the dead produced many ironic and surprising twists. The religious establishment which opposed Jesus in the name of obedience to the will of God is now actually seen as disobeying God in its rejection of Jesus! What it regarded as violations of the Law by Jesus are in fact the correct observance of the Law. The curtain of the Temple was ripped into two from top to bottom (Mk. 15:38). The Holy of Holies was thus exposed to public view and access. A new kind of worship which celebrates God's presence with His people—Immanuel—and provides unhindered public access to God's grace came into being through the death and resurrection of Jesus Christ! The cross by which condemned criminals were put to death and, in the case of Jesus, was the means for the most grievous miscarriage of justice, became *the* way through the sacrifice of Jesus by which sins are forgiven, sinners are acquitted, and humankind reconciled and restored to God! At the foot of the cross, a Roman centurion who took part in crucifying Jesus was the first pagan human being ever to confess that Jesus was truly the son of God (Mk. 15:39). On the basis of his vindication through his resurrection, Jesus as risen can now publicly claim without hesitation: "All authority in heaven and on earth has been given to me" (Mt. 28:18).

We return to the basic issue in relation to which we discussed lengthily the criticism against Jesus, namely, the issue about community. It seems that the most effective way to destroy a community in any form is to undermine the center that holds it together, namely, its source of power, authority, and vitality. A jugular assault on life-together must aim at what holds it together as a community, and what this is can only be the source of its power and the seat of its sovereignty. When the center cannot hold any longer, things will certainly fall apart.[1] A coup d'état at the center of power is all that it takes! The authorities of Judaism knew this, and they tried to break the hold of Jesus upon his people by undermining this authority. While they succeeded brutally in removing him from the human scene, they failed miserably in their attempt to destroy the source and nature of his authority which was *from* God and *of* God and *for* the purposes of God! And so instead of collapsing into ruin, the community brought about by life-together with Jesus experienced a rebirth and surged forward in fresh vitality from a center of life-giving power vindicated and resourced by no less than God Himself who raised Jesus from the dead!

We may conclude this section with the reminder that mission evangelism is nothing unless it is a call to follow Jesus and to be with him—two dimensions of discipleship we have considered so far. But the one who is followed and with whom one is joined in fellowship is an active, dynamic, and explosive reality. Jesus was a man with a mission; he was actively engaged in fulfilling that mission on a variety of fronts. He was a man on a missionary journey, and so he traveled tirelessly and fearlessly in his mission. He launched an assault on the kingdom of Satan by his "mighty works" of healing and exorcism. Through his preaching and teaching, he sought to persuade people to see his vision of life in the kingdom of God. Through his prayer life he modeled for his disciples a new relationship of intimate trust in God as their heavenly Father! He successfully met the challenge of those who questioned his activities and undermined his authority. By his own decision he went unflinchingly to his own death, ultimately entrusting himself and his destiny into the God whose nearness in His reign he boldly proclaimed and who seemed, ironically, to have abandoned him in the hour of his utmost need for Him (Lk. 23:46; Mk. 15:34).

To follow Jesus is to follow *him in action;* to be with him is to be drawn into *his mission* and eventually to become an active participant in it. To follow him and be with him today is no different. The mission is the same, although the setting may be different. The battle against evil is the same, although the frontlines may be different! The saving power is the same, although the needs may be different! One comes to know him by being with him in his mission activity, for he becomes who he is in his activity. He appears in what he does; he reveals himself in what he achieves. One comes to know him not simply as another fellow human being with leadership qualities, nor merely as an outstanding leader with extraordinary powers by which he achieved unusual feats, but rather as one in and through whom God Himself is effectively at work in revealing the glory of His coming reign by redeeming His people. And so in being with him, one comes inevitably also to be with the God who is at work through him. By being with Jesus, one gains sure access to the same intimate personal relationship in which as son he calls God *Abba,* Father! *Being with Jesus is being with the God who is with him. That is the kind of life-together into which one is drawn irresistibly in following Jesus and being with him.*

Note

1. William Butler Yeats, "The Second Coming," reprinted in *Understanding Poetry*, ed. Cleanth Brooks and Robert Penn Warren (New York: Henry Holt and Co., 1950), p. 506.

CHAPTER 7

BEING WITH OTHERS IN JESUS

We must now consider a third aspect of the nucleus of the new community which Jesus formed as a decisive part of his total strategy for social transformation. This is the sense of community that was forged among those who heeded the call of Jesus to follow him and be with him. The community of discipleship has two dimensions. One is vertical; it relates one directly with Jesus by following him and being with him. The other is horizontal; it relates one directly with those who follow Jesus and are with him. Those who are with Jesus are also with one another. The community of discipleship is *being with others in Jesus.* There is no way one can avoid this. There are those who say one can follow Jesus and be with him without being with the others who likewise follow Jesus and are with him in response to his call. They are wrong! To be with Jesus is at the same time to be with those who are with him! Being with Jesus is being with his people! And this constitutes a new way of life-together with others. In what way is it a new community? This is the issue we shall address in what follows.

To be sure the synoptic tradition shows that seldom was Jesus found alone by himself. *He was always with others.* Some of those who accompanied him were few, some were many, some were in fact "great" multitudes. Many of these others were those who came to him on their own. Then there were those who found a bone to contend with him. He welcomed their questioning and was undaunted by their criticism. He was honest, fair, and full of candor in his dealings with them. Then there were the crowds that gathered around him (Mk. 2:2, 13; 3:7, 20; 4:1; 5:21, 24; 6:34; 8:1-2; 10:1). They were attracted by his teaching and his readiness to help. It became "his custom" to teach them whenever they gathered around him (Mk. 10:1; cf. 2:13; 4:1; 6:34) and to heal the sick who came to him. His characteristic attitude towards the crowds was compassion (Mk. 6:34; 8:1-2). For the most part they were composed of the poor, the outcasts, the sick, the so-called "dregs of society."

While he welcomed their gathering around him and allowed them to crowd him he, nevertheless, put a certain distance between himself and them (Mk. 2:2; 3:7–9:20). The scene reported in Mark 4:1 is rather revealing. As the great crowd gathered, Jesus deliberately "got into a boat and sat in it on the sea; and the whole crowd was beside the sea on the land" (RSV). On one occasion, he asked his disciples to have a boat ready for him just in case he had to remove himself from the crowd that was pressing on him (Mk. 3:7-9). Jesus was *with* the crowds; he had compassion for them. He taught them and helped them. But he put himself at some distance from them. He was not with them in the same way as he was with his disciples. *His intimate way of being with his disciples gave rise to a new way of life-together among themselves.* What is new and special about this community of disciples?

The Family and the New Community

We can begin looking for an answer to this question by probing an incident about Jesus and his family (Mk. 3:20-21, 31-35). Concerned about his welfare and rumors about his mental health, the mother of Jesus, together with his brothers, sought him in order that they might take him home and care for him (Mk. 3:20-21). This was a most natural thing to do in a family. The crowd around Jesus appreciated this family concern for Jesus. Some of those in the crowd passed on to him his family's solicitude for him: "Your mother and your brothers are outside, asking for you" (Mk. 3:32 RSV). The concern of the family of Jesus is now joined by the crowd around Jesus. Such an expression of solidarity is also quite natural. Could Jesus resist such a natural family concern for his welfare, coming now as it does directly from his mother and brothers and joined in by the crowd around him? What stronger sense of community is there than the one expressed by a caring family and fellow townmates? Would Jesus not have behaved naturally and most fittingly had he gone home with his family and acknowledged their concern for him? Was it not his filial duty to obey and preserve family solidarity?

How did Jesus reply to this solicitude of his family for his welfare? The text of his answer reads: "And he replied, 'Who are my mother and my brothers?' And looking around on those who sat about him, he said, 'Here are my mother and my brothers! Whoever does the will of God is my brother, and sister, and mother' " (Mk. 3:33-35 RSV; cf. Mt. 12:46-50; Lk. 8:19-21). The answer of Jesus appears very hard-hearted, especially when viewed in the light of both his family's loving concern for him and the setting in which it was given. On the face of it, it seems that Jesus rejected his family and ignored and depreciated their sincere effort to do well by him. Moreover, by doing this in the presence of many people who knew him and his family, he added insult to injury by publicly shaming his mother and brothers, for no fault but expressing a loving concern for him! Such an uncalled for behavior evokes consternation and merits censure! It could certainly break the bonds of family no matter how strong they were. Jesus must have had some very good reasons for going this far. We must look more carefully into his reply to see if he indeed had motivations that would put in better light what he did!

First of all, it is to be noted generally that in his reply there is a clear indication that Jesus was envisioning a new community, a new form of life-together. Moreover, he believed that he had something to do with the formation of such a new community. Jesus still expressed in figurative language the bonds of such a new community in terms of family ties and relationships, such as having a mother and brothers. The question, "Who are my mother and my brothers?" is answered by the declaration "Here are my mother and brothers" in the text. He used the phrase "mother and brothers" in both instances. In short, the new community Jesus was envisioning closely resembles family cohesion, and for good reasons. There is no doubt that the bonds of family are what a sense of community should be: strong, cohesive, intimate. They express open communication, mutual concern, loving care for one another, loyalty to the family interest and welfare to the point of sacrificing personal welfare. The family is a model of human community. By using the strongest bonds of family life—being a son of a mother and having brothers—to express the ties that bind his vision of a new community, Jesus was affirming his family and the family generally!

Furthermore, the ties that bind a family together are *common bonds.* The members of a family may be different persons. They may be endowed with different talents and exhibit different interests. But they all share a *natural sense of community,* and what it shares naturally is as strong as the bonds of nature!

The family is also bound together by *common cultural ties*. The relationships within it are lived in specific ways determined by culture, handed on by tradition, and internalized through socialization, education, and practice. A mother's concern for a son expressed in a specific way, such as looking for him and asking him to come home, is affirmed by the values of the community. Such cultural appreciation can only reinforce the cohesion of the family. The family is a *cultural community* and what it shares in terms of values and norms and forms of behavior are deeply embedded in tradition and community consciousness!

The family is also knit together by *common historical experiences*. It shares common memories that shape its identity and give its pilgrimage in time a sense of continuity and meaning. Family reunions celebrate shared experiences that have the effect of holding the family together in spite of separation and generation gaps. The family is a *historical community* and what it shares in common remembrance, whether of joy or sorrow, binds it together through time and circumstance!

Finally, the family is a special unit of larger communities, such as a tribe, a clan, a race, a nation. With these larger natural communities, it would normally share common elements such as customs, laws, language, social structures, economic systems, a national territory, and political authority. What it shares in common with the larger society may affect its sense of cohesion for ill or good, depending on what is happening to the larger society. Massive social change may weaken family ties and change its shape and character. But as the basic social unit, the family is expected to contribute to the nurture and promotion of a sense of unity in society. Even in periods of social upheaval the family is expected to provide a sense of social cohesion and stability. It is therefore under pressure to embody a sense of community under all circumstances. The family is a *social community* and what it shares with the larger society is precisely its capacity to embody and model an elemental sense of social cohesion!

From what has been said, it can be seen that the family embodies all the basic elements that make for a strong sense of community. It gathers into itself common binding elements in natural, cultural, historical, and social communities. No doubt there are other ways of forming communities besides the family sense. Communities are organized around common activities, such as professional associations; common interests, such as labor unions; common goals, such as political parties, and so forth. But the sense of community embodied and fostered by these secondary forms of human association is not as elemental and binding and enduring as that embodied and nurtured in the family. In modeling the new community that Jesus envisioned upon the family and its ties, Jesus was expressing a firmly held conviction that its sense of togetherness must not be less than what makes a family into a community. Did Jesus then reject his family? How could he, if he used his family and his experience of family life as a basis for modeling the new community that was part of his vision for human life in the coming reign of God!

A Community More Inclusive Than the Family

The question we must ask, however, is this: Is the community enshrined in the family good enough? Jesus was prepared to affirm the family model as far as its capacity to unite can go. But is it enough for the sort of human community he envisioned? Apparently *it is not*. Can the family model *fully express* the community that Jesus had in mind? Apparently *it could not*. With this observation, we must now consider a *second aspect of the reply of Jesus*. According to the text, Jesus looked around at those who were sitting near him and he pointed to them and said, "Here are my mother and brothers" (Mk. 3:34 RSV). It is clear that he did not point to his natural mother and brothers. By not doing so, he was in effect saying that the sense of community they represented— which is that of the natural family—cannot fully express the kind of community he had in mind, and so it is not good enough. Instead, he pointed to those who were near him and he called them his "mother and brothers." In Mark's Gospel it is not clear who these were. It is simply pointed out that they were those "who sat about him" (Mk. 3:34). In Matthew's Gospel, however, these were definitely identified as "his disciples" (Mt. 12:49). This clearly indicates that *the community Jesus had in mind is the community of disciples who were called by him, gathered around him, and sat at his feet, and who now found themselves to be together in Jesus.*

What is lacking in the family community so that it cannot fully embody and express the discipleship community? And what is there in the community of discipleship that cannot be fully embodied in the family community? We must deal with these questions one after the other.

It has been pointed out earlier that the sense of community in the family is based on what is elementally common. It is what is shared mutually—what is common—that unites and forms community. This is true. And the strength of the family model is precisely its ability to express and foster the community-forming power of what is common and shared mutually. Secondary forms of human community in their varying intensities of cohesion, such as interest groups, political entities, and diplomatic practices, are based on the same principle.

But while this is indeed the strength of the family model it is also its Achilles' heel. *It is unable to include within itself as a constituting element of community the fact of otherness, difference, diversity, conflict.* The family not only unites, it also excludes at the same time. And it excludes those who are *not* family. That practically covers all of humankind! It can only take them if they *"join* the family" through ways that are themselves prescribed by the family. That means that those who join a family allow themselves to be *taken into* the family by agreeing to conform to what is common at the expense of suppressing their otherness. Communities that are modeled upon the family—tribes, races, nation-states, secondary human associations—do the same. They include as well as exclude at the same time, and the criterion for the one and the other is the principle of commonality! The family model of community is a closed one, and for this reason it is not inclusive enough! Could this be the reason why Jesus did not find it adequate for his vision of community? Is there a principle of community that embraces constitutively both commonality and otherness, unity and diversity, agreement and difference, the one and the many?

What the family model seeks to exclude is precisely what Jesus seeks to include in his vision of community. When Jesus pointed to his disciples as his "mother and brothers," *he was in fact laying claim to otherness as an essential component of the community of discipleship.* There are in fact strong indications to support this view. For one thing, his disciples *were not* his natural family. They belonged to *other* families. He was not their family, either. And yet he claimed them to be his "mother and brothers." Difference—not merely commonality—was the other basis of his community-forming claim! However, it was not his disciples who were "joining" his family. It was rather he who was calling them *his* "family." He was making himself a part of them rather than they becoming a part of him. Either way there was no attempt to suppress personal individuality and integrity. Otherness is affirmed! Furthermore, while there were members of families in the company of disciples, they had in fact broken away from their families upon the call of Jesus to follow him (Mk. 1:16-20). And although they were still referred to as brothers, they were not in the company of Jesus as brothers but as disciples of Jesus. Family solidarity has been broken and family relationships have lost their merely natural claims in the community of discipleship.

Still further to be noted as specially significant is the fact that in the company of Jesus were two people who would not normally find themselves together in peaceful terms. These were Simon the Zealot and Levi (Matthew) the tax collector. As their respective identifications indicate, these were not merely different individuals. They represented two mutually exclusive groups with radically different commitments and styles of life. Simon, before he became a disciple of Jesus, apparently belonged to a party designated as Zealot. The root sense of this word in Hebrew meant both zeal and jealousy. The one who is zealous is often intensely jealous of something he regards as of paramount importance, and the one who is jealous of something is often fanatically zealous. Intensity of commitment and uncompromising fanaticism make explosive company, and they both characterize the Zealot movement and the temper of its members! Simon, the Zealot, was a model member of this movement; the name of his group became his identity!

And what was this movement about? Palestine was at the time a colony of imperial Rome. The Jews were regarded everywhere in the empire as a subjugated people under military rule. They deeply resented their humiliation and oppression and looked longingly to the day when liberation and vindication would come! There were those among them who were ready to translate the hope into action. They formed liberation movements in rebellion against Rome. The Zealot movement was one such revolutionary organization. Many of its members came from people who regarded themselves as zealous agents of God and who were jealous for His Law. They believed that God's sovereignty must be vindicated against all forms of idolatry, apostasy, and transgression of the Law. Their wrath was specially directed against those among their own people who had become "hirelings" of Rome, namely, the tax collectors. And Levi was such a tax collector. When Jesus called him, he was sitting at the tax office (Mk. 2:14). As a tax collector, he collected levies from his own people to fatten the coffers of Rome and in the process he took care to make a profit for himself. Thus, from the viewpoint of a zealot, all the grievous sins against God and His people are represented by the tax collector. In serving Rome, he was serving the pagan gods of Rome; he was therefore an idolater. In turning against his people by serving Rome, he had become a traitor and apostate. And in making a profit for himself from his tax-collecting for Rome, a tax collector was robbing his own people. Tax collectors were, therefore, lawbreakers to be cast out together with sinners and prostitutes and robbers! In his jealousy for God and his zeal for God's Law, a zealot is ready and capable of killing a tax collector if he met him! A tax collector would serve himself well by avoiding a zealot. And the two met in Jesus! Could they have come together peacefully as family?

To be sure, in coming together in Jesus, the disciples found something common to all of them in spite of their otherness, difference, and conflict, namely, Jesus. It was their coming together *in him* that formed them into a community of discipleship. Is this not proof of the fact that it is still what is shared in common that invariably makes for community? Of course, there is no denying this fact. But one must also realize that what they shared in common is someone who is radically different from them. The *unique otherness of Jesus* was unmistakable from the beginning. He had "authority" unlike those who were normally regarded as having authority. He had powers of healing that enabled him to perform "mighty" works! He had a special relationship with God that was so close and intimate that calling Him *Abba*, Father, seemed all so natural and appropriate.

Jesus was not only "different" in a special sense, *he also transcended his disciples*. It was he who called them and demanded absolute commitment to himself. They sat at his feet and acknowledged him as their Lord. They sensed that he was what he claimed to be, namely, as the one in whom the coming reign of God has broken through into the midst of human life to heal and redeem and liberate! *It is precisely by being different from them and by transcending them in his power and presence that he is common to them!* It is as the disciples gathered around him and sat at his feet so that he became common to them in his otherness and transcendence that he forged them into a community of discipleship! *He represented indeed a power and a presence that can form into living community not only commonality and otherness among human beings, but also human communion with what is uniquely different and unconditionally transcendent!*

With this observation, we are led to consider a third element in the reply of Jesus. The text records Jesus as saying: "Whoever does the will of God is my brother and sister and mother" (Mk. 3:35). This is said following his claim that his disciples are his family. With this word *Jesus has in fact made his vision of community all-inclusive.* To appreciate this, we must see the logical buildup that leads to this saying as the climax. First, he does not deny his natural family which models a community on ties that are mutually and commonly shared. Second, he adds to "his family" the company of his disciples who are *other* than family and are *different* from each other, and some of whom may even be *hostile* to one another! Although his disciples only meet each other by being with him and so "share" him in common, he is nonetheless uniquely different from them and unconditionally transcends them. He, therefore, adds otherness and diversity as component elements of his vision of human community.

Love as the Basis of a More Inclusive Community

And now he throws wide open the parameters of human community to make it all-inclusive! He does this by simply using the word *whoever.* This literally means anybody. Jesus makes the point that his *whoever* includes women. The word *sister* which now appears in the last remark of Jesus does not appear in the first two parts of his saying about family relations. There, only the words *mother* and *brothers* are mentioned. In the third part of his remark which makes community all-inclusive, he pointedly adds *sister.* Although it is mentioned as an aspect of family relationship, it calls attention to another dimension of otherness which must figure as a constitutive component in Jesus' vision of an all-inclusive community. This aspect of otherness is *sexual differentiation,* and it must be viewed as something other than the relationship of motherhood, which is a natural family relation. The community of discipleship includes women, otherwise it is not all-inclusive! Sexual difference is the most basic and universal difference. It is God Himself who instituted it at creation (Gen. 1:27).

There is only one operating criterion that sets out the parameters of *whoever,* that is, the doing of God's will. Obviously this criterion applies to all and anyone, and is therefore common to all: *whoever does the will of God* is the brother and sister and mother of Jesus. But at the same time, however, one must not forget that this criterion is not a natural or social or human universal norm. It is *God's will;* it is God and His will, and not the human being and his will, which are denoted. This criterion is therefore something radically different from, and transcendent to, all human universal norms of community. Indeed, *what makes Jesus' vision of community all-inclusive is precisely the fact that he now bases it upon nothing more or less than the doing of God's will.* We must now consider the meaning of this criterion in the context of Jesus' vision of community!

It is, of course, necessary to distinguish between God's will and the doing of it. The will that is to be done is that of God, and not of the human being. But it is also clear that the doing of it is by the human being as agent. This distinction exposes a difficult problem: how can God's will, which is not that of the human being, be done through human agency? Given the difference between God's order of being and that of human existence, can human agency accomplish what is not in its nature both to will and to do? Nonetheless, no matter what difficulties this difference may entail, there is also absolutely no question of the fact that God's will must be done, for *His will is quite simply what He wants done!* "Thy will be done on earth as it is in heaven" is the unqualified petition of Jesus in the prayer he taught his disciples! It appears that applying the norm for an all-inclusive community is fraught with difficulties. If anything, it seems to render doing it impossible!

In the faith and practice of Israel the term "will of God" referred to the Law, the *Torah,* a word which in its root sense means "to direct" or "point the way." God points His way for Israel as His covenant people by revealing to her His will through the giving of the Law through Moses. The Law, therefore, expresses the will of God. The Law eventually came to mean the whole five books in the Jewish scriptures, which are attributed to the authorship of Moses. At the heart of the Law are the Ten Commandments, which were given to Israel through Moses at the inauguration of the Covenant (Ex. 19:1–24:18; Deut. 5–6). They embody God's requirements in making Israel become His people. It is through the Law that God directs and guides the way of Israel in the world. Since the Law is God's will for Israel and is given both as instruction and requirement, it must be obeyed by Israel. The will of God is revealed in order to be done; the Law of God is commanded to be obeyed. Doing is in obedience and obedience is by doing!

Since the Law is the will of God, it follows that every portion of it is to be regarded as equally valid and must be equally obeyed. Normatively no distinction about which is primary and secondary, first and second, greater or lesser was permitted about the Law in Jewish practice. But a close look at the Ten Commandments will show that they readily classify themselves into two types of requirements, one pertaining to God (Ex. 20:1-11; Deut. 5:1-5) and the other pertaining to human beings (Ex. 20:12-17; Deut. 5:16-21). For purposes of instruction, however, this distinction was permitted. But as early as the composition of the Deuteronomic Law, there was a reinterpretation of the Ten Commandments that went beyond this distinction. Already in Deuteronomy 6:4-5 the four commandments pertaining to God have come to be understood in terms of *loving God* wholly with heart, soul, and might. From here on, it was not difficult to regard the six commandments dealing with fellow human beings in the same light, that is, as *love of neighbor* (Lev. 19:18).

What is decidedly new here is not the distinction between God and neighbor, which is presupposed, but the understanding that *the doing of the Law is to be executed as love.* Loving God means doing the first four commandments; having no other God besides the Lord, not making and serving any graven image of Him, not taking the name of the Lord in vain, observing the Sabbath to keep it holy! By the same token, loving the neighbor means doing the next six requirements pertaining to fellow human beings: honoring one's parents, not killing another human being, not committing adultery, not stealing, not bearing false witness against one's neighbor, not coveting anything that belongs to one's neighbor. Thus, *the essence of obedience to the will of God and of doing the Law is love of God and love of neighbor.*

When one of the scribes, who were the authorized interpreters of the Law, came to test Jesus concerning his understanding of the Law, the question he asked was: "Which commandment is the first of all?" (Mk. 12:28). In answer Jesus merely declared what seemed to be the official understanding, which included the distinction between God and human being and doing the commandments pertaining to them in terms of love. As far as this goes, Jesus and the scribe apparently had no difference of opinion at all (Mk. 12:28-34; cf. Mt. 22:34-40; Lk. 10:25-28). In fulfilling the Law, which means correctly understanding it and fully obeying it, did Jesus then not go beyond the official interpretation of it? Does doing the will of God as a criterion for membership in the new community He envisaged require no more than what was expected of an ordinary devout Jew? The evidence in the record seems to indicate rather strongly that he did go beyond "the righteousness of the scribes and the Pharisees." Where he differed from the official interpretation was in radicalizing the depth and range of both the understanding of the Law and the doing of it in terms of love!

For the devout Jew the Law stood mediatingly between the human being and God. The relation between God and the human being and the relation between the human being and God are both through the Law: God giving the Law and the human being obeying it. Thus, for both God and the human being, the Law *is* the thing! Both are bound to the Law. Their freedom is within the Law. They both live by the Law—God in being faithful to it and upholding it as an expression of His being and His relationships, and the human being in obeying it as the raison d'être of his or her existence. *What Jesus did was to abolish the Law as mediator between God and the human being.* By so doing, he exposed into the open God's free readiness to be personally near by directly relating to the human being and graciously pouring upon man and woman alike the blessings of His reign, which creates, sustains, judges, saves and redeems! For Jesus this is the meaning of God's love which initiated the making of the covenant with Israel and prompted the revealing of His will through the Law. Love is the driving force of both Covenant and Law! It is the essence of God's relationship to the human being and to all of creation. For Jesus, this too is the meaning of the proclamation that the kingdom of God has drawn near through him—in what he said and did and lived and died for—and is now in our midst (Lk. 11:20). The word of Jesus that directly and assuredly relates God to His people is: "Fear not, little flock, for it is your Father's good pleasure to give you the kingdom" (Lk. 12:32 RSV).

Reading the mind of Jesus, Paul comprehends God's action in Jesus Christ in terms of love: "God shows his love for us in that while we were yet sinners Christ died for us. . . . There is therefore now no condemnation for those who are in Christ Jesus. . . . For God has done what the law, weakened by the flesh, could not do: sending his own Son in the likeness of sinful flesh and for sin, he condemned sin in the flesh, in order that the just requirement of the law might be fulfilled in us" (Rom. 5:8; 8:1-4 RSV). The writer of the First Epistle of John perceives the nature of God quite simply as love: God is love (1 Jn. 4:8, 16). It is the same love with which He relates to us and the world through Jesus

Christ to save us: "In this the love of God was made manifest among us, that God sent his only Son into the world, so that we might live through him. In this is love, not that we loved God but that he loved us and sent his Son to be the expiation for our sins" (1 Jn. 4:9-10 RSV; cf. Jn. 3:16).

For Jesus then and for the rest of the New Testament, love reaches to the very depths of God's being: His nature is love. Love also ranges over all His works from beginning to end. It is in love that He relates to humanity in Jesus Christ and so in love he creates and sustains, He judges and forgives, He saves and transforms, He redeems and glorifies! "So we know and believe the love God has for us. God is love, and he who abides in love abides in God, and God abides in him" (1 Jn. 4:16 RSV). Here the Law is abolished as standing between God and the human being. What is between them is love, and love does not intervene or stand between; it rather unites the diverse. It is that in which both the common and the different and that which transcends them both abide, and abiding in it they abide in each other!

If then the nature of God is love, and love is behind and over all and also the end of all His works, and in love He comes to reign and relate to us in Jesus Christ, and if love is the essence of His will and is therefore the fulfillment of the Law, then we may ask: what can "loving God" as the doing of His will possibly mean? *To love God in the light of all this is most certainly not to do the commandments first.* To the human being enslaved to sin and under judgment, which is the universal human condition, the Law does not command; it condemns! Indeed, it has condemned him/her already! There is no way of fulfilling the Law out of having been condemned already, for this is precisely the effect of the Law. To fulfill the Law under condemnation is to serve fully the sentence of the Law, which is death. Salvation is not in death by death but *from* death through life. But this is precisely what the Law cannot do (Rom. 8:3). Paul cries out the anguish of all humanity under sentence of death by the Law on account of sin: "Wretched man that I am! Who will deliver me from this body of death?" (Rom. 7:24 RSV). And his answer is: "Thanks be to God through Jesus Christ our Lord" (Rom. 7:25). Here the cry of anguish is replaced by the joy of doxology. What intervenes between the one and the other is the saving action of God in Jesus Christ, which redeems from condemnation and saves from the sentence of death. "There is therefore now no condemnation for those who are in Christ Jesus" (Rom. 8:1). And in John: "For God sent the Son into the world, not to condemn the world, but that the world might be saved through him. He who believes in him is not condemned; he who does not believe is condemned already, because he has not believed in the name of the only Son of God" (Jn. 3:17-18 RSV).

To love God as fulfilling the Law is first of all to respond to the call demanded by the drawing near of the coming reign of God, namely, *to repent,* to turn away from doing the Law under judgment and so out of condemnation. It is *to believe* in Jesus Christ, that is to acknowledge the reign of God in him, to come under his Lordship and so into the sphere of God's coming rule, *to respond to his call to discipleship* by following him and being with him in his presence and in his activity, and *so to be with those who are with him!* It is to *trust* God as the Father of Jesus Christ and so to ask Him in prayer for everything in life and in death and in what lies beyond death. *It is to depend upon Him* as the One who makes possible for us what alone is possible with Him, including our future in His promise of raising the dead by the same power by which He raised Jesus from the dead into life eternal. *And in repentance and faith and trust one immediately discovers the freedom and the power both to will and to do the will of God as given in the form of the commandments.* Within God's enabling grace and liberating love in the sphere of His rule, the human being discovers that he can indeed "do the will of God." But only then and not before!

If what has been said above is anywhere near the truth, then it is clear that doing the will of God in the perspective of the Kingdom is quite different from doing it as commandment in the perspective of the Law. The one is the basis and possibility of the other. But if that is true, *then mission evangelism as the call to repentance and faith and discipleship in view of the nearness of the coming reign of God is precisely the key that opens the door to the all-inclusive community envisioned by Jesus!*

Love as the Ethos of the New Community

What does it mean "to love the neighbor" in the sphere of God's rule? There are, of course, two related issues in this question. One has to do with who is neighbor, and the other with what it means to love him. In Jewish faith and practice, that is, in the sphere of the Law, the neighbor is clearly one's *kinsman,* in contrast to the foreigner. At the core of the kin circle of community is the natural family. It is extended to fellow

Jews whose racial and religious purity is beyond question. The *neighbor* is the one with whom one shares a natural family affinity and a racial and religious pedigree whose purity is without blemish. It is obvious that community here is based strictly on the principle of commonality. Jewish society has been known throughout history as an exclusive community. One can join it only by converting into it.

To love a neighbor who is a kinsman means doing what is required in the *Torah,* the core of which are the six commandments dealing with a fellow human being, that is, a fellow Jew. Except for the commandment to honor one's parents, the rest are formulated in negative terms, and are based on the ethical principle of nonmalfeasance. That is to say, they forbid rather than permit; they state what not to do but not what to do. Moreover, they aim at preventing the doing of harm or injury to another whether willful or unintentional, but they do not stipulate the good that must be done to others. To love a neighbor, it is enough to do him no harm. Faced with a choice, on the one hand, of doing good and in the process violating a prohibition, and on the other hand, keeping a statute and doing no harm, there is no doubt that the devout Jew would opt for the latter. Keeping the Law and doing no harm to another is so much better than violating the Law in order to do good!

The principle of racial and religious kinship identifies not only the neighbor but the non-neighbor as well. Viewed in this light, non-neighbors are of three kinds. The first, obviously, is the non-Jew, the foreigner. He belongs to the "uncircumcised" and is excluded from the community of the "circumcised" (cf. Eph. 2:11-12). The second are the racially impure Jews who because of this do not feel bound to observe the Law as devoutly as the pure Jew. Their racial pedigree and religious purity are under question. The Samaritans are a good example of this type of "foreigner." They, too, are excluded from the Jewish community. A pure Jew would have no association with them! Finally, there is the racially pure Jew who has broken the Law. A pure Jew who does not observe the Law is a contradiction. He is a "sinner" who must be cast out of the community. In contrast to the foreigner, he belongs to the community of Israel by race; but since he willfully violates the Law which constitutes Israel's identity, he is to be regarded as an outcast from the community. The foreigner is an "outsider" who cannot get inside the Jewish community unless he converts into it; the "sinner" is an insider who has been cast out of the community and cannot get in again unless he/she repents and becomes clean again. For as long as the foreigner and the lawbreaker are not members of the community of Israel, they are not "neighbors." They can be treated as "enemies" and be the object of hate (Mt. 5:43). For good community-preserving reasons the devout Jew need not observe the prohibitions enjoined in the Torah with respect to "enemies," let alone do good to them.

From what has been said, it is clear that if this is what Jesus meant by loving neighbor as doing the will of God according to the Law, then the new community he envisaged can never become all-inclusive. Loving the neighbor in the light of the Law is based on what is essentially common or mutually shared—such as racial purity, family kinship, a shared faith, common identity. Community based solely on what is common is unable to affirm and appreciate essential difference and real diversity as constitutive of life-together. For Jesus, on the other hand, these are also elemental to the community he envisaged. Moreover, where difference breaks out into conflict and generates deep-rooted enmity, a sense of community based merely on commonality is unable to provide healing and reconciliation and restore wholeness in terms demanded by the Law. Where these are not met, the ultimate social consequence is expulsion from the community. It is by making an "outcast" of the "foreigner" and the "offender" that community is preserved. The criterion of "whoever does the will of God" would operate by exclusion rather than by inclusion. Obviously, this is contrary to the intention of Jesus. This leads us to look for another interpretation of "loving the neighbor" besides the one available in Jewish understanding. Who would my neighbor be, and how might I love him, from the perspective of the coming reign of God which has drawn near?

For an answer it would be helpful to consider the parable of the Good Samaritan (Lk. 10:25-37). It is the classic source for an answer to this question. A lawyer came to Jesus to test him by asking what he had to do to inherit eternal life. Jesus asked him in turn about what he understood of the Law. This was the context best understood by the lawyer because he functioned in this milieu. So the lawyer quoted the summary of the Law in terms of loving God and the neighbor as oneself! Intending to put Jesus to the test, he soon found himself ironically the one being put to the test when Jesus told him, "You have answered right; do this, and you will live" (Lk. 10:28 RSV). Desiring to prove himself still in the right, he asked Jesus a second question: "And who is my neighbor?" The question is logically entailed by the admonition of Jesus. In asking it, the lawyer was following through on what Jesus told him. One must know unequivocally the neighbor whom he is to love! But that is exactly the problem: one does not know who the neighbor is! This is an issue debated among the scribes. The prevailing position believed that Leviticus 19:18 meant only fellow Jews. A small minority held that neighbors included Gentiles and Samaritans, that is, foreigners! Both positions assumed, however, that the Jew is under obligation by the Law to love his neighbor, whoever he is!

In answer to the lawyer's question about who is the neighbor, Jesus now tells the parable. He frames the issue no longer in the perspective of the Law but in the light of the coming reign of God which has drawn nigh. The kingdom of God is the subject of the parables of Jesus. The parable tells of a nameless man who is waylaid in the ditch by robbers who strip and beat him and leave him half dead, completely helpless and alone in a deserted place. Since the victim is traveling from Jerusalem to Jericho, the presumption is that he is a Jew. As the story unfolds, the answer to the lawyer's question seems to be portrayed by Jesus. It does not appear to be any of the answers traditionally debated: the neighbor is not the fellow Jew, nor the Gentile, nor the Samaritan. It seems that the *neighbor is rather the hapless victim needing immediate help whom one chances to meet in daily life.* By the way the story describes the victim, identifying the neighbor does not seem to be all that difficult. Although he neither speaks nor moves, the victim is so obviously the object of concern. The lawyer had no reason to quibble in seeing him described in a way that makes him appear unmistakably to be the neighbor.

But as Jesus goes on in telling the story, it soon becomes clear that there is something much more important than merely knowing who is the neighbor. What appears to be the real point of Jesus *is whether one is ready to be neighborly to anyone in need.* Being a neighbor to someone is much more important than merely knowing who your neighbor is. Knowing your neighbor does not necessarily make you behave neighborly to him or her. And behaving neighborly to him or her includes far more than identifying him as your neighbor. The *real neighbor is the one who is neighborly. It is by being neighborly that one makes the person in need one's neighbor.* And the neighborly can either be in need or not. Even those in need are not exempted from being neighborly. This is a more difficult issue because it concerns not just know-ing but acting on what one knows. It is a matter of _being_ a neighbor, not _knowing_ a neighbor. One can debate an issue intellectually such as who is my neighbor without bearing on reality or making a moral com-mitment to be neighborly. But when one acts upon reality in the light of knowledge or vision, one comes up against the hard facts of life which either resist or facilitate action. Practical options are existential, not intellectual.

The parable indicates the various options of acting neighborly or not. Both a priest and a Levite go down the same road. Both are Jews and so kinsman to the victim. Both are in the helping profession and are therefore expected to help the victim. Both see the victim as he lay help-less in the ditch. Both had the qualifications and the opportunity of being neighborly! With all these facts going in his favor, would not the victim rightly have expected the priest and the Levite, who are the paragons of Jewish virtue, to help him? But what did they do, instead? Both the priest and the Levite "passed by on the other side" of the road (Lk. 10:31-32). Not only did they not help the victim, they also avoided him as one unclean and who could make them unclean!

Now a Samaritan comes along and comes to where the victim is and sees him! The Jewish audience listening to the story would surely not expect the Samaritan to help the victim who is a Jew. There is a long and bitter story of hatred between Samaritan and Jew! A string of events formed that history. Following the Babylonian exile, the Samaritans opposed the restoration of Jerusalem. In the second century B.C. they sided with the Syrians in the war against the Jews. In 128 B.C. the Jew-ish high priest burned the Samaritan temple on Mt. Gerizim. In the early part of the first century the Samaritans defiled the Jewish temple and prevented the Passover feast from being celebrated by scattering the bones of a corpse in the Temple during the Passover, thus rendering the Temple unclean. The Samaritans did not fully recognize the authority of the Law and they did not observe it as devoutly as the Jews. To the Jew the Samaritan was an apostate who defiles. So Jews and Samaritans were mutually bitter enemies (Mt. 10:5; Lk. 9:51-55; Jn. 4:9). And yet it was the Samaritan enemy and religious apostate who helped the victim and behaved neighborly towards him. By being neighborly, he made the victim his neighbor and loved him. Consider his series of action:

1. When the Samaritan saw the victim, _he was moved with compas-_

sion, and he stopped in his journey and went to him. This is an act of inward sympathy for, and outward solidarity with, the victim. Compassion is love reaching out to the other to share in his or her suffering.

2. He bound up the wounds of the victim, pouring oil and wine. This would assuage the pain, bring healing and comfort to the victim. This is an act of salvation, of making whole!

3. He did not leave the victim in the ditch. Instead, he sat him on his own beast, brought him to an inn and stayed with him and cared for him through the night. He did not only see to it that the victim received medical care, he shared himself by being with him, providing him the comfort of his presence and solicitude! This is an act of self-giving in reconciliation and fellowship, which are formative of community.

4. The next day, he paid the innkeeper the rent of the room. This is an act of assuming responsibility for the good or welfare of another, even one's enemy!

5. Before leaving him to continue on his journey, he made sure that the innkeeper would take care of him, and pledged that he would pay the innkeeper whatever the cost in taking care of the victim! Having been robbed of his money and being helpless and away from home, the victim could not have paid the cost of the rent and his recuperation. For this reason, he could be sold to slavery for indebtedness and so he would be deprived of his independence and robbed of his future as well. This is an act of ensuring the dignity and the future of a fellow human being.

6. Finally, it is not unreasonable to claim that by what the Samaritan did, he created peace where there was enmity, reconciliation where there was alienation, community where there was hostility and separation.

Compassion and solidarity, healing and comfort, self-giving and personal care, provision for recuperation, protecting the dignity and securing the future, reconciliation and peace—these constitute loving the neighbor and behaving neighborly towards him or her! These are positive deeds, not negative prohibitions! They model the good to be done, not the harm to be avoided!

The climax of the story is the dramatic exchange between Jesus and the lawyer. Jesus now asked the lawyer: "Which of these three, do you think, *proved neighbor to the man* who fell among the robbers?" The lawyer answered him: "The one who showed mercy on him." And then

Jesus said to him: "Go and do likewise" (Lk. 10:36-37 RSV). This dialogue is the most critical part of the parable, for it is the teaching point. It reveals the revolutionary impact of the parable upon the hearer, and it urges him to act on his own insight and so participate in the realization of truth. We may note the following points:

1. Jesus asked the lawyer to answer his own question about who is the neighbor by forcing him to make his own judgment based on the evidence presented to him in the parable. By asking him to do his own thinking in answering his own question, Jesus removes the lawyer from the framework of the Law and so he could no longer rely on the authority of the Law. He has been placed in the realm of freedom which is the sphere of God's reign where he has to decide for himself what is right and good based on events brought about by the presence of the reign of God! He has to determine his answer in the light of both tradition and its answers on the one hand, and changes in the human situation—the changing facts of life—brought about by unexpected events, on the other hand. He must be prepared to lay aside what is merely prejudice and abandon what is palpably false, and decide only for the truth as he sees it happening before his eyes in ways he did not anticipate!

2. It is a credit to the lawyer that he was open to the parable and allowed it to make an impact on him. His answer reveals that he correctly perceived the truth and stated it "like it is," in spite of the constraints of tradition and prejudice. His answer correctly described the essence of what the Samaritan did: *he showed mercy on the victim*. He brought himself to acknowledge that it is the Samaritan foreigner, the religious apostate and outcast and enemy, who did this good! It was not the priest and Levite, the victim's kinsmen who were in the profession of being and doing good and so were under obligation "to love the neighbor." There is here a reversal of values: the bad doing the good; the good doing the evil by failing to do the good!

3. Having answered his own question through his own insight into the truth, the lawyer is now admonished by Jesus to "go and do likewise." God's will has been perceived and known. The mere knowledge of it by itself gives rise to the responsibility to obey it. The will of God happens by being done and it is done by human agency! Although it is God's will and seems humanly impossible, *it is nevertheless by doing it that it becomes possible. Merely contemplating it makes it impossible!* The power to do the impossible becomes available precisely in the doing of

it. It is by acting in obedience to what is the will of God, which seems impossible for human agency, that God in His reign makes it possible to happen. Jesus exhorted his disciples about doing the impossible with these words: "Have faith in God. Truly, I say to you, whoever says to this mountain, 'Be taken up and cast into the sea,' and does not doubt in his heart, but believes that what he says will come to pass, it will be done for him. Therefore I tell you, whatever you ask in prayer, believe that you receive it, and you will" (Mk. 11:22-24 RSV). *Faith in God is asking in prayer for what is possible with Him; and in doing what we pray for, He makes it possible for us to achieve it!* This is the solution to the difficulty about the human agent doing what in his nature he is not capable of willing and doing! Thus, the exhortation to "Go and do likewise" is not premised on obedience to the Law but on the obedience of faith in the God who makes possible the doing of His will as the expression of His reign. Being neighborly in a situation of long-standing enmity seems humanly impossible. Yet by the sheer act of doing it in faith as the will of God it can and does happen! It is the obedience of faith and not of the Law that makes the doing of the will of God the norm for an all-inclusive community.

We shall conclude this section by summarizing some of the ways in which "love of neighbor" understood as the will of the God who has drawn near to reign in Jesus Christ founds and builds up a new and all-inclusive community. First of all, we note that it affirms and builds upon the community-forming power of what is mutually shared in common. In this sense, love affirms the Law and builds upon it. Second, love respects and appreciates essential difference and real diversity and incorporates these into life-together as constituent elements. The "foreigner" as representing distinct and irreducible otherness must be embraced by love. He/she must not be "cast out" of the community on the principle that he/she is an "alien," and an "other." Nor must he/she be incorporated into the community because he/she has something in common with the community. Rather, it is precisely as an "other"—as someone really different—that he/she is to be taken in and affirmed as a member of the community. The unity of love includes not only the unity of the common but also equally the unity of the diverse.

Third, love is neighborly. It creates community where there is none and where it does not seem naturally and historically possible! To love neighborly is to love the enemy, to pray for his/her welfare, to do good to him/her, to forgive him/her and reconcile with him/her, to make peace peacefully where there is only enmity, to restore wholeness where relationships have been broken and people have become alienated from each other. Neighborly love is the act of self-giving to another for his/her benefit. It is the drive towards reunion with the separated (Paul Tillich).

Finally, this love has become humanly possible because God has drawn near in His reign precisely as love. We can love one another with this kind of love because God has loved us with this love in the first place. It is *in* this love that God calls us all to live and move and have our being. Therefore, it is *possible for us* to be and live and move in this love. Because it has become a possibility of life and of life-together for us, it is commanded of us. It is commanded as the will of God which has become possible for us to do through God's reign of love in Jesus Christ. Therefore, we can obey this command. To obey it one has simply to do it. It is as we do it in obedience that God makes it possible for us to achieve it. That which we can do because it is possible is done precisely by doing it. *And faith in God, which is also love of God, is nothing more or less than simply doing what God has made possible for us to do.*

All this only shows that neighborly love has the form and is the ethos of discipleship. It is a grateful response to God's gracious call which makes it possible. Because God in Christ has drawn near in love unconditionally and commands us to love all-inclusively, we can love in a way that makes of us all members one of another in the one body of Jesus Christ! Life-together in this love is as such an expression of faith, repentance, and discipleship! It is a possibility entailed necessarily by the proclamation of the gospel in mission evangelism.

CHAPTER 8

THE SIGNIFICANCE OF "THE TWELVE"

A Unique Community

That Jesus succeeded in forming his disciples into a distinctive community is strongly suggested by the fact that the disciples are often referred to as "the Twelve" (Mt. 10:2, 5; 20:17; 26:14, 20, 47; cf. 10:1; 11:1; Mk. 4:10; 6:7; 9:35; 10:32; 11:11; 14:10, 17, 20, 43; Lk. 8:1; 9:1, 12; 18:13; 22:3, 14, 47). This term has in fact assumed the significance of technically designating the disciples as a definite group. For one thing, it indicates that the disciples are *a unitary* group. Their names are mentioned not primarily as distinct and separate individuals but as constituent members of a group formed as one by a unity peculiar to itself.

For another thing, this term describes the disciples as possessing an *identity* as a group that distinguished it from other groups, even from the others with whom Jesus had some association. That identity derives from the relationship of Jesus to them and their relationship to one another in him. Although Jesus appears in the company of many others on some occasions, his being with his disciples is seen as something different. When one of his disciples is mentioned for something he has done to Jesus, it is in connection with his membership with "the Twelve" that he is mentioned (Mk. 14:10, 20, 43; cf. 26:14, 47; Lk. 22:47). Moreover, the number of the disciples is fixed: it is Twelve. Later on we will reflect on the significance of the number, but here we note its definiteness because it indicates that the group of disciples is special and irreplaceable. When one of them (Judas) died by hanging himself because of remorse for betraying Jesus, he was replaced so that the number "Twelve" would remain intact (Acts 1:12-26). The Twelve as a distinct group of disciples was never replaced when it passed away into history.

Finally, the group remained internally intact and gave this impression to those on the outside even when incidents occurred which might normally destroy the sense of unity of an ordinary group. Since it was the relationship between them and Jesus which was the binding core of their life-together, any shortcoming or failure to hold to this center would have threatened to disrupt their unity.

There were many such incidents of failure. Most basic is their *lack of understanding of Jesus*. After having revealed to them the "secrets of the Kingdom" Jesus was dismayed to find out that his disciples still did not understand (Mk. 4:10-13; cf. Mt. 13:10; Lk. 8:9-10). Their lack of understanding was compounded by their lack of faith in Jesus and their cowardly fear (Mk. 4:35-41; cf. Mt. 8:23-27; Lk. 8:22-25). In spite of being eye-witnesses to the power of Jesus in doing "mighty works" and of being given a share in this authority (Mk. 6:7), they "still did not perceive or understand" nor did they remember how "five loaves" were broken to feed five thousand people and still there was a surplus of twelve baskets full of uneaten food. And Jesus tells his disciples plaintively: "Do you not yet understand?" (Mk. 8:14-21; cf. Mt. 16:5-12). The root of their incomprehension, fear, and lack of faith is exposed by Jesus when he rebuked Peter in the hearing and presence of his disciples, saying "You think as men think, not as God thinks" (Mk. 8:33). Would not this mean that the disciples had failed miserably to see things in the light of the kingdom of God in spite of the fact that they were now in the sphere of the Kingdom precisely by being with Jesus?

There were many other more grievous failings which, taken individually or together, could have ended an ordinary relationship. At the moment of his most crucial decision in his career which could mean life or death for him, he took Peter, James, and John with him to pray in the Garden of Gethsemane. He needed the comfort of their company and had told them: "I am deeply grieved, even to death; remain here and keep awake" (Mk. 14:32-34). Did they keep awake with him and pray? They did not; they slept instead! Three times Jesus besought them to watch with him, and each time Jesus found them sound asleep. They failed to sympathize with Jesus in his agony and did not foresee the tragic destiny that awaited him! Then there was Judas who for a sum of money betrayed Jesus with a kiss so that the priestly authorities could arrest him (Mk. 14:10-11, 43-46). To underline the tragic irony of Judas's act of treachery and betrayal, he is always identified in the text as "one of the Twelve" (Mk. 14:10, 20, 43). And Peter, who professed that even if he had to die with Jesus he would never desert him nor deny him, did in fact desert him and deny him three times before the cock crowed twice (Mk. 14:28-31, 66-72). At the scene of the crucifixion itself, there is no mention of the disciples being anywhere near their fallen master. That is because "all the disciples deserted him and fled" (Mt. 26:56).

Instead, it is some women, among whom were Mary Magdalene, Mary the mother of James, and Salome, who were there at the crucifixion "watching from a distance" (Mk. 15:40). It is the same women who were privileged to be told and to hear the good news of the resurrection of Jesus from the dead (Mk. 16:1-8). The disciples had to receive the news about the resurrection through the women. According to Luke the eleven "apostles" regarded the news from the women as "an idle tale, and they did not believe them" (Lk. 24:10-11). The risen Jesus had to stand among them and urged them to "touch me and see me," had to show then "his hands and feet" and ask why they had to doubt, and had to eat in their presence before he could convince them to believe him as risen (Lk. 24:36-43).

Although the disciples responded wholeheartedly to the call of Jesus, the record in Mark shows that there is much to be desired in their understanding of Jesus and of his mission. In spite of his determined effort to share himself and his vision with them through word, deed, and intimate relationships the disciples fell short of what their master expected of them. Misunderstanding, lack of sympathy, treachery and betrayal, denial and desertion—all this would have destroyed the unity of an ordinary group! But what kept it together?

It was not only their relationship to Jesus which was threatened with disruption. Their sense of unity *with one another* was also imperiled. These three Gospels record at least two occasions that indicate that their sense of community among themselves in Jesus was not all that stable. One is a heated argument as to who among them is the greatest (Mk. 9:33-37; cf. Mt. 18:1-5; Lk. 9:46-48). The point of their controversy is who among them is the first in rank, importance, and prestige. Their understanding of "greatness" is what is found and practiced among Gentiles and their view of leadership is in terms of power and authority (cf. Lk. 22:24-27). Jesus tells them that this view of greatness and leadership has no place at all in the sphere of God's rule, and as his disciples they are not to regard themselves in this light at all! (Lk. 22:26). Instead, they are to understand and practice discipleship as servanthood and leadership in terms of service. Jesus points to himself as being among them "as one who serves" (Lk. 22:27; cf. Mk. 10:45). This controversy about greatness is clearly not only a dispute among the disciples but also between them and Jesus!

A somewhat similar incident is recorded in Mark 10:35-45. It has to do with the request of the Zebedee brothers, James and John, to sit in the centers of power in Jesus' kingdom (10:37). The text is quite frank in recording the response of the other disciples to the request: "When the ten heard this, they began to be *angry with James and John*" (10:41; the REB rendering is more direct and stronger: "When the others then heard this, *they were indignant with James and John*" [emphasis added]). Personal ambition and rivalry, the exercise of leadership in terms of rank, power, and prestige, and lordship over others, stood in the way of unity among themselves and between them and their Master. Are there some things more likely to destroy a sense of community than these? Jesus repeats in no uncertain terms that the community of discipleship is one of servanthood. "Whoever wishes to be great among you must be your servant, and whoever wishes to be first among you must be slave of all. For the Son of Man came not to be served but to serve, and to give his life a ransom for many" (10:44-45).

If the sense of community among the disciples as a group depended upon their attitude to Jesus and to one another, it would not have taken long for their life-together to founder and be wrecked upon the treacherous shoals of misunderstanding, betrayal, self-seeking ambition, and will to power. Fortunately it rested on a foundation stronger than human weakness and larger than human ambition. It was the unswerving faith of Jesus in his disciples, his unfaltering patience and understanding of their failures, his persistent effort at teaching them, his firm conviction that they could be changed and won over to the ways of the Kingdom, his unwillingness to give up on them that held them together from beginning to end. Having seen them in their worst, Jesus nevertheless looked beyond their frailties towards what they could yet become. His first word to them following his resurrection was *to send for them to a reunion with him in Galilee* where his drama with them all began in the first place (Mk. 28:16-17; cf. 24:36-43). How does one best interpret this act of Jesus? Is this not an initiative of love and goodwill on the part of Jesus which overflows in forgiveness and reconciliation and so effecting a happy reunion between him and his disciples, and thus restoring the bond of unity between him and them and among themselves? Is this not a dramatic example of the "sinned against" taking the initiative in forgiving and reconciling the sinner so that alienation may be healed and community restored?

But Jesus went beyond forgiveness and reunion. He entrusted his mission and its future to his disciples and frankly expressed his faith that they would not fail him because they would be empowered and accompanied by the Spirit clear through to the end (Mt. 28:18-20; Lk. 24:44-49). It is the commitment of Jesus to them and the mission to which he sent them, instead of their mere loyalty to him, that held them together as a community of discipleship! They were the Twelve because Jesus held them steadfastly as such!

Prefiguring the New People of God

The term "the Twelve" did not only signify the unity of the disciples as a unique and irreplaceable group; *it also prefigured the new people of God whose nucleus is precisely the twelve disciples as a specific unitary group.* In this formulation of a New Testament idea, several layers of symbolic meaning are in fact presupposed. In order to appreciate the symbolic richness of the number "twelve," it is helpful to probe briefly the association of this number with the people of God. First of all, we may note the fact that the number "twelve" referred to the *twelve tribes* of Israel which originated from the *twelve sons* of Jacob (Gen. 35:22-26; Ex.1:1-5). The twelve tribes of Israel, *signified the whole covenant people of God. It symbolized both the ancestral origin and covenant formation of Israel as a historical people.*

Moreover, when the Northern Kingdom fell in 722 B.C., the ten tribes which constituted it were "lost" through exile, resettlement, and intermarriage in other countries. There arose in this context the hope that Israel as a whole will someday be restored historically as a people of God. The term "the twelve tribes" continued to be in use even though only two of the original twelve still existed as constituting the Kingdom of Judah. The intention was to maintain in consciousness and hope the vision of Israel as a whole people of God even though historically this was no longer so!

When the Kingdom of Judah itself fell in 587 B.C. and the majority of the leading citizens were deported into exile, the hope of returning to the homeland and being restored as a whole people of God intensified and the use of the term "the twelve tribes of Israel" to symbolize this hope technically became prevalent. The hope of restoration included such ideas as the reassembly of scattered Israel (Ezek. 34, 37) under the leadership of David (Ezek. 47:13–48:29); the rebuilding of the Temple (Isa. 44:28; Ezek. 40–43); the Gentiles acknowledging Yahweh to be the Lord, accepting His word, learning His Law, and joining His people in worshiping Him in His Temple in the royal city (Isa. 54:3; 56:1-8; 60:3-16; 61:6; 66:18-24; Micah 4); liberation from foreign oppression and the restoration of Israel's sovereignty.

It is to be noted that the hope of restoration in the midst of exile, dispersion, and foreign oppression included some basic ideas which enriched the symbolic meanings of the term "the twelve tribes of Israel." There are three of these ideas worth mentioning. There is, first of all, the idea of *redemption*. The elements of liberation from foreign oppression, return to the homeland, reassembly around a rebuilt Temple are gathered up together as an act of redemption or salvation which restores the status of Israel historically as a people of God.

Second, there is the sense of *reconstitution,* that is, the provision of a new basis and a consequent recomposition and reordering of relationship as may be seen, for example, in Jeremiah 31:31-34 or Ezekiel 36:24-36. This is a realistic way of coming to terms with the historical realities at the time and of keeping faith with the hope of Israel. Ten of the original tribes had been lost and the cream of the members of the remaining two had been exiled; the monarchy had been dissolved; and the Temple was destroyed. There was no way for Israel to be restored to its original historical basis and composition. At the same time, faith in the promise that Israel shall be God's people endured and the hope that God will fulfill His promise was undiminished. And so the reconstitution of Israel was for the purpose of its restoration as the people of God.

Finally, there was the firm belief that this restoration was to take place at some *future time* to be determined by God Himself. Instead of enshrining only a *memory*, the term "the twelve tribes" now points to a *promise* and its fulfillment. In addition to recalling the ancestral past by pointing to the origin of Israel, the term now also has a future reference, since only in the future may the restoration of Israel take place. In addition to the remembrance of the covenant formation of Israel into a people, the term now also holds out the promise of a *new* covenant in which the law of God is known and obeyed *from within the heart* and God is known by all from *the experience of His grace in forgiveness and reconciliation* (Jer. 31:31-34; Ezek. 36:24-36). Thus, insofar as it carried the sense of restoration, *the term the "twelve tribes" signified the eschatological gathering and salvation of the whole people of God.*[1] The continued use of the number "twelve" formed the consciousness of Israel as the people of God by its power to evoke the memory of its origins and to nurture its hopes for a more blessed future in the promises of God.

This complex of ideas that formed Jewish restoration eschatology forms the immediate background of Jesus' choice of "the Twelve" (cf. Acts. 1:6). The fact that he called together *twelve* disciples is evidence strong enough to suggest that he shared in some measure the Jewish restoration hopes which were prevalent in his time. E. P. Sanders writes: "The expectation of the reassembly of Israel was so widespread, and the memory of the twelve tribes remained so acute, that *'twelve' would not necessarily mean 'restoration.'* "[2]

But Jesus radicalized this hope in ways far beyond the expectations of classical prophecy or normative Judaism. For one thing, his vision of a new people of God called for its *reconstitution* upon something more basic than, and therefore presuppositional to, Law and Covenant. *That new basis is the kingdom of God as now at hand.* The Twelve are formed by the call of Jesus to discipleship in view of the coming kingdom of God which is now at hand, not by tribal progeny and covenant formation. Moreover, he *revised* the timetable of Jewish eschatology by demonstrating through who he was and what he said and did that God's coming reign is already at hand, and people may enter now into its sphere by faith and repentance and discipleship, and not by obedience of the Law. The response of *the Twelve* to the call of Jesus is precisely the way people may enter the sphere of the Kingdom. Furthermore, the *reassembly* of the new people of God will not be around the old Temple and its worship which will be destroyed (Mk. 3:1-2), but *around him as the Son of God who came as the Son of Man to serve, and not be served, and to give his life as a ransom for many* (Mk. 1:1, 11; 10:45) *and who subsequently will be worshiped as the crucified and risen Lord* (Mt. 28:17); cf. Jn. 4:22-24). Being with Jesus is what forms the Twelve into a community. Additionally, *the inclusion of the Gentiles* in the new people of God is already prefigured in the love-command practiced by Jesus as the fulfillment of the Law. It is the practice of a love which knows no bounds and requires no preconditions and so creates the community of discipleship into a fellowship far more inclusive than any that Israel ever dreamed of. Finally, Jesus rejected the motivations of violence embedded in the political and military dimensions of Jewish restoration eschatology not only by what he said (Mt. 5:3-11; 26:51-54) but by how he lived and died. The Twelve is to be a peacemaking community because it has itself received the peace of the Lord (cf. Jn. 14:27).

A Community with a New Future

All this leaves no doubt that the formation of "the Twelve" is based ultimately on eschatological presuppositions quite different from those of Jewish restoration hopes. Not only were "the Twelve" constituted on a more radical basis in the at-handness in Jesus of the coming reign of God, but—precisely because of this—they were put on tract towards a new vision of the future which far transcended Jewish expectations. This logically leads to a consideration of the eschatology of Jesus. Treatment of this important theme, however, will be reserved for later discussion. It is enough at this point to note briefly the outline of the new future that is promised to "the Twelve" by Jesus.

Matthew reports a conversation of Jesus with his disciples which seems to promise to "the Twelve" a new future quite different from, although not unrelated to, the Jewish hopes for "the twelve tribes of Israel." The conversation is as follows: "Peter said in reply, 'Look, we have left everything and followed you. What then will we have?' Jesus said to them, 'Truly I tell you, at the renewal of all things, when the Son of man is seated on the throne of his glory, you who have followed me will also sit on twelve thrones, judging the twelve tribes of Israel. And everyone who has left houses or brothers or sisters or father or mother or children or fields for my name's sake, will receive a hundredfold, and will inherit eternal life. But many who are first will be last, and the last will be first' " (Mt. 19:27-30).

Several important points directly relevant to our purpose here are worth noting briefly. Let us first note the *structure* of the text. The context shows that this text is a part of a larger conversation between Jesus and his disciples (Mt. 19:23-30). The subject of this conversation is discipleship. Peter speaks of himself and his colleagues and of their discipleship when he said: "We have left everything and followed you." Jesus acknowledges this fact when he said in his reply, "you who have followed me." He widens the scope, however, when he includes in his reply "everyone who has left houses or brothers . . . for my name's sake"; but the substance is the same, namely, discipleship.

The specific point about discipleship which Peter raised directly with Jesus, however, is its reward: "what then will we have?" The sense of the question about reward is indicated in verse 25 which asks: "Then who can be saved?" The fact that Peter's question is about the "reward" of discipleship and is asked in the context of who can be saved clearly implies the future. Peter in short is definitely asking about *their future as a community of disciples* and so of the reward of discipleship itself.

We must also note the fact that Peter asked this question *not before* he became a disciple *but after* he had committed himself fully to Jesus and had been following him faithfully for some time. If the question of reward were asked before he became a disciple, it would be difficult to resist the suspicion that selfish motives of personal benefit were percolating in Peter's mind as he weighed carefully the pros and cons of following Jesus. But after deciding to follow Jesus and having lived as a disciple for some time, it is only fair to ask the future of such a mode of life. It does not appear in the records that Jesus criticized Peter for asking the question about the future of discipleship. We are entitled to regard the question as ethically proper.

The reply of Jesus speaks directly to the question of Peter. It reveals aspects of his view of the future as they relate to the future of discipleship. This is indicated in what follows.

Let us first consider the elements of the *content* of the answer of Jesus. For one thing, the *reward that saves* which is the future of discipleship is a possibility that clearly lies solely in the power of God and not in human beings (Mt. 19:26). It is definitely not a human possibility that can be had by human power or earned by human merit. It is for God alone to give in His power and mercy.

Moreover, the future of discipleship does not lie within the present temporal order of things. Rather, it belongs to "the world that is to be" (Mt. 19:28 REB). It is part of an order of reality which is different from the order of the world. Accordingly, its way of coming to be is different from the way the things of the world come to be. Therefore, *it cannot be* by the way things in the world come to be, which is through natural and human possibility. This is another reason why it is not a human possibility within the order of history.

Furthermore, in the "world that is to be" all things will be renewed. The Greek word *palingenesia* in Matthew 19:28, which is translated "renewal," means *renewal to a higher existence in righteousness* following the final crisis in the last judgment. And so it refers to life in a new order of existence and righteousness. In the perspective of the New Testament, this can only mean the fulfillment of the kingdom of God in the new creation at the end time, the beginning of which is inaugurated by the resurrection of Jesus Christ from the dead (cf. Lk. 22:30). This is further underlined by the reference to the reign of the Son of Man in glory which coincides with the renewal of all things: "when the Son of Man is seated on the throne of his glory" (Mt. 19:28). The renewal is of "all things." It is cosmic in scope. The reign of the Son of Man is over all of creation already transformed. This implies that the future of discipleship is an aspect of the reign of the Son of God. It is a dimension of the new creation in the fullness of God's kingdom. In rewarding discipleship the Son of Man is finally and fully exercising his reign in glory (cf. 25:21, 23).

In what does this reward consist of? The answer to this question is the climax of the answer of Jesus to the question of Peter. The reward consists of the fact that "the Twelve" will "sit on twelve thrones" (Mt. 19:28). That means "the Twelve" will share in the glory and in the reign of the Son (cf. Eph. 2:6). This sharing is done in terms of "judging the twelve tribes of Israel." The word "judging" here has the sense of "rule." To reign is to rule, and to rule is to judge. But we must not interpret this in the Gentile sense of exercising hierarchical authority over others (Lk. 22:25). Rather, it must be understood in terms of the rule of the Son of Man, which is self-giving service for the good and salvation of another (Mk. 10:45; Lk. 22:26-27). *The Twelve are to reign with Christ and share in his glory by serving no higher cause than the ultimate salvation of Israel as the whole people of God!* (cf. Rom. 11:25-32). But we must not miss the fact that the reply of Jesus about the reward of discipleship presupposes that the disciples will remain faithful and will persevere until the end. And he promises to accompany them until the end.

It is clear from what has been said that "the Twelve" as a symbol enshrines the eschatological destiny of the new community envisioned by Jesus. This destiny is implicit in the call to discipleship. The same promise is implicit in the call to discipleship made in mission evangelism.

In "offering Christ" there is implicitly offered the promise of a new future and a new destiny. What precisely is this new future and destiny, if something at all can be said about it? We can only reserve an answer to this question to a further work.

Notes

1. E. P. Sanders, *Jesus and Judaism* (London: SCM Press, 1985), pp. 77-98.
2. Ibid., p. 98.

CHAPTER 9

BEING SENT BY JESUS

Mission as Integral to Discipleship

Thus far, we have been exploring the elements that together make of people a new community in Jesus Christ. This is a dimension of the social experience of salvation, and it should become an essential element in any strategy of social transformation, as it was in the ministry of Jesus. We are searching for the elements that make for community by looking into the ways by which those whom Jesus called became a community in him. We have proceeded along this line on the assumption that the community of the disciples is the nucleus of the new people of God that later emerged following the resurrection of Jesus and the mission of his disciples. If this assumption is correct, and we have no reason to doubt it, it would follow that the elements that make for community among the disciples are more or less the same also for the church as the new people of God. Those factors that forged the disciples into a community are also constitutive for the community of the church. In other words, the church is quite simply but profoundly a community of discipleship. What constitutes life-together in Christ is discipleship. So far we have described four essential features in the community of discipleship. These are the call of Jesus, following after him, being with him, and being with others in him.

Following the texts on discipleship that we are studying, we now add a fifth element, namely, *being sent out on a mission by Jesus* (Mk. 3:13-14; 6:7; Mt. 10:5; Lk. 9:1-2; cf. 10:1-3).

From the way this element appears in the text, it necessarily goes together with the other elements. To follow after Jesus in response to his call, to be with him, and with others in him, inescapably means being sent out by him. One cannot have the first four elements without entailing the fifth one, and this latter one necessarily presupposes the former ones. They are all essential dimensions of the one indivisible relationship of discipleship to Jesus. However, there is a sense in which being sent out by Jesus on a mission is the *purpose* of the first four elements. This sending out of the disciples by Jesus appears in Mark as the last of a series and it is to happen yet in the future. It is difficult to avoid reading the text to mean: Jesus called disciples to be with him *in order that* he may send them out on a mission.

This, of course, does not in any way diminish the intrinsic value and meaning of each of the other elements of discipleship. But part of their intrinsic value is precisely to serve as *presupposition to mission*. Without being called by Jesus and being with him and with others in him, one cannot be sent out on a mission by Jesus. These are absolutely the conditions for knowing him and what he is about and learning obedience to him. On the other hand, is it not the case that an aspect of the intrinsic value of mission is precisely that it is the purpose for which the other four are in some sense a means, in the basic double sense of being *required for and useful* to mission? If one grants this, then one can hardly shirk the conclusion that being sent out by Jesus is not only an essential component of discipleship as all the others, but it is also a dimension of all the others. To know Jesus is to know him as one who has been sent out on a mission (Mk. 1:38-39; Lk. 4:43-44). To be with him and with others in him is to be with him in his mission. And the purpose of knowing him in this way, as one who is in mission, *is to be sent out by him to participate in his mission!* Mission is unavoidably an essential component of discipleship. The community of discipleship is a community of mission and so it is a community in mission!

In reflecting upon being sent out by Jesus on a mission as an essential aspect of discipleship, we shall consider two episodes together, the so-called "mission of the Twelve" (Mk. 6:6*b*-13; Mt. 10:5-15; Lk. 9:1-6) and the "mission of the Seventy" (Lk. 10:1-12, 17-20). Both episodes took place in the course of the earthly ministry of Jesus before his death and resurrection. They are to be distinguished from the sending of the Apostles, which took place following the resurrection of Jesus (Mt. 28:16-20; Jn. 20:19-23; Acts 6:7-8). On the one hand, the sending of the Twelve and the Seventy was by the earthly Jesus. It was temporary and limited in scope. The sending of the Apostles, on the other hand, was by the Risen Christ. Their commission was to remain in effect throughout their lifetime and its scope was universal and cosmic. There are, of course, profound similarities between the two sendings. Both are send-ings and commissionings done by the same Jesus Christ, although we must here bear in mind the distinction between the earthly Jesus and the Risen Christ. Both are continuations of the work or ministry of Jesus Christ, although we must remind ourselves that there is a historical dif-ference in form. Our primary purpose in considering the sending of the Twelve and of the Seventy is simply to show that the sending out on a mission is indeed from the beginning rooted in the ministry of the earthly Jesus and is an essential component of the relationship of disci-pleship as the appropriate response to the drawing near of the coming rule of God.

Jesus, the Lord of the Mission

We shall now point out the significance of these episodes for our pur-poses here. First, we note the fact that the *sending of the Twelve is by a decision or action of Jesus*. This act is separate from, although it presup-poses and follows upon, his choice of the Twelve and his call upon them to follow him. Sending the Twelve out on a mission *could* have been in the mind of Jesus when he called them, but he had to send them actually if they were to go out in mission. An actual decision of sending had to be made. There were many disciples of Jesus but only the Twelve were sent out on a mission. Does not this mean that while all missionaries are disciples, not all disciples become missionaries? To be sent out on a mission requires a commissioning by Jesus.

However, it is equally important to note that the decision to send was directed not to the disciples as individuals but to them as a particular community, as the Twelve (Mk. 3:14; 6:7). They were a special group precisely because they had been called by Jesus, they had followed him, they had been with him and with one another in him. It was as *this* community that they were sent out on a mission. Mission was an essen-tial dimension of the fact that they were a community at all. In short, they were a community of mission at the same time as they were a com-munity of discipleship. And if our argument is correct that the elements of discipleship are what constitute the church into a special community, is it far from the truth to conclude that the church is a community of mission precisely because it is a community of discipleship?

Next, we may not ignore the fact that *Jesus alone is the sovereign sub-*

ject of the action to send. He alone makes it. He alone authorizes it. And he alone commands it. It is he who establishes the mission and makes missionaries! In Mark 3:13-14 the action to send appears as a part of a series of actions in which Jesus alone is the subject. It is he who calls whom he wants, who appoints and names, and sends and authorizes. He decides whom to send.

The disciples could not have gone out on a mission on their own or by volunteering themselves and their service. No one becomes a missionary completely by self-choice. It was Jesus who originally decided that the disciples go out on a mission. And since a decision for them had been made, their only choice as the appropriate response to a command was to obey. Mark 6:12 records the response of the disciples to Jesus' command to send them out quite simply with these words: "So they went out. . . ." It was a response that was unhesitating, straightforward, and without reservation. The disciples *chose* to obey, and their obedience was *to carry out* their choice. Free obedience and obedient freedom are of the essence of discipleship; they are what drives the missionary and moves the mission.

We must note the fact that not only did Jesus alone decide to send and whom to send, but *he alone also determined what the mission was all about.* It was Jesus who constituted the nature of the mission. The texts specify that it was a mission to proclaim the message that the coming rule of God has drawn near, to call people to faith and repentance, to liberate people by casting out the demons or evil spirits that possessed them, and to heal people of their diseases and disabilities. One cannot escape noticing that these were the same messianic activities that characterized the ministry of Jesus. It is obvious, therefore, that the mission that Jesus was giving his disciples was a *continuation of his own messianic ministry.* He was asking them to do the same things he was doing. He was enjoining them to participate in his own mission.

Clearly this was no ordinary sending because it was not a simple human possibility. The mission of Jesus was to usher in the coming rule of God and this was entirely dependent upon God's sovereign initiative. The activities of Jesus' ministry were the messianic signs that the reign of God has broken through into the sphere of human life and history, thus transforming it into the promise of His own realm! In giving his disciples the opportunity to participate in this mission, Jesus was making them part of the sign-process by which the reign of God draws near to bring about faith and repentance, liberation and healing, and life in discipleship! And so their *own* activity in this participation assumed a messianic significance, which remained undiminished although the terms of their mission was temporary and limited, as will be shown below.

But now since the mission was no simple human possibility, is it fair to ask how was it possible for the disciples to do it? With what power and authority could they accomplish what they were sent out to do? Their unhesitating and obedient response though valuable and necessary was not enough. Enthusiasm and commitment are never a substitute for power, ability, and competence. This brings us to a *fourth* aspect of the sending out of the Twelve and of the Seventy, namely, *their empowerment*. Jesus did not only surprisingly offer the disciples the grand opportunity to participate in *his* mission, but he also *shared* with them unreservedly *the same power* by which he himself was carrying out his mission. *That* power astonished many who saw it operate. It gave Jesus' teaching astounding authority (Mk. 1:22). It enabled him to cast out unclean spirits and heal the sick (Mk. 1:25-27, 30-31). It was what attracted the outcasts, the sick, the demon-possessed, the disabled from far and wide to come to Jesus for healing (Mk. 12:12; Mt. 21:45-46). There was no doubt that this authority was unlike any that the people and their leaders had known before. This authority and its power were absolutely unique to Jesus! And they were his not by right of birth, or natural endowment, or education and training, but because they were conferred on him by the Spirit of God for the purpose of carrying out a specific mission, namely, the breakthrough of the kingdom of God into human life and its affairs (Mk. 1:9-11; Mt. 3:13-17; Lk. 3:21-22; Jn. 1:29-34).

But now Jesus was voluntarily sharing this authority with his disciples (Mt. 10:7-8). The explanation for this astonishing act seems to be that because Jesus sent them out to participate in his mission, he had to empower them with the only authority that could accomplish that mission! Did the disciples accomplish their mission through this authority and its power? Was it effective through them as it was through Jesus? The editorial comment in Mark 6:12-13 reads matter-of-factly: "So they went out and proclaimed that all should repent. They cast out many demons, and anointed with oil many who were sick and cured them" (cf. Lk. 9:6). The report of the Seventy to Jesus concerning their mission was more direct: "The Seventy returned with joy, saying, 'Lord, in your name even the demons submit to us!' " (Lk. 10:17).

The response of Jesus to this report expressed clearly his own assessment of the performance of the disciples and what it meant: "He said to them, 'I watched Satan fall from heaven like a flash of lightning. See, I have given you authority to tread on snakes and scorpions, and over all the power of the enemy; and nothing will hurt you'" (Lk. 10:18-19). This meant that what the Seventy did was clearly a continuation of the mission of Jesus. What Jesus saw as the result of what the Seventy achieved was precisely his mission being fulfilled, namely, the assault upon the power of evil over human life and its affairs. That assault did not consist merely in undoing the effects of evil upon its victims by healing them (such as disease, disability, demon-possession, etc.), but in overcoming evil precisely as power, and so causing it to fall swiftly and decisively—like lightning from heaven (cf. Mk. 3:22-27). And this was achieved no doubt by the power he gave them; it was an authority *"over all the power of the enemy."*

We must now add a *fifth* observation about the sending out of the disciples on a mission. *Jesus also determined the scope or extent of the mission.* It is the prerogative of the one who sends to decide where and to whom he sends someone. The instruction of Jesus to the disciples as recorded by Matthew indicated clearly both (a) where and to whom not to go, and (b) where and to whom to go: "Go nowhere among the Gentiles, and enter no town of the Samaritans, but go rather to the lost sheep of the house of Israel" (Mt. 10:5-6). This saying determines precisely the limits of the mission. Moreover, Matthew preserves a saying of Jesus which indicated that Jesus understood his mission as being limited to the lost sheep of the house of Israel: "I was sent only to the lost sheep of the house of Israel" (15:24; cf. Lk. 10:16). This meant that the scope of the mission given by Jesus to the disciples was in line with his understanding of the limits of his own mission.

To be sure, only in Matthew is this precise limitation of Jesus' mission to be found. Does it not contradict Jesus' own universalistic intent? Did not the kingdom of God include Gentiles and Samaritans? Should not their inclusion unmistakably signal that the coming reign of God has indeed drawn near? Why then limit the mission to "the lost sheep of the house of Israel"? Because of its embarrassing implication, the only reason it seems for Matthew to preserve these sayings of Jesus about limiting the mission to Israel was itself the authority of Jesus. Their embarrassing implication counts for the fact that they are genuine sayings of Jesus.

This limitation of the mission to the Jews, however, did not prevent Jesus from responding to non-Jews who actually turned to him for help (Mt. 8:5-10, 13; cf. Lk. 7:1-9; Mk. 7:24-30). In any case, our interest here is not primarily in the scope of the mission as such but in the fact that it was Jesus who determined it. Later on, the scope of the mission would include the Samaritans and the Gentiles, as indeed all nations in the *oikumene* (Mt. 28:16-20; Acts 1:8). But that was because the Risen Christ decided it to be so. This would only further confirm our argument that it is the one who sends that decides the limits of the mission, whether merely local and temporary, or universal, cosmic, and permanent!

In this particular episode as reported by Matthew, the scope of the mission given to the disciples was limited to "the lost sheep of the house of Israel." Geographically speaking, this meant that the mission was confined to Galilee. Samaria lay to the south, while Gentile territory lay to east, west, and north. Ethnically speaking, the mission was limited to Israel as a nation or people. But did this mean Israel as a whole in its "lost" condition, or only some parts of it. Joachim Jeremias suggests it is the whole of Israel as "lost" which is meant.[1] This reading is supported by the parallel contrast between Israel as a nation and the Gentiles and the Samaritans as "nations," and by the Old Testament allusion to Israel as a flock of sheep which had been led astray by its shepherds (Jer. 50:6), or "scattered" because the sheep had no shepherd (Ezek. 34:5-6; cf. Isa. 53:6).

At the same time the texts indicate that Jesus named specific types of people in Israel to whom the disciples were to go: the sick, the lepers, the demon-possessed, the sinners and outcasts (Mt. 10:7-8; cf. Mk. 6:12-13). Moreover, the placing of the sending of the Twelve in Matthew's Gospel follows directly upon an editorial comment describing Jesus' intense missionary activity (Mt. 9:35-37). In the course of this activity, Jesus was portrayed as follows: "When he saw the crowds, he had compassion for them, because they were harassed and helpless, like sheep without a shepherd" (Mt. 9:36). It would seem appropriate to conclude from the foregoing that Jesus thought of the whole of Israel and its religious leaders, including certainly the poor and the helpless and harassed within it, as "lost." The mission given to the disciples—which was part of Jesus' mission—was to bring to Israel the saving power and benefits of the Kingdom at hand and gather all of Israel into its sphere and under its reign, which is its true shepherd (cf. Mt. 23:37-39; Lk. 13:34-35).

But is not the picture of Israel and the crowds within it as lost, harassed, helpless, and without a shepherd a correct reflection of the lost state of the peoples of the earth as well? If this could happen to Israel as God's people, could it not also happen to other peoples who have no such elect status and destiny? Is not the same condition of being "lost" universally the immediate and compelling context of mission? If this is so, then is it not correct to conclude that in bringing the saving power and benefits of the kingdom of God to Israel, Jesus was in effect bringing them to all of humankind?

Besides being confined to a specific place and nation, the mission of the disciples (the Twelve and the Seventy) seems to have been limited also to a *time*. Although there was no definite word of Jesus covering the period of the mission, it ended when the missionary journey was finished and upon the return of the Seventy (Mk. 6:30; Lk. 9:10; 10:17). The next major series of activity of Jesus involving him and his disciples after he sent them out was teaching them that the Son of Man was to suffer, be rejected, killed, and after three days be raised from the dead (Mk. 8:31-33; 9:30-32; 10:32-34, and parallels). There is no evidence of further missionary activity by the disciples during this period. The temporary character of this mission is further confirmed by the fact that the Risen Christ replaced it with a mission that was to extend over the whole *oikumene* and was to last throughout the lifetime of the Apostles and beyond. This mission—although temporary—afforded them significant experience of what it meant to be an apostle of the Risen Christ later on. It was a sort of dry run for the more permanent vocation they were to receive later from the Risen Lord. This meant that the *sending of the disciples has permanent elements which are essential to mission as a dimension of discipleship*. Some of these elements are precisely those we have already considered.

To these we add a *sixth* element: *how Jesus perceived the mission field and how the disciples were to behave in their mission*.

Luke introduces the sending of the Seventy with two remarks of Jesus. The first one describes how Jesus perceives generally the situation to which they were being sent out: "The harvest is plentiful, but the laborers are few; therefore ask the Lord of the harvest to send out laborers into his harvest" (10:2). Matthew also has this saying. But he locates it not with the sending of the Seventy but in another connection—which also describes the mission-situation. Mark does not have this saying. The other remark of Jesus indicates the sense in which Jesus was sending out the Seventy: "Go on your way. See, I am sending you out like lambs into the midst of wolves" (Lk. 10:3). Matthew also records this saying, but he adds a proverbial advice: "so be wise as serpents and innocent as doves," which Luke does not mention (Mt. 10:16). The addition is helpful because it further elucidates the meaning of the main clause. Mark does not have this saying either. It is safe to say that the saying about the mission as "harvest" and the sending of the disciples as "lambs" come from Q, which both Luke and Matthew used as a common source in the composition of their Gospels.[2] This material puts us in touch as closely as possible with how Jesus saw the mission and how he expected his messengers to behave in it! Let us consider these two sayings.

Both sayings use figurative language. The first one likens the mission to a field planted with crops ready to be harvested. This assumes that somebody had already prepared the field and planted it with the crops which had also been cultivated and watered. Now the crops have ripened and are ready for harvest. The one who did all this was certainly not the laborers who were being sent out to do the harvesting. The one referred to as "Lord of the harvest" is also the Lord of the field and of the planting. It was he who prepared the field and planted it and cultivated and watered the crops until they ripened and were ready for harvesting. A genuine mission field has this characteristic: *it has already been made ready for harvesting by the prior or "prevenient" work of him whose mission it is.*

Moreover, *"the harvest is plentiful."* That is how every harvest should be, but is not always the case. There are times when the crops fail or are destroyed and so there is nothing to harvest. The reason the harvest is "plentiful" is that the "Lord of the harvest" has worked to make it so (cf. Mk. 4:26-32). The laborers who were sent to do the harvesting had nothing to do with making the harvest plentiful. All this was the work of the "Lord of the harvest." This is another characteristic of a genuine mission field: *it is always plentiful, not by the efforts of the laborers but by the blessing of the Lord of the harvest.*

Furthermore, those who are sent out to do the harvesting are called "laborers." This is in direct contrast to the "Lord" of the harvest. It is meant to emphasize the fact that "the laborers" do not own the harvest. It is the "Lord of the harvest" who owns it, and therefore he has full authority over it. He has the right of disposal over it. The only thing the *human* laborers could and must do is that of harvesting. But they could not even do this one thing on their own. They had to be sent and authorized to do it. And only the Lord of the harvest can send them. But by being authorized to do the harvesting, they are thereby given a share in, and thus a sense of ownership of, the harvest. Doing the task of harvesting is the human way of participating in the mission. But, of course, this is the most joyous portion of the work of mission. Is it any wonder then that the Seventy "returned with joy" to report on their mission to Jesus? (Lk. 10:17). *This is a further feature of a genuine mission field: it is joyous work because it is precisely only harvesting!*

Finally, while the harvest is plentiful, the "laborers are few." The human work of harvesting is never adequate in coping with what God has made ready for harvesting. And only He can supply additional "laborers" to the harvest. Those who labor, therefore, need not worry as to whether their effort is equal to the job at hand. It is the responsibility of the Lord of the harvest to see to it that the supply of labor is adequate and competent. The only concern of the laborers is to do their own and only part, which is to harvest the crop. The moment the laborers assume ownership over the harvest and begin to worry as to whether they could do the job adequately on their own, the more will their efforts become futile and fruitless. This is to take on a prerogative which is not theirs. *A genuine mission field is God's ultimate responsibility; and the laborers who are in that field doing the harvesting by God's own making are also a part of God's responsibility!*

The second saying of Jesus that is being considered here throws further light on his perception of the mission situation and how he expects his messengers to behave in it: "Go on your way. See, I am sending you out like lambs into the midst of wolves." Here the metaphor used to portray the mission situation is *"into the midst of wolves."* It stands in direct contrast to the picture of the mission as "harvest." In the metaphor of "harvest" the bright side of the mission is spotlighted. The grain is now ripe and it is plentiful. All that needs to be done is to harvest it and gather it into barns. Laborers have already been sent, and all they need to do is put the sickle to the crops. The mission field eagerly awaits human labor so that it may yield its abundant fruit. But now Jesus balances this bright side by pointing to the dark side of the mission situation. He uses the metaphor of "wolves" to do this. The disciples are "sent like lambs into the midst of wolves." This is an apt figure of speech. The favorite food of wolves is sheep flesh. Wolves hunt for flocks of sheep.

When they attack a flock of sheep, the sheep scatter. In the confusion, the lambs are left isolated, helpless, and utterly vulnerable. When wolves eat their prey, they devour them rapaciously. Active preying on the vulnerable and rapacious devouring of the helpless are the characteristics of wolves. For this reason, wolves are used in the Old Testament to portray the enemies of God's people. In Jeremiah 5:6, the enemy of Judah is represented by "a wolf from the desert." In Ezekiel 22:27 the "officials" of Israel are like "wolves tearing the prey, shedding blood, destroying lives to get dishonest gain" (cf. Zeph. 3:3).

In the New Testament, Jesus refers to "false prophets who come to you in sheep's clothing but inwardly are ravenous wolves" (Mt. 7:15). In John 10:12, the wolf comes to prey upon the sheep, scattering and snatching them. In Acts 20:29, "savage wolves" (referring to false teachers) will come into the church and will not spare it of false teaching and will cause dissension. And now Jesus warns the disciples that there are a pack of wolves lying in wait to prey upon them even as they go on their way in their mission! At work in the mission is not only the Lord of the harvest, ripening the grain and readying it for harvest and sending laborers to gather it into barns, but also the enemies of the Lord of the harvest who are ready to devour the laborers, prevent the harvesting from being done, and thus destroy all the work of the Lord of the harvest just exactly at the point when the fruits of his labor are about to be reaped. In fact, *this is another feature of a genuine mission field: it is one in which the enemies of the gospel are also actively at work.*

The ironic thing about a genuine mission situation is that knowing that it is full of predatory and rapacious wolves, Jesus still deliberately sends his disciples *"like lambs* into the midst of wolves." Is this not bull-headed foolhardiness? Does he not know that sheep are the favorite prey of wolves and lambs are vulnerable to the rapacity of wolves? In sending them to an inescapably wolfish situation, is he not thereby condemning them to sure destruction? Jesus must have known all this, since raising sheep is an important occupation of his people. But precisely because of this, Jesus must have known something about sheep and lambs which he thinks makes them specially fit for life in the midst of wolves! Jesus expects his messengers to behave exactly "like lambs" in a wolfish situation. What could this mean?

Sheep naturally gather themselves *into a flock*. A sheep not with the flock is a *stray*. Because it is lost, it must be found and brought back to the flock if it is to survive (cf. Mt. 18:10–14). A flock of sheep is thus a symbol of community. The disciples in mission are a community and must remain a community if they are to survive. Moreover, lambs are objects of affection as the ewe lamb in Nathan's parable (2 Sam. 12:1-6). Isaiah 53:7 portrays lambs as harmless, nonaggressive, and patient even in the midst of affliction: "Like a lamb that is led to the slaughter, and like a sheep that before its shearers is silent . . ." (cf. Jer. 11:19; Jn. 10:2-4). These qualities render sheep and lambs defenseless before wild and predatory animals like wolves and lions (cf. Mic. 5:8). Their helpless condition makes them in constant need of care and supervision (Num. 27:17; Ezek. 34:5; Mt. 9:36; 26:31). And so they need a shepherd to love them, lead them, feed them, care for them, and protect them (see Ezek. 34). *The need to be a flock led by a shepherd for the sake of survival is a characteristic of sheep which disciples in mission must emulate.*

Furthermore, the shepherd who leads the flock must be a *good shepherd*. He must do what a good shepherd should do as set forth for example in Psalm 23 and in Ezekiel 34. In John 10, the Good Shepherd knows, leads, feeds, cares, and protects his flock. Up to this point, he fulfills all that the Old Testament says about the Good Shepherd. But then in the Gospel of John, Jesus says something about the Good Shepherd for which there is no precedent in the Old Testament, not even in terms of the Suffering Servant. It is this: the Good Shepherd lays down his life for the sheep (Jn. 10:11-18). Jesus does not hesitate to send his disciples "like lambs into the midst of wolves" because he will be there as their Good Shepherd who will lead them, save them, and lay down his life for them. *Without Jesus as the Good Shepherd leading his flock in the midst of wolves, there is no genuine mission!*

Moreover, when a shepherd leads his flock as a good shepherd should do, the sheep respond to him in a most amazing way. They respond to him not simply because of their nature as sheep needing to cohere as a flock and requiring to be led by a shepherd, but because of his character as a good shepherd. The sheep will know the voice of the shepherd when they hear it. They will know when the shepherd calls them by their names. And when he leads them out, they will follow him obediently. They know that they are owned by their shepherd. If another shepherd calls them and leads them out, they will not follow because they do not know the voice of a stranger. And so they trust their shepherd completely and are loyal to him unreservedly. *The flock knowing its shepherd, hearing and knowing his voice, trusting and following his leading, being loyal to him in all circumstances, and being owned by him, are required qualities of a disciple community sent out as a lamb in the midst of wolves. They make of it a genuine missionary community.*

There is another important point worth noticing. While it is true that the sheep are in the midst of wolves, it is not their business to seek out deliberately the wolves and fight them. If they do this, then they behave as wolves, not as sheep. The business of the flock is to get on with its feeding, knowing of the likely presence of wolves but blissfully unmindful of them. But it does not feed as predators stealthily stalking their prey. It feeds as a flock of sheep trusting the shepherd to protect it against wolves and other wild animals. Similarly, while disciples in mission are in the midst of enemies, it is not their task to seek them out and pick a fight with them. Their commission does not say: "I am sending you as lambs in order for you to seek out the wolves and attack them." Their commission is to do the one thing they have been sent to do even as they are in the midst of those who would do them harm and seek to destroy them. Their one and only task is to proclaim the gospel of the Kingdom and bring its power and benefits to bear upon the people who have need of it in their situation. If this is done courageously, intelligently, and faithfully, it will itself constitute as the one and only way of dealing with evil as a power in human life and its affairs.

Of course, they know that there are other "powers" and "authorities" and "forces" at work in the same situation. They know that they do their mission in the midst of these enemy forces. They know that these enemies will behave like wolves which will hunt and prey upon the messengers of the gospel. But fighting them deliberately is *not* their business. They are not equipped for that kind of "struggle" because that is not the mission to which they are sent. It is the shepherd who is tasked to fight the wolves to protect *his flock;* so that the flock can get on with its feeding. *A genuine mission field is one in which the community in mission does its main task, aware yet unmindful of the dangers that may come its way, but trusting in the Shepherd of the mission for its protection.*

So far we have tried to describe qualities of sheep and lambs to indicate how disciples in mission are to behave. We must ask, however, whether this is all that is to be read in the symbolism of "lambs in the midst of wolves" which Jesus used. We have suggested all along that this symbolism signifies the mission as understood by Jesus and as given to his disciples in which to participate. What then is Jesus seeking to project by a mission that is portrayed in terms of "lambs in the midst of wolves"? Perhaps this is not an impertinent question to ask at this point.

The enmity existing between sheep and wolves is a natural one. In rabbinic Judaism, it has been transposed historically to symbolize the profound alienation between Israel as the people of God and the Gentiles. From the perspective of Israel, the Gentiles were without a messiah, "being aliens to the commonwealth of Israel . . . having no hope and without God in the world" (Eph. 2:11-12; cf. 1 Thess. 4:5; Col. 1:21). In prophetic eschatology, however, there was nurtured even right in the midst of this estrangement between Jew and Gentile the hope that the day will come when *"the wolf shall live with the lamb,* the leopard shall lie down with the kid, the calf and the lion and fatling together, and *a little child shall lead them"* (Isa. 11:6). The context in which this hope appears has to do with the coming reign of the Messiah as seen in the eyes of prophetic hope. That vision includes the healing not only of the enmity *within nature* but also *within history,* especially the estrangement between Jew and Gentile, and *between nature and history.* Not only shall the wolf and lamb live together, but "a little child shall lead them." In Isaiah 65–66 this vision of *shalom* is transposed to yet another level of hope; this time in the perspective of the beginnings of apocalyptic eschatology.[3] Here the living and feeding together of wolf and lamb (Isa. 65:25) appear in the context of the creation of the new heaven and the new earth in which the "former things"—including the enmity between Jew and Gentile—"shall not be remembered or come to mind" (Isa. 65:17-19). In the New Jerusalem that is to be created "as a joy and its people as a delight" (Isa. 65:18), *all the nations shall assemble and they will see the glory of the Lord.* God will even make priests and Levites of some of the Gentiles (Isa. 66:18-23). This is a remarkable vision. And all Israel awaits the coming of the Messiah and the *shalom* that comes with the creation of the New Heaven and the New Earth and the New Jerusalem!

When we come to the New Testament we find, however, that Jesus has foreshortened this waiting with his bold declaration that the coming kingdom of God has indeed drawn near, and its coming is connected directly with who he was and what he was doing and teaching, thus virtually claiming himself to be the coming Messiah for whom Israel awaits! He claimed that it was for this that he came; it was the mission of his person and of his life and work, and for which he died! (Mk. 1:38-39; Lk. 4:43-44). What Jesus was here doing was boldly transposing the hope of Israel into *a messianic hope* that is in process of being realized precisely through his person and mission. In and through him, Paradise is now being regained! And as we saw in the above, he made his disciples participate in mission. By sending them out "like lambs in the midst of wolves" he was making them participate in the very process of healing the enmity between lambs and wolves. In this participation, the disciples in mission were at the same time anticipating the final reconciliation of sheep and wolves and their living and feeding together in God's kingdom of glory! *Genuine mission is a participation in—and thus, an anticipation of—the final healing of the enmity within nature, within history and among peoples, especially between Jew and Gentile, and between nature and history, and the transformation of all into the New Creation!*

We are now ready to add a *seventh* observation concerning the elements that together form the mission of the disciples. *This one has to do with detailed instructions given by Jesus.* In considering this matter, we will use mainly Luke 10:4-12 and Mark 6:8-13 (cf. Lk. 9:1-6). These texts are independent of each other. The version in Luke includes material from Q. The Markan version and the Q material are both earlier than Matthew's version. Our use of them here rests on the assumption that the earlier texts stand closer to the Jewish practices that have to do with the relation of rabbis to their disciples and to the behavior of Jewish missionaries who went out on their own. It is further assumed that Jesus availed of these Jewish practices in the instructions that he gave to his disciples when he sent them out of a mission. The version in Matthew includes materials that reflect postresurrection incidents and apostolic experiences (i.e., 10:18-23). One could presume that this material was not part of the original instruction given by Jesus. This does not mean, of course, that the Matthean version does not refer to Jewish customs and practices similar to those mentioned in Mark or in the Lukan Q either. If this material in Matthew can shed further light on our considerations, we shall not hesitate to us it.

Having indicated his understanding of the mission and how he expected his messengers to behave generally in carrying it out, Jesus now gives more specific instructions to them about what equipment to bring along on their journey, how to conduct themselves on the road, what to do as they entered a house or a town, and how to respond if they were welcomed or rejected. These instructions are meant to spell out more clearly and concretely what is entailed in behaving "like lambs in the midst of wolves." The word used in Mark 6:8 (*paragellein*) in giving these instructions has the force of an order (cf. Mt. 10:5). It is the word for giving a military command. It is also the word a teacher or rabbi would normally use when he prescribes rules or principles of conduct to be observed by his pupils. It is also the word that a king or emperor would officially use when he gives a command or makes an order. Thus, the instructions of Jesus to his disciples have the force of a royal command and they are meant to be obeyed.

The first of these instructions is about what to bring along on the journey. Actually they were ordered "to take nothing for their journey . . . no bread, no bag, no money in their belts, no [extra] tunic," except what they were wearing (Mk. 6:8; Lk. 9:3; 10:4). The only things they were to bring is a staff and the tunic and sandals they were wearing. These are what will *put them on the road,* and anything else having to do with their personal comfort and material provision, such as extra clothing, food and money, is absolutely forbidden! They were forbidden to greet people on the road as this might stall them in their journey. Why is this? Did Jesus deliberately seek their discomfort or ask them to go hungry? By no means. On this instruction, Jesus was forcing his messengers to become single-mindedly aware of what they were about: they were on a journey, the journey is for a mission, and the mission is about the kingdom of God. This should be the first and only interest of the disciple sent on this mission. Therefore, his personal bearing and equipment must show this unmistakably. If he were after his personal comfort or is loaded with material things which could slow down his journey or draw attention away from what he was about, he would give the impression that he was more interested in these things than in his mission! Personal comfort and material possessions are the most likely competitors of the kingdom of God for the top rung in one's scale of values (Mt. 6:24). For a disciple in mission, there is only the one treasure of the kingdom of God at hand, and so his whole heart must be in it and in nothing else (Mt. 6:21).

But how will a disciple in mission then provide for his needs? The answer is: he does not! When a rabbi teaches, he receives no payment. That is because he did not also pay for what he teaches. The Law was given freely by God and it must be taught freely to God's people. Matthew reports Jesus as adhering to this rabbinic practice: "You received without payment; give without payment" (Mt. 10:8). In return for his teaching (which covers both the *task* and the *content* of teaching), however, it is the custom of Jewish households to receive a rabbi or teacher into their homes and share their hospitality with him or fill his meal bags with provisions (Lk. 10:7). Supporting a rabbi was considered by the Jewish community as both a privilege and an obligation. It was in this sense that "a laborer deserves his food" (Mt. 9:10; Lk. 10:7). There is here a symbiotic relationship between rabbi and community. On the one hand, *the rabbi is concerned only with his one task: namely, to teach the Law.* He must not be overly preoccupied with his personal comfort and material well-being. Least of all must he give the impression that he teaches the Law for personal and material gain. On the other hand, *the community considers it a privilege to receive a rabbi and an obligation to support him and meet his personal needs adequately.* And so when Jesus instructed his disciples to "take nothing on their journey," he was assuming that the households in the community will welcome them and will provide for their needs adequately in the same way they provided for the rabbis.

This customary symbiotic relationship depended, however, on a more basic but variable factor, namely, the acceptability of the rabbi in his person and teaching. In the Jewish community, this was not much of a problem. Rabbis were held in high esteem; seldom was a rabbi unwelcome because of personal reasons. Although there were different schools of interpreting the Law formed around great teachers who differed in viewpoints, still the task was basically the same and widely accepted. It was to teach the Law so that the community may be shaped and directed by it. There was fundamentally no reason to assume that the community will not normally welcome a rabbi and support him. Jesus took this practice for granted when he sent his disciples on their mission. There would always be those who would "share the peace" that his messengers would give (Lk.10:6; Mt.10:1-3). Once welcomed, they are to stay in that home until they leave and "eat what is set before you" (Lk. 10:8). They are not to "move from house to house" or they might give the impression that they are looking for better food and more comfortable accommodation. This will certainly diminish the community welcome for them and bring dishonor upon them!

Still there was always the possibility that a rabbi and his teaching or interpretation of the Law may not be acceptable and so he may be denied the customary hospitality. In the case of the messengers of Jesus the possibility of rejection was more than likely. They were sent out to teach one thing: "The kingdom of God has come near to you" (Lk. 10:9). This is not the theme of an ordinary lecture of merely public interest given to a general audience. It is preaching an hitherto unheard of message which comes home to roost precisely in the preaching of it. If, indeed, the medium is the message, then this was it! Moreover, it is not teaching about a general matter that would affect the people in a general sort of way. It concerns the "you" to whom it is addressed, and the "you" is under pressure to make a decision about the message put to him. Obviously, this is not the same as teaching the Law by a rabbi. *This is evangelization in its purest sense.* Because of this, it was more likely that the teaching about the Kingdom would not be received and the messengers would not be welcome! Jesus anticipated this (Lk. 10:10; Mk. 6:11; Mt. 10:14). *In a mission situation in which evangelization is the cutting edge, the possibility of rejection is more than likely to happen, and it must be anticipated.* What does one do in such a situation?

The response that Jesus recommends has three parts. The first is: leave the place and its people (Mk. 6:11; Lk. 9:5; Mt. 10:14). One must not stay where one is not welcome. Since the coming of the Kingdom is a time of opportunity, it is urgent that those who would welcome it are found and one should not waste valuable time with those who refuse it! Mission is a journey; a missionary does not tarry where one is not welcome. Moreover, it is by leaving that the refusal is acknowledged. It is the sign that the right to refuse is accepted. The gospel does not force itself into anyone's heart! Furthermore, leaving is an exercise of the freedom of the mission. Mission moves and the freedom to move is of its essence. *The freedom of the mission is precisely the freedom of the gospel. The gospel is free insofar as the mission that bears it is free and free to move on.*

The second advice of Jesus is: "shake off the dust that is on your feet as a testimony against them" (Mk. 6:11; Lk. 9:5; Mt. 10:14). This is a figure of speech that symbolizes Jewish and Gentile relationship. A Jew coming from Gentile territory shakes off the dust from his feet before he enters Jewish territory. The reason for this is that dust from Gentile soil is considered defiling to a Jew. It must be shaken and wiped off from one's feet. It must not be brought into Jewish soil. Gentile dust represents the godlessness of Gentile culture and its tragic fate, and it must not contaminate the purity of Jewish faith and jeopardize its hope.

When Jesus applied this practice of shaking the dust off the feet in his instructions to his messengers, he meant to express two strong feelings. First, it is a way of expressing strong protest against the refusal of the gospel. Rejecting the kingdom of God as having come near is a most offensive action, and it must not be taken lying down by the messengers of the Kingdom. While the *right* to refuse is to be respected, the response of *refusal* is to be protested because it is a response that is utterly inhospitable and palpably wrong. The messengers are advised to demonstrate their objection against this wrong response in the strongest possible terms. Second, Jesus was in effect telling his messengers to regard the people who refuse the gospel as *Gentiles living in Gentile territory*. Since they refuse to enter the sphere of the rule of God, they remain outside it and are to be treated as such. This refusal can only mean that they have identified themselves as being in the condition of the Gentiles—as godless and hopeless—in spite of being religious. They are, therefore, to be judged and condemned as such. *Refusing the gospel is not only offensive, it is ironically self-condemning. It is a fate-laden decision!*

This becomes clearer when we consider the third part of Jesus' advice. In Luke's Gospel, Jesus admonishes his messengers with the following words: "But whenever you enter a town and they do not welcome you, go out into its streets and say: 'Even the dust of your town that clings to our feet, we wipe off in protest against you. Yet [or nevertheless] know this: the kingdom of God has come near.' I tell you, on that day it will be more tolerable for Sodom than for that town" (Lk. 10:10-12). To put the matter in a nutshell, Jesus was saying to his messengers: Tell the people who refuse you, *their refusal does not get them off the hook!* The sense and force of the phrase "Yet know this" are meant to contradict whatever effect the refusal might have upon the coming of the Kingdom. And the whole sentence simply and flatly asserts that the refusal has no effect whatsoever upon the fact that the coming kingdom of God has indeed come near! The event of the nearness of the Kingdom is by God's initiative and action. No human refusal can nullify its happening nor diminish its significance. Ironically, a people's rejection of it is in fact telling evidence of its having come near them, for they could not have rejected it inhospitably unless it had come to them through the message and mission of the disciples, in the first place! And because of this fateful rejection, such a people's standing before God in the day of final judgment will be much worse than what befell Sodom and Gomorrah.

Why is this? In the Old Testament Sodom and Gomorrah were cities destroyed by divine judgment because of wickedness and impenitence (Gen. 19:24-26). Before they were burned "with sulfur and fire from the LORD out of heaven," Abraham had pleaded with God to spare them (Gen. 18:22-33). But they would not repent. God sent special messengers to warn them of the impending doom, but they treated the messengers inhospitably and rejected them (Gen. 19:1-11). In consequence of their wickedness, impenitence, lack of hospitality, and rejection of God's messengers, they were destroyed. This is the meaning symbolized by the cities of Sodom and Gomorrah in the New Testament (Lk. 10:12-13; 17-29; Mt. 11:23-24; Rom. 9:29; 2 Pet. 2:6).

Now, something greater than Abraham and the messengers sent to Sodom and Gomorrah has come. It is the coming kingdom of God drawing near through the Messiah in the person and work of Jesus. Its power and benefits are being brought to people through the message and mission of messengers sent by Jesus himself. If cities and towns like Chorazim and Bethsaida which Jesus specifically mentions (Lk. 10:13) treat these messengers inhospitably and reject their message, their fate in the last judgment would be far worse than what befell Sodom and Gomorrah. These cities of wickedness never had the opportunity of hearing the gospel of the Kingdom coming near and witnessing its saving power at work. If they did, they might have repented and thus, they "would have remained until this day" (Mt. 11:23). The fate of Sodom and Gomorrah in the Last Day pales into insignificance when compared with the destiny that will befall cities and towns that reject the gospel of the Kingdom! This means that rejection of the gospel and lack of hospitality to its messengers now determine one's fate in the *day of final judgment!* And unless the rejection is changed into faith and repentance, that fate will certainly consist of destruction. On the other hand, a decision made here and now that welcomes the gospel and is hospitable to its messengers not only opens up the future with hope but also throws wide open the gates of heaven for entry into the eternal bliss of God's glory! *That is the threat and the promise held out when the Kingdom comes near to anyone!* And it comes near to anyone through mission evangelism similar to the mission of the disciples!

We now come to the *final* point in our analysis of the elements of the mission of the disciples, namely, *their commission as authorized representatives of Jesus Christ.* If we ask why welcoming or rejecting the messengers of the Kingdom have a fateful significance, the answer is to be found in a remark of Jesus which appears as a kind of conclusion to the sending of the Seventy. Jesus is reported to have said: "Whoever listens to you listens to me, and whoever rejects you rejects me, and whoever rejects me rejects the one who sent me" (cf. Mt. 10:32-33, 40). This statement obviously implies that the messengers are the authorized representatives of Jesus who commissioned them, and Jesus in turn is the authorized representative of the One who sent him. Anyone who welcomes the authorized representative welcomes the one who commissioned and sent him, and anyone who rejects the representative rejects Him whom he represents. The concept operating here lies at the heart of a Jewish secular institution called *shaliah,* which is established upon the legal principle that the one who is commissioned is the authorized representative of the person who commissioned him.[4] The rabbis put the matter in a nutshell in the oft-quoted words: "The one a man sends is the equivalent of himself."[5] This rabbinic precept in turn rests upon an older Semitic principle which is the basis of the law of embassy: an ambassador or envoy fully represents the one who sends him, usually the king.[6]

An analysis of the operating principle in *shaliah* will show the following elements: (1) the critical point in the commissioning is the *conferring of authority,* not the fact of being sent nor the kind of task to be carried out. (2) The conferring of authority *empowers* the one commissioned *to represent* the one who commissions him. (3) The one thus commissioned is *sent out* to represent the one who authorized him *in some business or transaction* or relationship to be carried out *at some place away from where the sender is.* (4) To transact business with the authorized representative *is equivalent to doing business with the one whom he represents.* The rabbinic formulation puts it succinctly: "A king's ambassador is as the king himself."[7] A *sheluhim* (the equivalent word in Greek is *apostle*) is an authorized representative sent out to represent in person and action the one who commissioned him!

While *shaliah* is fundamentally a secular and legal term, it was used by extension by the rabbis on some religious parties who were believed to have been commissioned and authorized by God. This was especially true of the priesthood as a whole. Its authorized function was to represent God before the people and the people before God when it performed its cultic task. Some significant personalities, such as Moses, Elijah, Elisha, and Ezekiel, were also regarded in this light, not because of their prophetic calling, but because of certain abilities given them by God to perform some miraculous deeds which God normally reserved for himself.[8]

But the rabbis never applied the term *sheluhim* to the prophets, although it would have been most appropriate. Nor was it ever used in connection with Jewish missionaries.[9] The time of Jesus was a period of intense Jewish missionary activity. Those who went out in this mission did so, not by the commissioning of the community, but by voluntary personal initiative. And the motive was not to spread an essentially universal faith, but to earn merit for the reward that it entailed. This was true especially in Pharisaic circles where Jewish missionary activity originated.[10] There were no authorized Jewish missionaries in the sense of *shaliah*.

As far as can be ascertained, it was Jesus who by a stroke of genius originally applied the institution of *shaliah* and its operating principles upon the mission of the disciples. In this mission, it is very clear that it is Jesus who is powerfully at work and fully represented: he established the mission and determined its nature and limits; he chose whom to send, he commissioned and empowered them, he told them how to behave and what to expect in it; he made them believe they were participating in his own mission, and therefore they were representing him directly. He was present in and at work in what they were doing. And so to receive his messengers is to receive him. They stood in the position of their Lord, and so it can be truly said of them that "a disciple is not above the teacher, nor a slave above the master; it is enough for the disciple to be like the teacher, and the slave like the master" (Mt. 10:24-25). Jesus in turn is the authorized envoy or apostle of his Father who sent him. His sending is covered exactly by the same principles operating in the *shaliah*. What has been said about his messengers as fully representing him can be said about Jesus fully representing his Father. Alternatively, what is said about Jesus being powerfully present and at work in what the disciples were doing can be truly and equally said about God being fully present and effectively at work in who Jesus was and what he said and did (cf. 2 Cor. 5:18-20).

In 2 Corinthians 5:18-20 Paul makes a similar claim that follows closely the principles operating in the *shaliah*. Like Jesus he applies them upon the mission of God. We can summarize the elements of the claim as follows: (a) Paul speaks of the new creation as *all coming from God;* (b) that *God was in Christ* in reconciling the world to Himself; (c) that this ministry of reconciliation in Christ has been *entrusted to the apostles;* (d) and so the apostles are indeed *"ambassadors for Christ";* (e) as such, *God is making His appeal through them;* (f) and on this premise, Paul now *"entreats"* the Corinthians on behalf of Christ to be reconciled to God! There is here an unbroken chain of sending—a mission sending—from the Father to the Son to the disciples as apostles and to those who receive the disciples. The source of this unbroken chain of mission is the love which is the very heart of God. And that unbroken chain acts as a channel through which this same love travels freely until it reaches us where we are here and now! How we respond to that love in the here and now immediately registers its impact through the same mission channel upon the inner life of God. He feels our reaction, and He responds according to His character and purposes as a sending God. Although the chain of sending appears to span the distance between time and eternity, between earth and heaven, the link between the one and the other is instant and direct. That means God is sensitively and utterly responsive to what we do with His love! Our time and space—our location in history—do not intervene in His response to us, although His response determines our destiny. And so how we respond to the love of God as it reaches us in this chain of sending is fatefully decisive! It has immediate consequences *for now and for eternity!* This is why mission evangelism is the cutting edge of mission.

We bring to conclusion this lengthy treatment of the nucleus of the new community. We have described five basic elements that constitute it, namely, the call of Jesus, following after him, being with Jesus, being with others in him, and being sent out by him. In the process we also described the particular ethos of this new community as the ethos of love. The reason for doing this is the perception that these elements are also what constitute the community of the church. They constitute the nucleus of the church. In our analysis of these elements, we have stayed very closely to the form, substance, ethos, and structure of discipleship as these are disclosed in the formation of a discipleship group by Jesus. We have done this because the new community that was formed by Jesus is in fact a community of discipleship. He formed such a community because the life of discipleship is evidently called for as the appropriate response to the coming reign of God as having drawn near upon the human scene in Jesus Christ.

Our consideration of the nucleus of the new community of discipleship and mission is a part of our effort to identify and describe the essential components of what may be construed as the strategy of Jesus for social transformation. We have identified several elements of this strategy, namely, (a) the virtual replacement of the Law by the at-handness of the coming rule of God as the foundation of Jewish social existence; (b) the new possibilities of life and life-together made available in the sphere of God's rule; (c) the radical changes in the structures of society, lifestyles, and behavior demanded by the nearness of the kingdom of God; (d) the disclosure of love as the pervasive and compelling ethos of social existence because it is the essence of the rule of God; and finally, (e) the formation of a new community that demonstrates the new life of discipleship that is most appropriate in the sphere of the rule of God.

We have tried to identify and describe these components both in the ministry of Jesus and in those who have experienced the saving benefit of this ministry as portrayed in the Gospels, together with the tension it evoked among those who resisted it. Our reason for doing this is not primarily historical but missiological. The ministry of Jesus included the elements that we have mentioned. That ministry was an essential aspect of this mission. In fulfilling his mission through this ministry he made available to the society of his day the benefit of the drawing near of the coming rule of God upon the human scene. That benefit was received and experienced (in faith, repentance, and discipleship) by the people of his day, most notably the community of discipleship that he formed.

The ministry of Jesus and the human experience of its saving benefit as portrayed in the Gospels provide strong historical basis and credibility for the Christian community to continue the mission of Jesus in relation to social existence through the witness and service of mission evangelism. But such a credible basis can only function as such as it is taken up deliberately and faithfully in mission evangelism. The drawing near of the coming reign of God in the saving ministry of Jesus for human appropriation and experience is not simply a natural and human possibility that is latent in the nature of things and can be had for the taking! That it can become possible at all, however, is witnessed to historically and credibly by the ministry of Jesus and the human experience of his benefits. Its becoming possible today rests on the same initiative that made it come originally in Jesus, namely, God freely and graciously coming upon the human scene in His saving reign in Jesus Christ. It is this coming that creates the possibility of "offering Christ" for receiving him through faith, repentance, and discipleship.

But is not "offering Christ" for human reception precisely what witness and service in mission evangelism are all about? And if so, must not such an "offering of Christ" that is continuous with his ministry and the experience of his benefits, and still dependent upon the God who comes in His reign, include what we have construed as the strategy of Jesus for social transformation? Can mission evangelism do less? Is it not the case that the experience of salvation gives rise to mission evangelism, while in mission evangelism the possibility of experiencing salvation is indeed offered?

Notes

1. Joachim Jeremias, *Jesus' Promise to the Nations* (London: SCM Press, 1958), p. 26.

2. Q comes from the German word *quelle,* which means *Source.* Critical scholarship has established that both Luke and Matthew had access to material which they both used in the *writing of their Gospels.* This explains why their Gospels contain material that they share in common but not with Mark's.

3. I am here following the lead of Paul D. Hanson who traces the beginnings of apocalyptic eschatology to Hebrew prophecy, contra Gerhard von Rad (see Paul D. Hanson, *The Dawn of Apocalyptic*, Philadelphia: Fortress Press, 1979; Gerhard von Rad, *Old Testament II*, New York: Harper and Row, 1965).

4. Karl Heinrich Rengstorf, "Apostleship" in J.R. Boates and H.P. Kingdom, *Bible Key Words*, Vol. II (New York: Harper & Brothers, 1958), p. 14.

5. Ibid.

6. Ibid., p. 15.

7. Ibid., p. 16.

8. Rengstorf, op. cit., pp. 22-23.

9. Ibid.

10. Ibid., p. 21.

CHAPTER 10

THE KINGDOM OF GOD AND THE LAY MISSION OF THE RISEN LORD

The Ministry of Jesus as Lay Mission

It is hoped that from what has been written so far in this book, one may have some sense of the depth, scope, significance, and grandeur of the sort of transformation that Jesus sought to achieve in the society of his day in the light of his vision of the coming reign of God as having drawn near in his person and work. Would it not be a delightful but sobering surprise to realize that the person who single-handedly made the effort to accomplish this social transformation was a *layperson,* and that the ministry he unselfishly and faithfully rendered through his life and death was quite simply but profoundly *lay ministry? Jesus was a layperson and his ministry was lay ministry.*[1]

Jesus the Layman

According to Matthew 1:1-17 the tribal pedigree of Jesus is traced through Joseph to David to the royal tribe of Judah (cf. Lk. 3:23-34). This means that Jesus did not belong to the priestly tribe of Levi; he had no priestly pedigree whatsoever. Not being of priestly descent, Jesus belonged, therefore, to the category of Jewish "laity." Moreover, Jesus was raised in a devout Jewish lay family who lived in an obscure peasant village called Nazareth. He went to school in the local synagogue where he learned quite well the scriptures and religious traditions of his people.[2] Although he was known as a skilled teacher (a rabbi), there is no reliable tradition that he had gone to any established rabbinic school for a formal rabbinic education. His education was that of an ordinary rural layperson. Although a learned teacher of the Law, he was not an "ordained" teacher of the Law as the scribes were. Jesus not only taught the Law as a layperson, he also practiced the Law as a layperson.

He did not, however, join the lay movement that was dedicated to the perfect observance of the Law, namely the Pharisaic movement. Jesus was a lay practitioner of the Law but he was not a Pharisee. In fact he disagreed at many points with the way the Pharisees observed the Law. In other words, *Jesus taught and practiced the piety of the Law as an ordinary Jewish layperson!*

The one reference in the New Testament that directly tells us about what trade Jesus engaged in for a living is Mark 6:3*a*. Jesus is here referred to as a "carpenter." The definition of a carpenter today as a workman "who builds or repairs wooden structures, as buildings, scaffolds, shelves, etc." would fit Jesus.[3] Moreover, the Greek word *tekton* used of Jesus and translated "carpenter" did not exclusively refer to a woodworker. It could also include one who worked on "hard material that retains its hardness throughout the operation, e.g., wood and stone or even horn or ivory."[4] But the work of a woodworker in Nazareth— which Jesus most likely did—included the making of various types of furniture, such as beds, tables, stools, lampstands, as well as boxes, cabinets, and so forth.[5] The point of all this is to say that *Jesus was an ordinary Jewish layperson who plied a layman's trade that required skill, from which he earned an honest if modest living, and through which he rendered useful service to his community, until he gave it up to become an itinerant lay preacher!*

And yet it was in his situation as an ordinary layperson that Jesus had an extraordinary experience of God. He did not have to withdraw from the humdrum of daily secular life in order to search for God in some far-off or isolated wilderness untouched by human concern. He did not have to renounce the religious heritage of his people and culture in favor of something new or exotic or foreign. The term he used to convey the meaning of his experience of God, namely, "the kingdom of God," was a concept drawn from secular experience but with a religious undertone current in his time, although he made it bear the special meaning that derived from his extraordinary experience of God. And in communicating to his audiences that special meaning, he used stories, figures, and metaphors drawn from ordinary human experience!

In his experience, he saw God transcendent as reigning. That meant that God is real precisely as He reigns. Expressed in more philosophical language, one can say that the being of God is in His reigning. As reigning, God is the ultimate compelling power who executes His will and overcomes any and all forms of resistance to His reign in ways consistent to Himself as God.

But Jesus also saw this reign as an activity of God immanent in the world and directed towards the good of His people. It is the activity of a Father who seeks to benefit His children. And so Jesus saw God as reigning in the power of a love that knows no bounds and brooks no resistance in securing the good of His children as He himself sees and determines that good. There is, therefore, in Jesus' experience of God a vision of good for human life. God reigns precisely by achieving the good He desires for His creation and His people. Put in more philosophical language, one can say that the being of God in His essence as God is fulfilled (completed, perfected?) as He achieves the good He desires for His people! God does not become fully God until He achieves His good purpose for His creation and for His people (cf. 1 Cor. 15:24-28).

It is this determined effort on the part of God to achieve the good He desires for His creation and His people that is meant by God as loving. And so one can say that God reigns by loving and it is by loving that He fulfills His reign. *The being of God is in His reigning as love in the world.* Thus, the meaning of God as reigning is not to be discerned in any abstract speculation apart from its relationship to and activity in the world but precisely in the way it actually transforms the human situation in a decisively saving way.

Is it any wonder then that in order to exemplify God's reign as loving and to realize His vision of good for human life, Jesus determinedly engaged in a mission of lay ministry that entailed the transformation of the society of his day? It is a ministry of transformation because of several reasons. One such reason is the fact that the society of his day as ordered by the Mosaic Law was found to be wanting when measured in the light of the reign of God. The reign of God has dimensions of both beyondness and ultimacy (transcendence) and an inner pervasive nearness to the world (immanence). In drawing near at hand it has an inevitably evaluating effect (judgment) upon any and all forms of status quo. And so it stimulates a ferment for social change. *Jesus, the layman, stirred up this social ferment.*

Another reason is that there are new and better possibilities of life that are opened up by the drawing near of the reign of God. A new future has dawned upon the human scene (eschatology) and for those who have been deprived and marginalized and those who, having achieved what is best in the status quo and yet are dissatisfied and are yearning for something better, there is held out to both the hope of a new quality of life which only the reign of God can make available! The end time in which life is made whole and fulfilled has in fact drawn near. Since the end time of fulfillment is now in the midst of the present, the present is mobilized to move in the direction of its true future. *Jesus, the layman, brought a sense of hope for a new future to the struggle for life!*

A further reason is that in order to initiate a decisive movement of change towards the future that has now drawn near, it is absolutely necessary to engage in effecting specific changes in society of the sort that Jesus saw fit to do in his ministry. Those activities are *messianic* in character; that is, they are the sort that effect the change which anticipates the fulfillment of all things in the consummation of the reign of God. They are the activities that God's messianic agent (the Son of Man, the "anointed One") is to do if he is to usher in the messianic era, that is, the dawn of the new age, the end time breaking in upon the present (Isa. 11:1-10; 42:1-4; 61:1-3; Lk. 4:16-21). *This messianic ministry was achieved by Jesus, the layman.*

The Disciples as Laymen

The twelve disciples whom Jesus called to be with him were all layper-sons (Mk. 3:14-19; Mt. 10:1-4; Lk. 6:12-16). As far as it can be established, there was no priest or ordained rabbi among them. Four were fishermen (Mk. 1:16-20; Mt. 4:18-22), one was a tax collector (Mk. 2:13-14; Mt. 9:9; Lk. 5:27-32), and another a member of a nationalist party (Lk. 6:15). While the others figured in some incidents connected with the ministry of Jesus, none of these incidents gives any clue to any priestly or regular rabbinic activity on their part, although Jesus once used the work of a scribe as an analogy for the work of a disciple (Mt. 13:52). It is safe to conclude that all twelve were ordinary laypeople who lived in ordinary lay settings. It was to this motley group of laypeople whom Jesus trained that Jesus entrusted his mission and with whom he shared his authority. It was as laypeople that they took part in the mission of Jesus. *And so the mission of Jesus, begun by him as a layperson, was continued as a lay mission that was shared with, and participated in, by laypeople! It was carried out outside of the regular priestly and rabbinic establishment, and was perceived by its opponents as a dangerous threat to the priesthood and all that it stood for.*

Jesus' Ministry Rejected by the Priesthood

No wonder the relationship between Jesus and the priestly party in Jerusalem headed by the high priest was one of intense hostility. One incident in the synoptic tradition, illustrating the hostility in the setting of a controversy, is the dispute about the resurrection (Mk. 12:18-27; Mt. 22:23-33; Lk. 20:27-40). Unlike the Pharisees, the Sadducees (the priestly aristocratic party in Jerusalem headed by the high priest) did not believe in the resurrection at the last day. They tested Jesus by asking him about it in terms of a story about a woman who was married to seven brothers, one after the other, each dying with no children by her. The question asked was: "In the resurrection, whose wife will she be?" Jesus prefaced his answer with a stinging comment about their question and about them. First, he told them their question was wrong. Twice he said to them they were wrong, both at the beginning of his answer and at the end (Mk. 12:24, 27). And then he told them bluntly why their question was wrong: it was because they knew "neither the scriptures nor the power of God" (Mk. 12:24).

This hostile comment of Jesus reveals his contempt of the Sadducees. The priesthood in Jerusalem is supposed to be the guardian of the Temple and its religious traditions, including its beliefs and practices. The priests were supposed to know the Scriptures, through which God reveals Himself so that His people may come to know Him from the time of their Fathers, but unfortunately they did not. The priests were supposed to have a vital relation with God in such a way that they experience His power so that they know Him as the "God not of the dead, but of the living" (Mk. 12:27). But this was not the case, unfortunately! Their interest was more political and economic rather than religious and theological, for they controlled the levers of power in Jerusalem! It is ironic that Jesus, the layman, knew more about the Scripture and about God than the priests, and he did not hesitate to criticize them and expose their ignorance on such an important issue as belief in the resurrection.

If one were a priest and is being severely criticized for ignorance, exposed to public ridicule, and threatened in one's standing in the community, on an issue about which one is supposed to be knowledgeable, how would one feel? Is it any wonder that the attitude of the priesthood in Jerusalem escalated from unrelieved hostility to premeditated violence? Both in the synoptics and in John, the priesthood led by the high priest plotted "by stealth to kill him" (Mk. 14:1-2; Mt. 26:57-66; Jn. 11:49-50).[6] *The rejection of the ministry of Jesus by the Jerusalem priesthood confirms its character as a lay movement outside the religious establishment.*

Jesus Christ as High Priest

Since Jesus was not officially a priest in the sense of the Judaism of his day, and since his ministry was rejected by the established priesthood, does this mean that his lay ministry was without priestly significance? This is a question that is unavoidably implied by the way we have presented the ministry of Jesus on the basis of our reading of the synoptic tradition. Indeed, one can go so far as to claim that it is a question implicit in the synoptic record itself. But this issue is not considered one way or the other in the record itself. The one place in the New Testament where the issue is treated lengthily and profoundly is in the Epistle to the Hebrews. In fact, the high priesthood of Jesus is the central theme of this epistle. Among other things, Jesus is presented here as "the apostle and high priest of our confession" (Heb. 3:1). He is the "merciful and faithful high priest in the service of God" (2:17). He is a "great high priest who has passed through the heavens" (4:14). He is "a high priest forever according to the order of Melchizedek" (6:20). But even the author of this epistle clearly acknowledged that if Jesus "were on earth, he would not be a priest at all" (8:4) because he had no priestly pedigree since he belonged to the tribe of Judah (8:21), and because "there are priests who offer gifts according to the law" (8:4). From the perspective of the Mosaic Law and the Levitical priesthood, Jesus in his earthly life and ministry could not be a priest at all!

How then did Jesus come to be regarded as priest, and what is the character and scope of his priesthood according to the Epistle to the Hebrews? For obvious reasons, we cannot here give a detailed exegesis of this epistle. It will suffice to indicate a summary of some of the main ideas that establish the priesthood of Jesus. The first thing to note is that Jesus is made high priest by being called, appointed, and designated as such by God Himself as His Son (3:2; 5:4-6, 10; 7:28), "not through a legal requirement concerning physical descent" (7:16); that is, not through the Mosaic Law and not by Levitical descent. Moreover, the appointment of Jesus as high priest by God is "according to the order of Melchizedek" (5:6, 10; 8:20; 7:1-28). This order of priesthood is quite different from the Mosaic and Levitical one. The figure, Melchizedek, represents a priesthood that is "forever" in that he is "without father, without mother, without genealogy, having neither beginning of days nor end of life, but resembling the Son of God, he remains a priest forever" (7:23). The priestly order of Melchizedek is here viewed as the divine eternal priesthood. Since the designation of Jesus, the Son, as high priest by God is according to the order of Melchizedek, *his priesthood is thus divine, eternal, and forever. As such it is far superior to the order of temporary priesthood as determined by Mosaic Law and Levitical descent* (7:1-28). Finally, the designation of Jesus as high priest is sworn by God with an oath: "The Lord has sworn and will not change his mind: 'You are a priest forever' " (7:21; cf. 6:17-18). From this premise, the author of the Epistle to the Hebrews draws the inevitable conclusion: Jesus "holds his priesthood permanently, because he continues forever" (7:24). The last phrase in this quotation is directly in contrast to the Levitical priests who "were prevented by death from continuing in office" (7:23). There is here implied that the oath that God swore in making Jesus priest forever includes raising Jesus from the dead so that his priesthood is carried out "in the power of an indestructible life" (7:16).

Although the priesthood of Jesus is by divine calling and appointment, it was made perfect, nevertheless, by his own obedience, suffering, and achievement as a human being (2:10, 14, 18; 4:15). For one thing, he shared the same "flesh and blood" common to all human beings (2:14). "He had to become like his brothers and sisters in every respect" (2:17). He has been "in every respect tested as we are, yet without sin" (4:15; cf. 2:18). "In the days of his flesh, Jesus offered up prayers and supplications, with loud cries and tears, to the one who was able to save him from death, and he was heard because of his reverent submission" (5:7). He died the death which is the way of all flesh. In short, *Jesus lived a human life in complete priestly solidarity, not only with his own people, but with all of humanity.* Because of this full solidarity without any reservation, he is "able to sympathize with our weaknesses" and "be a merciful and faithful high priest in the service of God" (4:15; 2:17).

Moreover, although he is the Son yet living a fully human life, he "learned obedience through what he suffered" (5:8). His obedience made his priestly calling perfect and has thereby "obtained a more excellent ministry" (5:8; 8:6). In short, it can be said that the whole human life and lay ministry of Jesus is viewed in this epistle as priestly in character. *Jesus lived a priestly life and served a priestly ministry, and so he fulfilled the priestly office more perfectly than the one established by the Mosaic Law and by Levitical descent.*

A second thing to note in the perfecting of the priesthood of Jesus is that he freely and once for all offered his life as "a sacrifice of atonement for the sins of the people" (3:17). There is a great deal of meaning packed in this phrase. The death of Jesus was a consecration of his life in obedience to his calling to the priesthood. It is a sacrifice offered for the removal of sin, and therefore fulfills what is at the heart of Jewish Temple worship and sacrificial system, namely, the forgiveness of sins through the shedding of blood (9:22). This sacrifice was offered once and for all, making it effective for all and for all time, thus eliminating the repetitive ritual sacrifice in Jewish worship "that can never take away sins" (10:11; 9:24-26).

Not only does the self-sacrifice of Jesus remove sin, it also "destroys the one who has the power of death, that is, the devil, and free those who all their lives were held in slavery by the fear of death" (2:14). Thus, by the one and once for all self-sacrifice of Jesus, he removed the thralldom of sin, the devil, and the fear of death, which are obstacles in the way of approaching God directly. With their removal, Jesus Christ succeeds in fulfilling the aim of Jewish worship, namely, entry into the presence of God, which is what the Jewish high priest is supposed to symbolize when he enters the Holy of Holies in the Temple once a year (9:11-14, 24-26). *Jesus Christ is the perfect high priest because he "did not enter a sanctuary made by human hands, a mere copy of the true one, but he entered into heaven itself, now to appear in the presence of God on our behalf"* (9:24; cf. 3:14). Since the way to God's presence has been cleared once and for all, reconciliation and fellowship with God and life in His presence have become possible in Jesus Christ: *"He is able for all time to save those who approach God through him, since he always lives to make intercession for them"* (7:25).

The last phrase in the text just quoted brings us to the third factor to note in the perfection of the priesthood of Jesus, namely, his exaltation to sit at the right hand of God to make continuous intercession on behalf of all who approach God in and through him (1:3; 8:1-2; 10:12).

As high priest, Jesus did not only live in solidarity with his people and all of humanity and clear the way of direct access to God through the removal of the thralldom of sin, the devil, and the fear of death, by his self-sacrifice, *he also now sits at the right hand of God to make intercession for the salvation of all humankind.* Intercession is an aspect of the core function of priesthood. It is a mediating function that establishes an intimate relationship between two parties who would not normally be in such a relationship. Jesus Christ fulfills this function perfectly and permanently between God and humankind. He mediates a "new" and "better" covenant in which God is directly and intimately the God of His people, and the people are fully sanctified as God's people (8:6-13). On the one hand, he appears in the presence of God on behalf of the people, pleading for their eternal redemption (9:12, 25). On the other hand, since "he is the reflection of God's glory and the exact imprint of God's very being" he makes God vitally present to His people by sharing with them the mercy and grace of God that is their help in time of need (1:3; 4:16). As mediator-intercessor Jesus Christ is thus "the source of eternal salvation for all who obey him" (5:8).

From what has been said above, it is difficult to avoid the conclusion that in the perspective of the Epistle to the Hebrews the entire life, ministry, death, resurrection, and exaltation of Jesus is priestly in character and significance. Jesus did not serve a priestly office nor perform priestly activities in the Mosaic and Levitical sense. He is, however, high priest in his person, life, ministry, death, resurrection, and continuing lordship both by God's designation and by his own achievement. His priesthood is perfect: "For it was fitting that we should have such a high priest, holy, blameless, undefiled, separated from sinners, and exalted above the heavens" (7:26).

Two inevitable conclusions follow from the character and perfection of the high priesthood of Jesus. The first is that since the perfect and far more superior high priesthood of Jesus is now in effect, the old priesthood under the Mosaic Law and by Levitical descent and the whole system of Temple worship and sacrifice that it served are now abolished. That old priesthood and its system of worship are only a copy and shadow of the true priesthood and worship (9:24; 10:1), and they cannot make anyone perfect (9:9; 10:1). Since the true, genuine, and perfect priesthood is now in effect, the mere copy and sketch and shadow of it is thereby rendered obsolete and so abolished (8:13).

The second conclusion has to do with the appropriate response to a perfect priesthood that is now in effect. The epistle concludes the section dealing with the high priesthood of Jesus with the following exhortation: "Therefore, my friends, since we have confidence to enter the sanctuary by the blood of Jesus, by the new and living way that he opened for us through the curtain (that is, through his flesh), and since we have a great priest over the house of God, let us approach with a true heart in full assurance of faith, with our hearts sprinkled clean from evil conscience and our bodies washed with pure water. Let us hold fast to the confession of our hope without wavering, for he who has promised is faithful. And let us consider how to provoke one another to love and good deeds, not neglecting to meet together, as is the habit of some, but encouraging one another, and all the more as you see the Day approaching" (10:19-25).

This text divides itself into two parts. The first part, from verses 19-21, summarizes the achievement of the priesthood of Jesus. We have dealt with this matter lengthily above. The second part, from verses 22-25, describes what one has to do in response to the priesthood of Jesus. What is this response? *It is to live in the priesthood of Jesus Christ.* This simply means that life is to be lived and understood in the immediate presence of God as mediated by the intercession of Jesus Christ who now lives and stands before God on our behalf always. The priesthood of Jesus Christ paves the way for approaching God directly and it mediates the presence of God to those who approach Him through the way that Jesus himself has pioneered. Therefore, a life lived in the priesthood of Jesus is one that is in the posture and movement of approaching God in Jesus. In short, *it is a life shaped in the form of worship.* A life that is shaped as an approach to God in worship has the following features:

a) It is directed to God in posture and movement "in the full assurance of *faith*" and as forgiven and cleansed.

b) It holds fast without wavering to its *hope* in the promise of Jesus Christ who is faithful in fulfilling what he has promised.

c) It relates to others in *love* by doing what serves their good.

d) It anticipates a Day of reckoning which is one of celebration for those who live in the priesthood of Jesus Christ.

One can readily see from what has been said that *to be in the priesthood of Jesus is to live a priestly life of faith, hope, and love towards the future, that is to say, a life that mediates the presence of God because it is lived precisely in the immediacy and intimacy of that presence! It is a life available to all human beings because it is a life lived by the layman, Jesus Christ.*

The Mission of the Risen Lord

There seems to be no doubt that Jesus wanted his mission to be continued after his death. He had trained his disciples for this. He had sent them out to take part in his mission to the "lost sheep of the house of Israel" as a kind of preparation or dry run for what was to come. After being raised from the dead, the Risen Lord inaugurated the apostolic mission by sending his disciples as his apostles to continue his mission in all the world (Mt. 28:19-20; Mk. 16:15-18). According to the Gospel of John, Jesus understood this sending of the apostles as a continuation of the mission he was sent to do by his Father: "As the Father has sent me, so I send you" (20:21). What Jesus achieved in his life, ministry, and death was a mission from the Father who had sent him. This mission and its achievement appeared to have been defeated by its enemies when they crucified Jesus, but they have now been vindicated by the Father by raising Jesus from the dead.

The statement, "So I send you," by the Risen Christ in John's Gospel contains some profound theological affirmations that must be grasped. First, we must note the fact that the sender here is the Risen Christ. *He is, as it were, inaugurating his own mission as the Risen Lord.* Up to this point, he was only carrying out the mission of the Father. This is indicated quite clearly by the statement, "As the Father has sent me." What Jesus achieved in his life, ministry, and death is the mission of the Father. The sender of this mission is the Father; Jesus was merely sent out to do it all the way to his death. The "me" in the statement, "As the Father has sent me," is the Incarnate and Crucified One. He was the earthly, human, humbly obedient servant of God subject to the way of all flesh. But now the "I" in the statement, "So I send you," is the Resurrected One who is the risen, exalted, and reigning servant of God who is Lord of His people and of all peoples. This "I" is the sender of this mission; it is his own mission as the Risen Lord which he is now inaugurating by sending his disciples as his apostles in the world.

The second thing to note is that the mission of the Risen One is, nonetheless, continuous with the mission of the Father which was accomplished by the Incarnate and Crucified One. This is indicated by the relationship of "As . . . so." It is continuous because the way the Crucified One carried out the mission of the Father has been *vindicated* by the Father Himself raising the Crucified One from the dead.

God's vindication of Jesus by resurrection means a number of things. For one thing, it means that the verdict of the opponents of Jesus upon him and his achievement that he was a lawbreaker, a blasphemer, a rebel, and that his whole mission was not of God, is in fact absolutely wrong. The resurrection of Jesus irrevocably overrules and overturns that verdict. This reversal of the verdict upon Jesus by God is an exercise of divine sovereignty. The way this sovereignty is exercised in terms of raising Jesus from the dead is a demonstration of the power of the reign of God. The raising of Jesus from the dead is an act that only God reigning can do!

For another thing, by raising Jesus from the dead God the Father is confirming the achievement of Jesus that it is indeed His mission and has been carried out in accordance with His will. The resurrection of Jesus is God's certifying deed that Jesus did the right thing in carrying out what the Father sent him out to do! Finally, because the verdict of those who opposed Jesus has now been overturned, and since the way of Jesus has now been confirmed as the right one, then it must be continued and carried forward to its ultimate end and completion.

For accomplishing this task, Jesus claims he has been fully authorized. He has been given "all authority in heaven and on earth" to do it. The authority of Jesus in carrying out his mission as Risen is none other than the full authority and power of the reign of God. The continuation of the mission under the responsibility and authority of the Risen Lord is what the Risen Christ now inaugurates by sending his disciples as his apostles in the world: "So I send you." By continuing it, the Risen One makes as his own the mission of the Father which he himself accomplished as the Incarnate and Crucified One in obedience to the Father's will. *Therefore, the mission of the Father is now continued and carried forward universally—from Jerusalem to Judea to Samaria and to the ends of the earth—in and through the mission of the Risen Christ. In exercising full authority over this mission, the Risen Christ is thus the exalted*

Lord of this universal mission! In fact, because of the experience of the Lordship of the Risen Christ in his mission, there is a tendency in the early church, as evidenced by some later writing in the New Testament, to identify the Lordship of Christ in his mission with the kingdom of God (Eph. 5:5; Col. 1:13; Rev. 11:15; 12:10).

The last thing to note in the statement, "So I send you," is the fact that the ones being sent now are the disciples of Jesus. In being sent by the Risen Lord, the disciples become apostles of the Risen One, that is, as *his* commissioned representatives and authorized agents of his mission in the world. As apostles they become active and obedient participants in the mission of the Risen Lord. They do not thereby cease to be disciples. Rather, their discipleship is fulfilled in their apostleship, and their apostleship presupposes their discipleship and is carried out within its framework.

As agents of the mission, they are free to do what will affirm and forward this mission in the world as they are given gifts and opportunities to do so. And as the commissioned representatives of the Risen One who sent them, they are assured that the One who sent them is present to and is with them, and acts in and through what they do as inspired by him. And so those who receive the apostles receive him who sent them. *Thus, in participating in the mission of the Risen One, the apostles are in fact continuing the mission of God in the Incarnate, Crucified, and Risen One and carrying it forward to the ends of the earth and to the end of history! There is, therefore, an unbroken continuity expressed in different modes in the one mission of God: from the Father to the Son (Incarnate and Crucified) and from the Son (as Risen Lord) to the apostles and so to the apostolic community, the Church.*

As the apostles carried out their participation in the mission of the Risen Lord, two surprising developments took place. The first is that Jesus who proclaimed the message of the coming reign of God as having drawn near became himself the message proclaimed. Jesus Christ, Crucified and Risen, as Savior and Lord, is now the Good News! The other surprising development is the fact that the church came into existence.[7] Called into being by the Risen Lord, and founded upon the Apostles and Prophets, with Jesus Christ himself as the cornerstone, it shares in the reality of the Resurrection as its continuing witness, and agent (Eph. 2:20). In short, with the passing away of the apostles, the Risen Lord continues his mission in today's world through the Christian community as founded upon the witness of Apostles and Prophets, or upon the witness of both the New and Old Testament Scriptures.

It may be well to conclude this chapter with the reminder that the mission of the Risen Lord is *to and in the world as a whole*. Whereas, the mission of the Incarnate and Crucified One was to the *world* of Israel as God's people. The mission of the Risen One is to "all the nations" and "make disciples" of them (Mt. 28:19). Indeed, the mission is to make disciples of all the peoples, that is to say, to make all peoples into God's people in Jesus Christ. In this way, "the kingdom of the world becomes the Kingdom of our Lord and of his Messiah, and he will reign forever and ever" (Rev. 11:15; cf. 12:10). Thus, the mission of the Risen Lord is to the world at large, not to the church. The purpose and mission of the church, as it is called into being by the Risen Lord, is to participate in the mission of the Risen Lord as witness, agent, and sign. The universal mission of the Risen Lord remains prior in order and dignity to the participation of the church in it! The church is subject to the Lordship of the Risen Christ in its participation in the mission of the Risen Christ.

Notes

1. John P. Meier, *A Marginal Jew*, Vol. 1 (New York: Doubleday, 1991), p. 345: "One aspect of Jesus' family background was so obvious to his Jewish contemporaries that, as far as we know, neithter he nor they ever commented on it during his lifetime. Yet this aspect has been so overlooked or misunderstood by later Christians that it needs to be emphasized. It is the simple fact that Jesus was born a Jewish layman, conducted his ministry as a Jewish layman, and died a Jewish layman."

2. Ibid., pp. 268-78.

3. *Webster's Encyclopedic Unabridged Dictionary of the English Language* (New York/Avenel: Gramercy Books, 1994), p. 226.

4. Ibid.

5. Meier, op. cit., p. 281.

6. Meier, op. cit., p. 347: "No doubt many aspects of Jesus' background converged to put him on a collision course with Caiaphas and the Jerusalem priesthood: he was a no-account Galilean in conflict with Jerusalem aristocrats; he was [relative to his opponents] a poor peasant in conflict with the urban rich; he was a charismatic wonderworker in conflict with priests very much concerned about preserving the central institutions of their religion and their smooth operation; he was an eschatological prophet promising the coming of God's kingdom in conflict with Sadducean politicians having a vested interest in the status quo. But underneath many of these conflicts lay another conflict: *he was a religiously committed layman who seemed to be threatening the power of an entrenched group of priests*. That, as well as the other facets of his background, con-

tributed to the final clash in Jerusalem. In short, *that Jesus was a layman was not a neutral datum; it played a role in the development and denouement of his drama"* (italics supplied).

7. We cannot here detail the transition from Jesus as the proclaimer of the reign of God to Jesus Christ proclaimed as Savior and Lord, nor the theological rationale and historical causes for the emergence of the Church, as these would entail material which, if dealt with here, would make this work unduly long.

CHAPTER 11

FORMS OF LAY MISSION IN TODAY'S WORLD
—PART ONE—

Sharing in the Vision of Jesus

The Christian community is inevitably confronted with the issue of lay participation today in continuing the mission of the Crucified and Risen Lord and carrying it forward universally and globally. This matter will be addressed in this chapter and in the last one. What follows is to be taken as suggestions drawn from what we have learned about the strategy of Jesus for social transformation.

The underlying assumption of all that follows, however, is the conviction that the continuing mission in the world of the Crucified and Risen Lord remains as the mission of God continued and carried forward through the mission of the layman, Jesus Christ Crucified and Risen. Of course, this lay mission is now the established and official witness to the Crucified and Risen Lord who now bears all authority in heaven and on earth and sits at the right hand of God. *But it is established officially precisely as lay mission in the world.* Moreover, the participation in this lay mission of the Crucified and Risen Lord is *lay* participation, that is, as the participation of the *laos tou theou,* the whole people of God, as the apostolic community in the world. The people of God includes what is artificially denoted as "clergy" and "laity." Both are in fact members of the one people of God and in their respective "ministries" they share in the one common lay mission of the Crucified and Risen Lord as the laypeople of God.

We use the term *lay mission* to stress four important features:

a) The mission of the Crucified and Risen Christ was accomplished by him as a layperson.

b) It was continued initially in its universal scope by the Twelve Apostles who were also laypeople.

c) It is now being continued universally by the *people of God* which includes both "clergy" and "laity." In this sense, the clergy do not have a separate and distinct mission from the "laity," although they differ in their functions of serving the same mission. The term "the ordained ministry" refers to the distinctive function with which the clergy serves the one lay mission. Similarly, the term "lay ministry" designates the distinctive function with which the laity serves the one lay mission.

d) The mission is to and in the *world of peoples* for the purpose of making the peoples in their worlds God's holy people. The focus of the mission is on *world* in all its dimensions, not merely in its *religious* element, in contrast to the so-called secular one. In the light of this understanding, lay mission is a more comprehensive term than "mission evangelism." This term denotes the aspect of lay mission that presents the summons to "faith, repentance, and discipleship" as the appropriate response to the claims of Christ. In this sense, evangelism is the cutting edge of lay mission.

And so it can be asked: How is lay participation in the mission of the Crucified and Risen Lord to be carried forward today? The first and basic suggestion that could be made is *for God's people to share in Jesus' vision of the kingdom of God.* That they can share in this vision is possible. That this sharing is possible is grounded in the fact that by faith, repentance, and discipleship they are already in the sphere of the kingdom of God as having drawn near. The sphere of God's Kingdom is centered in Jesus Christ, in who he is and what he said and did, in his life, ministry, death, and resurrection, in his person as the incarnate, crucified, and risen Christ and Lord. The sphere of God's Kingdom extends to the mission of the Risen Lord in the world, and that mission includes the participation of the Apostles and of the apostolic community, namely, the church as the people of God. That the people of God are in mission is by that fact proof that they are in the sphere of God's Kingdom as having drawn near in the midst of the world. Thus, to be in the sphere of God's Kingdom is to exist in Jesus Christ and live as his discipleship-community, participating in his mission in the world.

The vision of Jesus is focused on *God as reigning.* Thus, to be in him as the sphere of the Kingdom is to have one's vision riveted to the vision of Jesus which is fixed and focused on God as reigning. It is God exercising His royal activity as creating, saving, caring, and fulfilling rule which is lighted and lifted up in this sphere. In short, *God is seen as the one who trusted, obeyed, and adored as King in the sphere of His rule!*

One beholds Him in His royal majesty and power. One acknowledges in praise and worship that there is none like Him. It is God reigning—only this and nothing else—which is seen in the horizon of the vision of Jesus.

But there are very serious difficulties in acknowledging God as King in His Kingdom both in the context of the early church and in today's world. As Christianity moved out of its cocoon in Judaism and spread into the wider Hellenistic world, it ceased using the phrase "the Kingdom of God" in its proclamation and witness. It is hardly mentioned in the writings of Paul and in John. The reason for this is that of the setting of the Greco-Roman world which was ruled by Rome, the term would be misunderstood as referring to a rival kingdom in the Roman Empire and its followers treated as traitors. This would be reason enough to extirpate them, and the Roman imperium did make the effort by brutally persecuting the early Christians. The early Christian community and its leaders took great pains to clear this political misunderstanding. Paul admonished the Christians in Rome to be subject to the governing authorities and pay taxes (Rom. 13:1-7). In John's Gospel, Jesus asserts before Pilate that his Kingdom is not from this world (Jn. 18:33-37). The term that seemed to have been preferred in the Hellenistic setting of the time is the *Lordship* of the Crucified and Risen Christ. But in explaining what this means, the early Christians had to tell "the story of Jesus of Nazareth as the Christ." This particular storytelling is what gave birth to the "gospel" as a distinctive literary genre.

In today's world there is an apparent widespread rejection of the phrase "Kingdom of God" among those who promote and think about God's mission and by the wider public. The reason for this is its connotation that God is a monarch, and as such His rule can be used to justify and promote all forms of political, social, economic, and cultural domination and oppression. Any concept of God that results in any ideology of imperialism is anathema in today's world. The various forms of liberation movements that aim at securing freedom, which is viewed as the essence of human nature and dignity, require an understanding of God that is nonmonarchical, and demand a corresponding ordering of social life that is thoroughly democratic. Of course, it is not always conceded that there is an intrinsic relationship between a concept of God and the form of social order. These two themes *can* be treated theoretically independently of each other. But can this be done appropriately in connection with the understanding of Jesus about the kingdom of God? We will deal with this question below.

For reasons such as those mentioned above, it may indeed be wise, missiologically speaking, not to use the phrase "the Kingdom of God," in today's lay mission. But certainly there are values in this term as Jesus used it that must be retrieved and incorporated into the language of witness in today's world. There is now a process of retrieval that is going on in New Testament scholarship.[1] The method of retrieval includes not only the acknowledgment that the language employed by Jesus in talking of the Kingdom is metaphorical (i.e., parabolic) but more important the recognition that the phrase "kingdom of God" is in itself a symbol. That is to say, the phrase itself metaphorically refers to a different reality besides what it literally signifies. Thus, to speak of God as reigning is to point that God relates to the world and this relationship is expressed in terms of what He does to and in it. Such a relationship and activity is somewhat similar to the way an earthly king relates to and does his work among his people. Moreover, it is within this relationship and activity that God comes to be experienced and known. The reign of God is the context for humanly experiencing and knowing God and His ways in the world. What we know of God as reigning, however, cannot be confined within or limited to the known ways of earthly kings. God reigning also *intends* to say that God *can* and *does* evaluate, reverse, or supersede those known ways, since such power and prerogative are aspects of what makes Him "King," and, therefore, He has the right to exercise them actively.

From what has been said above, it is clear that the phrase "the Kingdom of God" must be understood as a symbol that is open-ended: it makes God knowable and expressible in ways that profoundly affect the world; but it also points to, and safeguards, God's reality as free to express Himself in ways consistent with His freedom as God. This exercise of sovereign freedom may entail the reversal or replacement of what we already know humanly of God and His ways from models of earthly rule. The parables of Jesus about the Kingdom point to some aspects of God's royal activity in the world. But the symbol of "the Kingdom of God" as such also intends to point to the inexhaustibility and unpredictability of God's ways of expressing Himself in the freedom of His reign! This is the primary reason why in the effort to understand the "meaning" of the kingdom of God, it is not possible to define it. The kingdom of God lends itself to being "likened" to something it is not, but it resists being defined in terms of something it is not! It authenticates its own meaning in the contexts in which it appears.

God Seen from the Sphere of His Reign

What then can be said of God in the light of the symbol of the kingdom of God. For one thing, it can be said that *God is coming.* This seems to be a better way of speaking of God than saying that He exists. Of course, to say that God is coming already presupposes His existence. But His existence is not something that is bare and inert and incapable of arousing any expectation of Him. On the contrary, to say that God is coming already comes from expecting Him. This anticipation is stirred up precisely by the impact of His precedent reality. To expect God as coming entails searching for Him actively, anticipating His appearance, and alertly waiting for His arrival! To say that God is coming is another way of speaking of the prevenience of His presence and the antecedence of His reality to everything else!

For another thing, it can be said that the coming God *comes.* That He comes is an exercise of His initiative and power as God. If He does not or cannot come, He is not God at all because He does not have the initiative and the ability to come. That He comes is precisely an exercise of the power of His sovereignty. He is able to break through and overcome that which prevents Him from coming. *He reigns by coming.* Moreover, God becomes real to us by His coming. His reality is not out there waiting to be searched, discovered, and thought about speculatively. His reality is not a given datum that lies ontologically as the basis of all that is and can be probed metaphysically. Nor is He real because He is the necessary or logical conclusion of a given premise, or a plausible theory that makes sense of a pile of data! *God becomes real to us only as He comes,* that is, as He takes the initiative in authenticating Himself in His coming! To say that God comes is another way of saying that God freely reveals Himself as the God He is!

Furthermore, it can be said that the coming God comes *near.* To be near is why He comes. To be near means overcoming distance, separation, alienation, and obstacles that stand in the way. There is the distance between Him as God and what is not God, which in the first instance is nothing or nonbeing. In coming near what is nothing, God creates: He calls into being those things which are not. Creation itself is already the nearness of God. There is the distance between God as Creator and creation as creaturely. In coming near what is creaturely, God sustains, provides, and guides. Creaturely dependence upon God already rests on the nearness of God. There is the alienating distance between God and the sinner. In coming near the alienated sinner, God saves by forgiving, reconciling, and sanctifying. Salvation is the healing and reconciling touch of God's nearness. There is the disturbing distance between God and a frustrated, unfulfilled, and dissatisfied life. In coming near such a life, He promises new possibilities and inspires the effort to achieve them. The joy of achievement springs from the inspiring and enabling nearness of God. There is the daunting distance between God and being bound in life to time and space. In coming near what is temporal and temporary, God gives the assurance that the temporality of life is undergirded, sustained, and surrounded by the eternity of His immediate presence which is equidistant to all times and lifetimes. The Now of the Eternal is precisely the intimate nearness of God. There is the inescapably fatal distance between life and death, and death seems to overcome life finally! In coming near life that is overcome by death, God overcomes the power of death by the power of His life: He gives life to the dead. Resurrection life is the nearness of God that overcomes the power of death! To say that God comes near is another way of saying that God is gracious and merciful, and it is His desire that we enjoy the benefits of His grace, that is to say, of His nearness.

Another thing that can be said of God in the light of the symbol of the Kingdom is that the coming God comes near _from the future_. To us human beings, the future is beyond the horizon of our sight; it is unknown and uncertain. It is from the mystery of the future that the coming God steps out in coming near. Even as He comes near to be known, He enshrouds Himself in the aura of mystery; He surrounds Himself with the majesty of transcendence, He shines through in the glory of ultimacy. It is precisely when He is near as coming from the future that we are able to say, He is far while being near. God does not lose His mystery, His transcendence, and His ultimacy in coming near. It is _as God_ that He comes near, and it is in being near that He _becomes God_ to us!

God comes near from the future that is His. The future of God is the consummation and fulfillment of His reign when God shall be all in all and through all and above all (1 Cor. 15:28; cf. Rev. 21). It is He who alone consummates His rule, so that He as God in the fullness of His being is *in* and *through* and *above* all things. This is still future to God and this future is His future. God's future, however, is *not* our future until He makes it our own and fulfills it in us and in all things. Therefore, His future is not a possibility of our present. Our present, therefore, does not inexorably move into and arrive in the future of God. Rather, it is God's future which He makes our own which comes, and comes near, to our present. God's coming near from His future has the character of an *advent:* it comes *from* His future *to* us in our present. In this way, He makes His future become our future. We do not arrive at this future as though it were the predetermined end of our temporal journey. But since the future is for us also the source of the possible, God makes Himself in His future possible to us so that His future can become our future! The future that He makes possible for us is our true future.

This true future of ours brings with it—when it comes to us—a judging activity. It exposes our present as burdened with the past—its mistake, its sin, its guilt, its missed opportunities, its crippling paralysis, its future without hope. It reveals the truth about us and compels us to admit it in penitence! *But the future that comes from God judges the past in the light of new possibilities that it provides.* And so in breaking upon our present, God's future, which He makes our own, offers to correct the mistake, to forgive the sin, to cancel the guilt, to break the paralysis and liberate from it, and opens up a new horizon of possibilities, and at the same time inspiring the effort to realize them! Moreover, the future that comes to our present does not consign to the garbage heap the gains of the past. The wisdom crystallized from experience, the maturity born out of trial and triumph, the achievement accomplished through sweat and struggle are all incorporated into the possibilities given to the present.

In liberating the present from the past, in supplying it with new possibilities, in providing it with a sure sense of direction, the advent of the future shakes, mobilizes, and moves the present towards the fulfillment of its true future, which is given it by God from His future! Centered in the Incarnate and Crucified Christ, and under the authority of the Risen Lord, this movement cannot be other than a missiological one that is participated in by the agency of the people of God. The advent of the future upon our present, therefore, means decisive changes in our personal, social, and historical life and its conditions and direction. These changes are what are thematized by faith, repentance, and discipleship as the response to the advent of the reign of God! The realization of these changes in the world at large is what lay mission is all about until He is all in all!

But God's coming from His future into our present does not exhaust the future and its possibilities which are His. That is why God's coming near in Jesus Christ is always "at hand." There is always more to the future as it comes from God to us and our world because God is the inexhaustible source of possibility. The coming God comes, and is always coming to come. There is always more to come of the coming God until He is all in all!

Finally, it can be said that *this God is the Father of the Lord Jesus Christ.* The King in the Kingdom is a Father. God reigns as the Father! *He reigns as Father in His love. His reigning is simply the expression of His loving, and His loving is what is achieved in His reigning.* Love is behind and in and through and above all the activities of His reigning. The coming God, who comes near from the future in Jesus Christ to our present, providing it with its true future and mobilizing and moving it to fulfill that future, seeks to meet His people in the sphere of His rule in the world as quite simply a loving Father! He reigns by achieving the good He intends as a Father for His children! He reigns as the humble servant of His people! This in some measure sums up what can be seen and spoken of God as one shares in the vision of Jesus Christ!

In conclusion, it may be asked, What is the point of sharing in the vision of Jesus? For one thing, one cannot help it, if one is a Christian. One cannot be in Jesus Christ without being placed in the horizon of his vision, and being turned around to the focal point of that vision. That vision is fixed single-mindedly on God who is perceived and understood in a particular way. Because God is the kind of God as Jesus sees Him, He graciously offers "life abundant" that is nowhere else to be found except in Him. For another thing, if one engages in lay mission as one must if one is a disciple of Jesus Christ, what is it that one can share with others that will make a real difference for good in their lives and in the way they perceive the world? Is it not the vision of Jesus Christ and his faith in the God who sent him all the way to the Cross and vindicated him by raising him from the dead, thereby making possible a new life, a new humanity, and a new creation? What else can a Christian share with fellow human beings, except this?

Moreover, if one is to participate in the lay mission of the Risen Lord, one must engage in doing certain activities. Are not the activities of lay mission those that witness to and, in some measure, realize in the world of today, the possibilities of the new that are offered in the vision of Jesus? Lay mission is applying concretely in the world of today the vision of Jesus. That is exactly what Jesus did in the world of his day. What is there to apply if one does not share in the vision of Jesus?

Note

1. See Norman Perrin, *Jesus and the Language of the Kingdom* (Philadelphia: Fortress Press), 1976; Bernard Brandon Scott, *Hear the Parable* (Minneapolis: Fortress Press, 1989); Bruce Chilton, *Pure Kingdom, Jesus' Vision of God* (Grand Rapids, Michigan: Wm. B. Eerdmans Publishing Company, 1996); Robert W. Funk, *Parables and Presence* (Philadelphia: Fortress Press, 1982).

CHAPTER 12

FORMS OF LAY MISSION IN TODAY'S WORLD —PART TWO—

Following the Risen Lord into the World of Today

A second suggestion for lay participation in the mission of the Risen Lord, besides sharing in the vision of Jesus, *is to follow its movement in today's world, using as a model Jesus' lay mission of social transformation.* We have already seen that God's reign relates Himself actively in the world. Who He is can be discerned from His activity of reigning. His reigning also includes a vision of good for human life. His reigning seeks to achieve this vision of human good. His work of realizing this vision has been modeled by Jesus in his lay mission. The aim of Jesus' mission—as he put it himself—is simply to seek first the kingdom of God and its righteousness in everything. In what areas of social life did Jesus seek the reign of God? The answer to this question would spell out various possibilities of lay participation in the mission of the Risen Lord in today's world. Lay mission today would do no better than simply follow the mission of the Risen Lord as it moves into our world today on the basis of the model of his earthly ministry. The proposals that follow deal with basic issues rather briefly and generally.

Establishing Society

For one thing, Jesus sought the reign of God in what established and constituted the society of his day. He saw that Jewish society was founded on the Mosaic Law. He believed, however, that there is something more basic and primordial than the Mosaic Law, and this is his vision of the kingdom of God. Accordingly, he sought to found even the Mosaic Law upon the reign of God. The kingdom of God and its righteousness must be "first" in what establishes human society.

It seems that this is a clue to one significant move of lay mission in today's world. Like the Jewish society of Jesus' day, most societies today are established and constituted by some form of law, whether in terms of a written or unwritten constitution which enshrines a political theory, or by way of the basic principles of a dominant ideology, which are determined and applied by its political party. Moreover, most forms of law are understood as autonomous, that is, as self-legislated, either in the form of a "social contract" ratified by a people, or a party "consensus" imposed upon a people by the party of a dominant ideology. As autonomous they do not have a transcendent reference beyond themselves and the "contract" or "consensus" that spawned them. Law is a form of self-rule. The "rule of Law" is self-referencing. The day when the law of the state is an earthly reflection of the law of heaven or of the order of the gods is long gone, and rightly so. Most states today are secular, with the exception of Islamic theocracies. They thus reflect the secularity that has become a dominant characteristic of most modern societies.

To be sure, some states constitutionally provide for religious freedom and the separation of church and state. This allows for the free practice of religion, although the degree or extent of religious freedom varies, depending upon the law or state in question. For the most part, this has come to mean, however, the practice of "purely" religious activities. It is assumed that such activities are nonpolitical and they should not deal with the affairs of the state. Indeed, any attempt to draw out in practice the political implications of a religious perspective, assuming that it has any, is invariably frowned upon by the secular public! The practice of religion, although free in varying ways, is relegated to the private sphere, far and away from the public arena. If it does enter the public arena, it is tolerated as undue interference. Religious freedom is understood by the secular public as religious tolerance. What is tolerated is not quite right, and yet it would be a greater wrong to remove it forcibly. Or what is tolerated is quite harmless, and there is no point in paying attention to it. Toleration in the senses just described expresses, of course, a condescending attitude, and it reflects the measure in which the status and practice of religion have lost their public significance in secular societies.

In this connection, one area into which the mission of the people of God in secular society may go, in following the mission of the Risen Lord, is in establishing the basis of society in its proper foundation. In the view of Jesus, the reign of God is more primordial than the rule of Law. For this reason, Law must be grounded in the reign of God and must be regarded as expressing it in some measure. There cannot be, however, an identification of the reign of God with the rule of Law. The kingdom of God cannot be another Law, and the Law cannot be the kingdom of God. The Law, however, requires a reference transcendent to itself which is not itself Law. That transcendent reference must be in the form of a vision. According to Proverbs 29:18 (KJV), without a vision, a people will perish. But such a vision—properly so-called— must transcend the limits of sight, although it must be perceived within the horizon of sight. The vision of the kingdom of God is such a vision. It must be witnessed to in lay mission as such a vision. In relation to what constitutes society, it must be interpreted symbolically as being more primordial than any form of law, although it is not itself Law and cannot function as Law. In the light of the vision of the kingdom of God, Law cannot be self-referencing and completely autonomous so that it is not accountable to anything but itself. Otherwise, it becomes an idol.

Of course, a great deal depends on how the kingdom of God is kept alive as a vision in the constitution of society. If it were presented in the form of another Law, or functions as Law, or is continuous with Law, so that there is virtually no distinction between kingdom and Law, as is the case in Islamic theocracies, the kingdom of God loses its character as a vision and cannot function as a symbol. It will be another self-referencing Law that rules by itself as Law, with no accountability to any reference beyond itself. And so it becomes another idol. But how is this to be avoided?

The Critique of Law

This question leads into another arena in which lay mission may participate in the mission of the Risen Lord in today's secular societies. If the vision of the kingdom of God were seen as primordial to the rule of Law, *it can then function symbolically as a critical frame of reference for evaluating any form of law that establishes and orders society.* Again it is Jesus who provides the lead in this enterprise. He judged the Mosaic Law in the light of his vision of the reign of God. He relativized this Law, he pointed to its deficiencies, affirmed and fulfilled its values and advantages, and led it beyond itself to horizons of new possibilities. The same can and should be done today as an aspect of lay mission.

Most modern societies use their constitutions or ideological and moral principles for self-criticism. This is an important source of social renewal, and it must be encouraged. Nothing is more legitimate and healthier than for a society to measure itself against its own fundamental law, which presumably embodies its vision for itself. A critical dialogue can take place within a society as to how it can best improve itself on the basis of its own ideals and aspirations which are embodied in its basic law and moral principles.

But by what measure or in the light of what critical framework are the basic law and the ideological and moral principles *themselves* to be evaluated? In secular societies there is no provision for meeting this need, if it is seen at all as a need. The best that can be done is to make critical but relative comparison among the basic laws and ideological and moral principles of states or peoples. Although this is to be encouraged, the same question as to what transcendent frame of reference may these various basic laws and principles be evaluated can still be rightly and compellingly asked. It is not far from the truth to claim that there would be no forthcoming answer from a thoroughgoing secular perspective!

Into such a secular vacuum, the vision of the kingdom of God could enter in the form of lay mission and be a partner in a dialogue between itself and the basic laws and ideological and moral principles of any state or society. It can present its evaluation of those fundamental laws and principles in the fivefold way suggested, namely, relativize them, expose their deficiencies, affirm and appreciate their values, and show further possibilities of improvement, and make a case for the validity of such an evaluation. It is assumed here that the evaluation and the case made for it derive from sources in the transcendent vision itself and not from what is being evaluated.

The best possible scenario, which such a presentation may provoke or help create, is a critical dialogue between the transcendent vision and the fundamental legal, moral, and ideological assumptions of a society. A process of mutual questioning takes place. A dialogue between critical frames of reference ensues. This is what happened between Jesus whose frame of reference was the kingdom of God and the scribes and Pharisees whose frame of reference was the Law. If this intensive dialogue between critical frames of reference happens simultaneously with the dialogue taking place within a society based on its own frame of reference, there would be a ferment for social change such as Jesus provoked in the society of his day.

The worst that can happen is for those who have a stake in the status quo to feel threatened, and because of fear they might not listen at all to the substance of the dialogue, let alone participate in it. In such a case, the usual reaction is to nip the dialogue in the bud by asking the question: "By what authority" does one presume to enter into this conversation? Such a fear born out of threat can easily and quickly escalate into violence, which is what the Jerusalem priesthood and the Roman authorities inflicted upon Jesus! Such a possibility has to be risked in lay mission for that is where the lay mission of Jesus finally led him.

The Mission of People-Making

So far we have identified two ways of following the mission of the Risen Lord into the secular societies of our time. These have to do with advocating that the reign of God is primordial to Law that establishes society, and that as a vision it functions as a critical frame of reference for evaluating society in its basic law and principles. To this we add a third, namely, *the thrust of the reign of God in people-making*. There can be no doubt that one aspect of the purpose of the reign of God is the making of human beings into becoming God's people and be His witnesses in the world. God created the human being in His image so that the human being is a reflection of the reality and truth of God. God redeemed Israel and made a covenant with her so that Israel shall be His people and He her God. The Law as the expression of His will was given to Israel through Moses so that by obeying it Israel shall indeed be made into His people and be a "light to the nations."

In the drawing near of the coming kingdom of God in Jesus Christ, one of the things Jesus did was to evaluate how Israel has fared in becoming God's people under the aegis of the Mosaic Law. What he saw gave rise to the program thrust of his ministry. He exposed the victimizing effect, that is, the injustice, of the Law; he ministered to the victims of injustice *in* and *of* society; he sought to overcome the evil forces that plagued people and stunt their development as human beings; he appreciated the achievement of those who rose to the best that was available in the Law, but, at the same time, showed them what they still lacked. He formed the nucleus of a new community that is discipled around the reign of God. In other words, Jesus carried through in his ministry the people-making thrust of the reign of God.

This ministry is being continued today by the mission of the Risen Lord. Lay participation in this mission can do no better than carry it forward universally in today's world. One aspect of people-making is the right ordering of human relations. People are made in and through relationships. The right ordering of human relations is the aim of Law. Where this is not achieved and there is distortion in human relations, injustice occurs. This harms people and is inimical to people-making. *And so one aspect of lay mission is precisely the exposure of injustice in society.*

Law intends to secure and establish justice (righteousness). This is its purpose both in conception and application. But the conception of Law in its form and substance is never perfect, and the way it is applied, as thus conceived and according to the procedures it itself provides, is also never perfect. The measure of imperfection both in the conception and application of Law represents a measure of injustice. Thus, although justice is the aim of Law, it never fully realizes this aim; the extent of the failure is a measure of injustice. There is always, therefore, a degree of injustice in any justice system conceived and established by Law.

Discerning and exposing this injustice of the justice system is never easy. Perhaps the injustice resulting from the failure in the application of Law may easily be seen and most likely readily rectified because the criteria for recognizing it are already provided in the substance, form and procedures of the Law. But by what terms is the Law itself as whole to be evaluated to determine the extent of its imperfection so that the measure of injustice it necessarily entails may be discerned and possibly rectified? The Law as currently conceived and established can only regard itself as perfect. It can, therefore, evaluate itself only in terms of itself, and for this reason it may not see its own imperfection. Is there no other term of reference in the light of which Law may be judged for its imperfection, and the measure of injustice it bears may also be discerned? Moreover, the justice envisioned by Law is only possible within the Law. Is there no justice beyond the Law, and therefore is not yet possible within the Law as presently conceived and established?

Jesus exposed the injustice of the Mosaic Law in terms of a "higher righteousness" made available in the kingdom of God. This ministry of

Jesus is being continued today by the Risen Christ. Though difficult, the people of God in their ministry are called to participate in this mission of exposing injustice. They can do so because they share in the vision of the kingdom of God and its righteousness. It is this righteousness, which is "higher" than the righteousness of the Law, which gives them the transcendent criterion for evaluating any justice system established by Law, and provides them with resources and possibilities for the reconception and reform of Law, so that it may deliver a more just system of justice! If such a "higher righteousness" is brought to bear upon Law and the justice it envisions, the best that can happen is a healthy dialogue between the higher righteousness of the kingdom of God and the righteousness of the Law. It is hoped that such a dialogue can result in a more perfect Law and a more just delivery of justice.

When society is ordered by Law, as indeed it must, two fundamental things happen. On the one hand, the justice envisioned by Law in its degree of perfection is thereby established. On the other hand, the injustice resulting from the imperfection of Law unfortunately also becomes effectively operational.

Social ordering by Law is both just and unjust. What does one do to the victims of injustice not only *in* but *of* society as ordered by Law? In a court of Law, justice is secured retributively. There are those who win and there are those who lose in a case that is adjudicated. Those who win are rewarded. Those who lose get their desert, and they are not always the guilty ones. They are either made to pay damages or consigned to prison.

But suppose the whole society were a court of Law. Does not justice here also operate retributively in that there are those who win and there are those who lose? The only difference between a court of Law and the whole society viewed as a court of Law is that in a court of Law there is a clear verdict and a definite sentence rendered by a judge, although it may not be the right verdict or the correct sentence. Whereas, in society at large the injustice of the Law operates imperceptibly yet effectively, and with equally palpable results, as evident in the victimization and marginalization of innocent sectors of society, although there is no sitting judge rendering the decision.

What is inescapably tragic in this situation is that the victims of the injustice of Law cannot be "saved" by the Law itself because they are the consequence of its own imperfection. There is no hope of redress from the imperfection and the injustice that produced their situation. They can only be saved if Law and its obedience are perfect. But what Law is perfect? What application of Law is perfect? What obedience to Law is perfect? If Law is perfect, it would be perfectly just; and if so, then there would be no victims of injustice. Thus, it can be claimed that Law bears within itself a measure of injustice, and so there are inevitably victims of injustice!

Again, it is appropriate to ask: What is to be done with the victims of injustice? The answer to this haunting question will always remain a challenge to lay mission. People-making requires redeeming people from what dehumanizes and "de-peoples" them. The first basic thing to do is, of course, to make the Law as perfect as possible so that it will deliver a more perfectly just system of justice. This is precisely what has been advocated above. But this is not enough because the victims are people who have *already* been victimized, and people who suffer from injustice require something more than correcting an unjust justice system, important as this is. These people need to be saved from the consequences of having been institutionally ravaged and structurally marginalized. They need to be rehabilitated and revitalized for a new lease on life!

But can they be saved through the Law when it is the Law that victimized them in the first place? Are they not rather to be redeemed *from* the Law, and for this reason, they have to be saved *outside* of the Law? Is this not exactly what Jesus did? He put in place and carried out a ministry of salvation from, and outside of, the Law of his time! His ministry of finding the lost, forgiving the sinner, healing the sick, liberating the poor, befriending the tax collector, restoring the outcast, and loving the enemy, was carried out against the Law and with resources made available, not by the Law, but by the reign of God. His ministry to the elite of the society of his day—the elite righteous and the elite rich and powerful—went beyond what the Law required. What they lacked in their obedience of the Law could be discerned and met, not from the Law itself, but from what was outside of the Law, namely, the coming reign of God as having drawn near. The call to faith, repentance, and discipleship was not to return to the Law but to enter the kingdom of God already at hand in Jesus Christ.

It is not far from the truth to claim that this people-making ministry of salvation from the Law and outside of the Law is being continued and carried forward universally today in the mission of the Risen Lord. The people of God in their ministry are being called upon to participate in it in today's world. The participation, however, is to be done responsibly in relation to the problems, prospects, and opportunities that are to be found in contemporary societies. Today there are serious attempts to conceive justice that liberates from the institutional injustices of imperialism, racism, sexism, classism, ethnocentrism, and "ideologism." These injustices are the deplorable consequences of imperfect and unjust legal systems. The resources being tapped for the revisioning of justice lie for the most part outside of the already established imperfect forms of law and the inadequate justice systems they envision and deliver. This reconception of justice in larger terms is forcing the reform of Law in many societies today. Moreover, the many forms of help that are being organized to bring healing, comfort, and hope to the victims of contemporary injustices make use of resources voluntarily made available by different groups, many of them religious, civic, and nongovernmental.

All these developments in the reform of Law and the healing of injustice are evidence to the eye of faith that the Risen Lord continues to move universally in mission in today's world. And much more can be done. It may well be that the people of God in their lay mission need not look far to discover opportunities of participating in the people-making mission of the Risen Lord. These opportunities are just around the corner, and they can be seized and programmed from where the laypeople are placed!

The Reform of Social Structure

There is a fourth dimension of the thrust of the reign of God as exemplified in the ministry of Jesus. This has to do with *the reform of social structure for human community.* It has been shown that there are two dimensions in social structure. One is the *elemental,* and the other, *behavioral.* The elemental are gifts of God in creation and in salvation. Jesus identified some of them in the Sermon on the Mount. These are the gifts of life and its value; of sexuality and gender; of the other person in marriage and the blessing of family; of the capacity for language and truth telling; of the grace to love even the enemy; of relating to God in human ways; of treasuring or valuing objects of true value; of the ability to judge and to distinguish between good and evil, right and wrong, truth and falsehood; of the freedom to be and to choose the way of being in the world. This list is meant to be illustrative, rather than exhaustive.

As gifts of God, they are meant to express the love of God in His reign. They signal His basic, gracious, and intimate relationship to His creation, and so they are continuing activities of His reign. In receiving these gifts, the people of God respond in worship, gratitude, praise, and continuing dependence upon God's grace expressed in prayer and joyful discipleship. The elemental dimensions of social structure thus provide a fundamental reason for celebrating the reign of God precisely in the midst of natural, social, and historical life.

Moreover, the elemental dimensions in social structure are universal and they run through all societies. No society is without them, since without them no society is possible. The elemental factors, thus, provide the basis for the rise and development of the *behavioral* in social structure and of social structure itself. The behavioral is an aspect of culture and has to do with human behavior in at least three forms. The first deals with the forms and ways of interaction among human beings. The second refers to the behavior of human beings in relation to their natural/cosmic environment. And the third has to do with the behavior of human beings, together with their environment, in their relationship to God. All three forms of human behavior must intend to express and celebrate the reign of God since they arise from the elemental dimensions of social structure.

The intention of the reign of God in His elemental gifts is to make human community possible! Social structure is the form in which the elemental and the behavioral are brought together in varying degrees of integration across time in society. Social structure crystallizes and organizes aspects of human behavior, which would otherwise remain defused in the wider culture, around the elemental dimensions as nodal centers. Patterns of behavior organized around these nodal centers are forms of social structure. There is, for example, human behavior centered on the fact of life, on sexuality and gender, and so forth. Forms of social structures are handed on from generation to generation, and so they become formative and normative in human behavior. They are thus the institutional forms of human community.

From the foregoing, it is possible to derive a set of criteria for evaluating forms of social structure and for resourcing their possible reform. The criteria may be expressed in the following questions:

1. Do they acknowledge the presence of God and celebrate it as the basis of human community?

2. Do they make possible the development of human community?

3. Do they deal with the environment in such a way that it makes human community possible and celebrate God's presence in it?

Of course, the overall criterion is the one question as to whether social structure to some degree expresses and celebrates the reign of God in people-making and community building! In evaluating and reforming social structure, the focus is necessarily on the behavioral component. If, as an aspect of its mission, lay ministry would evaluate and reform social structure in contemporary societies, in the light of the criteria indicated above and using as resources what Jesus said in the Sermon on the Mount, it would find its hands full. Doing justice to this agenda is a tall order. Certainly it is not possible to develop here a full blown social ethics. What follows is to be taken only as hints of what can possibly be done in order to leave ample room to the creativity of human agency in lay mission in responding to the many opportunities of social reform appearing today, especially in the area of social structure.

Most societies style themselves today as secular in the sense that they eschew as a matter of fact any reference to any form of ultimacy that is transcendent and critically meaningful. Put more bluntly, the idea of God is merely that—just an idea. If the idea is pressed to refer to something in any way resembling what is indicated by the idea, such as God existing, then the idea makes no sense because no such thing as God exists. The consequence of such a view is the disappearance of any aura of the sacred in the way things are. The human in its natural, social, and historical life is understood and treated as having no religious dimension at all. If vestiges of the sacred still remain in human consciousness, they are taken as on the way to sure extinction and are without essential significance in any case. The practice of religion in society may still exist, but it is only one aspect of the many components of society, and is therefore relative to all the others, and is in turn relativized by them. It cannot claim ultimacy for what it represents, since the impossibility of such a claim is precisely what makes society secular.

From the perspective of lay mission, which is born out of sharing in the vision of the reign of God, such a view of society as secular is a contradiction in terms. Societies exist with social structures; no society is without them. Moreover, social structures necessarily contain for their basis elemental dimensions which are unconditionally given and they run through all societies. No social structure is possible without them, and so without them no society is possible.

This means that society necessarily presupposes foundational, unconditional, and absolutely given features which cannot be made to disappear by the proverbial mere snap of the fingers, or by simply ignoring them as though they did not exist, and thereby making them cease to operate. To be sure, society has many features which are best understood and treated as merely secular, such as its injustices, its vices, its corruption, and so forth, together with the behavior that goes with them. Moreover, society promotes values which are best desired and acquired as merely relative goods, and to that extent are secular, such as social status, economic security, military strength, and so forth, together with the behavior that they entail. Furthermore, society has many ways of doing things, such as the methods of science and technology, which are best accomplished without sanctimoniously involving the name of deity or any of its properties.

The secularity of all the factors just mentioned, however, does not mean that the elemental dimensions of social structure which make society possible are not present in society, and that by ignoring them they are thereby banished from reality. If the secularity described above, which is essentially behavioral, appears to be an inevitable, but not necessary, feature of society, since no society seems to be without it, then its possibility as a cultural form depends upon the fact that society as such exists. In short, the prior existence of society is the premise of its secular, behavioral feature, while the existence of society as such is premised upon the elemental dimensions of social structure. Secularity may be a relatively cultural and behavioral characteristic of society; it is not *of* the elemental dimensions of society as such.

If this analysis is anywhere near the truth, then it follows that making secularity as the measure of social reality is, to say the least, shortsighted. More bluntly put, it is wrong and "foolish" in the biblical sense. If it were not for its pervasive attraction in the world of today, lay mission should not even dignify it with its attention, let alone consider it as worthy of serious challenge. But societies, like individuals, can become foolish, too. Like the fool mentioned by the psalmist (Ps. 14:1; 53:1), they can say "in their heart: 'There is no God,' " and then go on behaving like fools and organizing social life accordingly! The real fool is not the *theoretical* atheist who uses his intelligence to argue that God does not exist, and then behaves as though God really exists. This atheist argues the wrong issue intelligently, but he lives prudently and wisely. There are not too many of them since only a few would devote their intelligence passionately to argue a wrong issue. The existence of God is a wrong issue to argue because it cannot be settled finally by argument one way or the other.

The real fool is the *practical* atheist who simply assumes in his heart, without further intelligent consideration, that God does not exist, and then lives accordingly. Paraphrasing Dostoyevsky, if God does not exist, then everything is permitted, and so one must live freely without God. There are now far too many of these practical atheists since their style of life is very attractive and one does not have to prove the validity of its premises. Some societies have in fact simply evolved as practical atheist. They have become "foolish."

Any responsible lay witness that is faithful to the good news of the reign of God cannot allow such a situation to go on without challenging it. The challenge which lay mission can put to societies which style themselves as secular is at least twofold, namely, to expose their self-contradiction and "foolishness," and to celebrate the elemental dimensions of society as signs of the reign of God for the purpose of generating human community. None of the social forms through which the elemental dimensions express community should be identified, however, with the kingdom of God!

The reform of social structure as an aspect of the lay mission of the Risen Lord in today's world also entails *the refinement of behavior in human interaction for the purpose of promoting human community*. This particular behavior is a basic cultural component of social structure. Its purpose is precisely the same as that of the elemental dimension in social structure, which is to develop human community. It is, therefore, appropriate to evaluate it as to whether it promotes human community. Does the behavior in human interaction, institutionalized in social structure, contribute to the development and refinement of human community? Answering this question is a major task of lay mission. Obviously, a detailed answer to this question is not possible here because concrete and detailed answers have to be contextual. It seems sufficient to indicate a general direction which may serve as a guide in the search for contextual answers. This direction may be found in the intrinsic relation between behavior in human interaction and the formation of human community as its essential purpose. This intrinsic relation may be seen in the overall intention of Jesus in what he said about behavior in the forms of social structure which shaped the context of his remarks.[1] We will deal with four of these forms of social structure to illustrate our point.

1. Human behavior centered in human life must not only prevent the taking of life, but must actively promote valuing it as a gift of God, and should therefore be celebrated in worship. In the perspective of worship, human life is seen as a most precious good in human community. Without it there cannot be human community. To promote valuing of life would entail such behavior as appreciating it in itself, nurturing its growth, respecting its rights, meeting adequately its needs, developing its potentialities, providing it with an environment that is life-supporting, and honoring it gratefully as indeed a precious gift from God! What promotes the valuing of life enhances human community. What degrades life and results in the rise of a "culture of death" destroys human community. The active promotion of the valuing of life in societies for the enhancement of human community should be a primary concern of lay mission today!

2. Human interaction around sexuality to promote human community is a major issue in today's world. In the mind of Jesus, what should be expressed generally in human interaction around sexuality is not lust, but love for the other. It is love as an act of deliberate goodwill that can relate together male and female in mutual respect for each other's difference in person, role, and dignity. Gender difference—being male or female—is the most basic differentiation among human beings. There is no consensus among societies and cultures as to what this difference means for human community. Some cultures and societies are male-dominated; others stress the female and maternal dimension of sexuality. However, there is a growing consensus that human community requires that what are essentially different must be appreciated as such, and at the same time valued in their mutuality and unity. Only love as deliberate goodwill, which is doing to others what you would like others do to you, can unite the different. When sexual and gender interaction is viewed in the light of human community, can the conclusion that there is much wrong to overcome and so much more good yet to be done be avoided? Surely not! Perhaps lay mission today can participate in overcoming what is wrong, and in doing what is right and good, in this area of human interaction!

3. Marriage and family life institutionalize a form of human interaction that seeks to establish a love-relationship that is freely entered into, binding, lasting, intimate, caring, and mutually self-giving for one another's welfare and for the common good. It requires behavior that expresses trust, commitment, faithfulness, respect, integrity, patience, generosity, forgiveness, self-sacrifice, and much more. Is there any doubt that these behavioral traits are absolutely essential, not only in marriage and family life, but also in human community as a whole? Is it not the case that the most conducive environment to nurture and practice them habitually is family life? What builds up marriage and family life is also what strengthens and ennobles human community. What breaks up marriage and family life in the end destroys community among human beings.

And yet today marriage and family life are under assault! Vice and widespread addiction to substance abuse, new forms of sexually transmitted disease (such as AIDS), the increasing rate of divorce, single parenthood, both parents with separate careers or working for a living, the reordering of roles of husband and wife, of male and female, in the family as a result of gender equality and appreciation—to mention but a few—are making a tremendous impact on marriage and family life. Do the effects of these factors on the family mean that the behavior that makes for marriage and family life, and for human community as well, is no longer adequate and should be changed? What new form of marriage and family life is evolving in today's world, and what kind of behavior does it require? What implications do these questions have for human community? Can lay mission afford to be a gallery spectator in this contemporary drama around marriage and family and its impact on community among human beings?

4. Human community depends upon truth, not on falsehood and deception. The form of truth is language. The reason for this is the fact that it is through language that reality is grasped and told as it is and as to what it means. Unless reality is discerned, apprehended, and described in the way it is and in what it means, it is as good as useless for human community. This activity is achieved through language, which is a distinctively human ability. Language is, therefore, truth-telling. As such it binds human community to its foundation in reality.

Moreover, human community also depends upon the fact that there is something that connects by communicating. Without this connecting by communicating, there cannot be human community because human beings differ from each other, and they protect their difference and demand that it be respected and valued. It is language that connects by communicating. It is thus the medium through which human community is formed and maintained.

Language, however, connects only when it communicates a shared message that binds. The message that binds and is shared through language that communicates is truth. Language is thus both the *form* and *medium* of truth in the making of human community. The essential virtue of language is that it is quite simply truth-telling. It tells, and so it communicates and connects. It tells *the truth,* and so it binds and builds up community in truth.

And yet, strangely enough, it is also through language that lies are formed and communicated. And so community can also be destroyed by language! In today's world, there is much lie-telling and truth-hiding. Language ironically is also used to communicate this evil. The manipulation of information, the making of propaganda, the efforts at persuasion by revealing only the half-truth, the justifying of a wrong through a process of reasoning that is claimed to be right, the making of legal fiction, and so much more, have become systematically promoted in modern societies through language! Does the use of language in widespread lie-telling and truth-hiding result in the building up of human community? This is very doubtful, to say the least! The essential purpose of language is to build up community by telling the truth! The terse advice of Jesus is: "Let your word be 'Yes, Yes' or 'No, No'; anything more than this comes from the evil one" (Mt. 5:37). Must not lay mission participate in achieving this essential purpose of language in human interaction?

There are other forms of social structure that urgently and vitally require reform for the sake of human community. We can only mention some of them here. Unfortunately, we neither have the time nor competence to discuss them in a way that would do justice to their complexity and importance. For example, there is human behavior in relation to the natural environment. It has been a source of security for ages to assume that the natural environment is always *there* to support life in its diversity, including human life, no matter how it is treated by the human being. Today this assumption can no longer be made. The reason is that it is now human behavior that is threatening to destroy the environment and its ecosystem, and thereby undermining its ability to support and sustain life. What kind of human behavior would both "till and keep" the earth and its ecosystem and preserve nature as God's creation? What is the proper role of the human being in relation to the earth and its ecosystem? Is it to exploit it, to dominate it, to be subordinated to it, or to care for it as a steward of God while being a part of it? This is a new challenge to lay mission today. Can it shirk the challenge?

Another form of social structure that seems to require reform is the behavior revolving around the human relation to God, or the practice of piety. This is already a vital issue within any form of religion, as it was in Jesus' day and in ours. The issue, however, is exacerbated by the fact that in today's world there is a variety of ways of practicing piety. There is the Hindu, the Buddhist, the Islamic, the Taoist, the Christian, and so on, including their different versions. These different ways of practicing piety encounter its other in significant ways in today's world. How does one behave in relation to any of these forms of piety in a way that promotes human community and at the same time makes one faithful to one's own religious convictions? Is it by persecution, condescending tolerance, aggressive conversion, intensive but irenic dialogue, cooperative activity for the common good? Again, this is a new challenge to lay mission in today's world! Can the challenge be ignored?

We have been suggesting how lay mission might participate in the mission of the Crucified and Risen Lord in today's world. We have indicated that this participation might be done by sharing in the vision of Jesus Christ and sharing the same vision with others, and by following him as he moves as the Risen Lord in our world today. We specified some areas of social life where we might find him engaged in social transformation: in founding and constituting society in its proper basis, in the critique of Law as a form of social order, in people-making by exposing injustice and saving its victims for a richer and fuller life, and in reforming social structures for promoting human community. We are fellow workers with him in achieving his mission of social salvation.

There are other forms of lay mission that we have not been able to explore because of lack of competence and space considerations. However, the multifaceted strategy of social transformation entailed by the vision of the kingdom of God as seen by Jesus provides the searchlight for discerning and exploring new opportunities and meeting new challenges for lay mission in today's world. The people of God will undoubtedly have the courage, the faithfulness, and the wisdom to respond to these opportunities and challenges. The promise of the Risen Lord to his disciples as he sent them forth into the world was: "And remember, I am with you always to the end of the age." The Christian community of today relies confidently in the same promise.

Essentially we have tried to do two things in this book. We have sought to describe the strategy of Jesus for social transformation, and upon this strategy we have sought to model forms of lay mission which could make a difference in today's world. Social ferment is taking place today, both locally and globally. The Christian community has always played a significant role in the reform of society. There is no reason to doubt that God's people will continue fulfilling this role today, especially through its laypeople. The social ferment that is taking place everywhere provides them with a missionary opportunity that does not happen frequently in human history. Moreover, their knowledge of what Jesus did in helping transform the society of his day provides them with a wealth of insight to make a contribution in the remaking of society.

According to Jesus, God's people in the world are there to be "the salt of the earth," and "the light of the world" (Mt. 5:13-14). Salt has to be mixed with what is to be salted if it is to salt. Light makes a difference only in darkness. And both salt and light work quietly but effectively in their respective contexts. They are noticed as effective only in terms of the difference they quietly make. Salt and light are vivid metaphors for illuminating the way God's people may do their work in today's world. They are placed in their respective contexts but quietly make a difference in social transformation. Of course, the aim of all this is simply and only for "the praise of your Father in heaven."

Note

1. See chapter 4.

BIBLIOGRAPHY

Achtemeier, Paul J. *Mark*. Philadelphia: Fortress Press, 1986.

Bornkamm, Gunther. *Jesus of Nazareth*. New York: Harper & Brothers, 1960.

Braaten, Carl E. *The Flaming Center*. Philadelphia: Fortress Press, 1977.

———. *The Apostolic Imperative*. Minneapolis: Augsburg Publishing House, 1985.

Bultmann, Rudolf. *Jesus and the Word*. New York: Charles Scribner's Sons, 1958.

Chilton, Bruce. *Pure Kingdom: Jesus' Vision of God*. Grand Rapids, Michigan: Wm. Eerdmans Publishing Company, 1996.

Conzelmann, Hans. *An Outline of the Theology of the New Testament*. London: SCM Press LTD, 1969.

Crossan, John Dominic. *In Parables*. New York, Hagerstown, San Francisco, London: Harper & Row Publishers, 1973.

Dawe, Donald G. *Jesus: The Death and Resurrection of God*. Atlanta: John Knox Press, 1985.

Danker, Frederick W. *Jesus and the New Age* (A Commentary on Luke's Gospel). Philadelphia: Fortress Press, 1988.

Donahue, John R., S.J. *The Gospel in Parable*. Philadelphia: Fortress Press, 1988.

Green, Michael. *Evangelism in the Early Church*. Grand Rapids, Michigan: Wm. B. Eerdmans Publishing Company, 1970.

Funk, Robert W. *Parables and Presence*. Philadelphia: Fortress Press, 1982.

Furnish, Victor Paul. *The Love Command in the New Testament*. London: SCM Press LTD, 1973.

Goppelt, Leonard. *Theology of the New Testament*. Trans., John Alsup. 2 Volumes. Grand Rapids, Michigan: Wm. B. Eerdmans Publishing Company, 1981, 1982.

Hahn, Ferdinand. *Mission in the New Testament.* London: SCM Press LTD. 1965.

Hanson, Paul D. *The People Called.* San Francisco: Harper & Row Publishers. 1986.

Harvey, A. E. *Jesus and the Constraints of History.* Philadelphia: The Westminster Press, 1982.

Interpreter's Dictionary of the Bible. 4 Volumes. Nashville and New York: Abingdon Press, 1962.

Jeremias, Joachim. *Jesus' Promise to the Nations.* London: SCM Press LTD, 1958.

———. *Jerusalem in the Time of Jesus.* Philadelphia: Fortress Press, 1969.

———. *New Testament Theology.* Vol. I: The Proclamation of Jesus. London: SCM Press LTD, 1972.

Jewett, Robert. *Letter to Pilgrims.* New York, New York: The Pilgrm Press, 1981.

Käsemann, Ernst. *New Testament Questions of Today.* London: SCM Press LTD, 1969.

Keck, Leander E. *A Future for the Historical Jesus.* Nashville and New York: Abingdon Press, 1971.

Kingsbury, Jack Dean. *Matthew As Story.* Philadelphia: Fortress Press, 1988.

———. *Conflict in Mark.* Minneapolis: Fortress Press, 1989.

Kittel, G. and Friedrich G., Eds. *Theological Dictionary of the New Testament.* Trans. and abridged into one volume, Geoffrey W. Bromiley. Grand Rapids, Michigan: Wm. B. Eerdmans Publishing Company, 1985.

Lebacqz, Karen. *Six Theories of Justice.* Minneapolis: Augsburg Publishing House, 1986.

———. *Justice in an Unjust World.* Minneapolis: Augsburg Publishing House, 1987.

Mealand, David L. *Poverty and Expectation in the Gospels.* London: SPCK, 1980.

Meier, John P. *A Marginal Jew* (Rethinking the Historical Jesus), Vols. I and II. New York: Doubleday, 1991, 1994.

Mitchell, Basil. *Law, Morality and Religion.* London: Oxford University Press, 1967.

Moltmann, Jurgen. *the Crucified God.* London: SCM Press LTD, 1974.

———. *The Trinity and the Kingdom.* San Francisco: Harper & Row Publishers, 1981.

———. *The Way of Jesus Christ.* London: SCM Press LTD, 1990.

Murphy, Frederick J. *The Religious World of Jesus*. Nashville: Abingdon Press, 1991.

Pannenberg, Wolfhart. *Theology and the Kingdom of God*. Philadelphia: The Westminster Press, 1969.

Perrin, Norman. *Jesus and the Language of the Kingdom*. Philadelphia: Fortress Press, 1976.

Rawls, John. *A Theory of Justice*. Oxford, New York, London: Oxford University Press, 1978.

———. *Political Liberalism*. New York: Columbia University Press, 1993.

Sanders, E. P. *Jesus and Judaism*. London: SCM Press LTD, 1985.

Schillebeeckx, Edward. *Jesus: An Experiment in Christology*. Trans., Hubert Hoskins. New York: The Seabury Press, 1979.

———. *Jesus and Christ*. New York: Crossroad, 1982.

Schrage, Wolfgang. *The Ethics of the New Testament*. Trans., David E. Gree. Philadelphia: Fortress Press, 1988.

Schweizer, Eduard. *Jesus*. London: SCM Press LTD, 1971.

Scott, Bernard Brandon. *Hear Then the Parable*. Minneapolis: Fortress Press, 1989.

Segovia, Fernando F., Editor. *Discipleship in the New Testament*. Philadelphia: Fortress Press, 1985.

Senior, Donald and Stuhlmueller, Carroll. *The Biblical Foundations for Mission*. SCM Press LTD, 1983.

Strecker, George. *The Sermon on the Mount*. Trans., O. C. Dean, Jr. Nashville: Abingdon Press, 1988.

Thompson, William M. *The Jesus Debate. A Survey and Synthesis*. Mahwah: Paulist Press, 1985.

Waetjen, Herman C. *A Reordering of Power*. Minneapolis: Fortress Press, 1989.

Williamson, Lamar, Jr. *Mark. Interpretation: A Bible Commentary for Teaching and Preaching*. Atlanta: John Knox Press, 1983.